152

HERBERT NEIE
THE DOCTRINE OF THE ATONEMENT IN THE THEOLOGY OF WOLFHART PANNENBERG

THE DOCTRINE OF THE ATONEMENT IN THE THEOLOGY OF WOLFHART PANNENBERG

BY

HERBERT NEIE

WALTER DE GRUYTER · BERLIN · NEW YORK

1979

THEOLOGISCHE BIBLIOTHEK TÖPELMANN

HERAUSGEGEBEN VON
K. ALAND, C. H. RATSCHOW UND E. SCHLINK

36. BAND

232.3X
N316
80021924

CIP-Kurztitelaufnahme der Deutschen Bibliothek

Neie, Herbert:
The doctrine of the atonement in the theology of Wolfhart Pannenberg / by Herbert Neie. —
Berlin, New York : de Gruyter, 1978.
  (Theologische Bibliothek Töpelmann ; Bd. 36)
  ISBN 3-11-007506-7

© 1978 by Walter de Gruyter & Co., Berlin 30 (Printed in Germany)
Alle Rechte, insbesondere das der Übersetzung in fremde Sprachen, vorbehalten. Ohne ausdrückliche
Genehmigung des Verlages ist es auch nicht gestattet, dieses Buch oder Teile daraus auf
photomechanischem Wege (Photokopie, Mikrokopie) zu vervielfältigen.
Satz und Druck: Walter de Gruyter, 1 Berlin 30 · Einband: Fuhrmann, 1 Berlin 36

PREFACE

The title of this book might sound pedantic to potential readers and deter some. It was meant to be unassuming and to the point. Yet it might conceal the degree to which I was intrigued and enthralled by Pannenberg's thought at large. My efforts at an analysis of his mode of understanding the cross led me to attempt to familiarize the reader with the major aspects and tenets of this theologian's systematic design. I got carried away. Thus, as a contribution both to the discussion on Pannenberg and to a contemporary understanding of the cross, my study at the same time wishes to facilitate a thorough grasp of Pannenberg's thought for those familiar with his works and to entice those not familiar to turn to this author. For it is my conviction that Pannenberg represents an important option in contemporary Christian philosophical and doctrinal theology.

Of my esteemed teachers of student days who started me off on my theological journey and spurred my interest in the atonement I gratefully mention Arnold B. Come (now president of San Francisco Theological Seminary) and Wolfgang Trillhaas, Professor Emeritus of the University of Göttingen. I am deeply indebted to the chairman of my doctoral committee at the Graduate Theological Union, Berkeley, Benjamin A. Reist, who gave my research unselfish interest, untiring encouragement, and absolute independence. A. Durwood Foster wisely guided my research. Bernard M. Loomer opened my eyes for Process modes of thought. For this and their friendship I wish to thank them. I am grateful to Professors Kenan B. Osborne, O.F.M., James McClendon, and Gerard Caspary for what I learnt from them.

I must not omit to give thanks to many non-professionals who helped me to experience and pass on reconciliation as a living reality: my parishioners and students, foremost my parents and family to whom I dedicate this book.

I gladly acknowledge the generous doctoral grants of the Graduate Theological Union and the substantial financial support of Mrs. Thomas R. Clark of Elk River, Minn., during the years of my research. Equally, I thank all who contributed financially to the printing of this, above all the Evangelische Kirche von Kurhessen-Waldeck, Germany.

While writing this I was indefatiguably assisted by the patient and cheerful services of Mrs. Louise Beck, librarian. Unforgettable is the fellowship of the San Francisco Seminary community who graciously extended their hospitality to me and my family.

The cross of Christ is our salvation according to our faith. May this treatise be of some help when we try to understand why and how.

Fulda, August 1978　　　　　　　　　　　　　　　　　　　　　　　H. N.

TABLE OF CONTENTS

Introduction 1

Chapter I:
Introduction to Pannenberg's Doctrine of the Atonement 5

  1. The General Theological Setting of the Doctrine 5
  2. The Biblical Understanding of Jesus' Death 6
  3. The Epistemological Criterion: Historicity 10
  4. A Preliminary Statement on Pannenberg's Presuppositions of His Epistemological Criteria 16
  5. The Hermeneutical Criterion: Contemporary Wirklichkeitsverständnis 18
  6. The Application of the Epistemological Criterion to Jesus' Death   22

Chapter II:
Jesus' Divinity Established 24

  1. The Proleptic Character of Jesus' Pre-Easter Ministry 24
  2. The Resurrection of Jesus as God's Confirmation of Jesus' Identity   28
  3. The Resurrection of Jesus as Abrogation of the Law 31
  4. What Does the Conception Resurrection of the Dead Mean? 33
  5. The Evidence for the Historicity of Jesus' Resurrection 37
  6. The Proleptic Character of God's Confirmation in Jesus' Resurrection 44

Chapter III:
Jesus' Divinity Defined and Pannenberg's Concept of Revelation 48

  1. The Concept of Revelational Presence 48
  2. The Concept of Retroactive Ontological Enforcement 54
  3. The Unity of the Man Jesus With God 58
  4. Jesus' and the Father's Divinity 60
  5. The Relation of Divinity and Humanity in Jesus 63

Chapter IV:
Jesus' Identity as the Son of God 73

   1. Jesus' Personal Community with the Father and its Function 73
   2. Jesus' Indirect Identity with the Son of God 74
   3. The Concept of Dedication to God and the Final Step Toward Jesus' Identity as Son of God 77
   4. The Mutual Dependence of the Noetical and the Ontological Foundation of Jesus' Identity as Son of God 80
   5. Some Consequences for Theological Anthropology 85

Chapter V:
Analysis of the Determinative Concepts of Pannenberg's Theology as a Whole 88

   1. Three Motives of Pannenberg's Theology 88
   2. Important Systematic Influences 94
   3. The Biblical Foundation of Pannenberg's Ontology 101
   4. The Corroborative Anthropological Evidence 104
   5. The Concepts of God and Being 110
   6. The Existence of God 122

Chapter VI:
The Significance of Jesus' Death on the Cross 129

   1. The Relationship of Jesus' Death to the Law 130
   2. Can We Speak of an Expiatory Character of Jesus' Death? 136
   3. In What Sense did Jesus Die for Humanity? 140
   4. The Concept of Inclusive Substitution 145

Chapter VII:
The Significance of Jesus' Death on the Cross (II) 151

   1. The Critique of Three Soteriological Theories 151
   2. The Significance of Jesus' Freedom and Sinlessness 156
   3. The Evaluation of the *Officium Sacerdotale Christi* – Doctrine 168
   4. Intermediate Result 171

Chapter VIII:
Critique of Pannenberg's Staurology 180

1. The Old Israelite Understanding of Expiation 180
2. Ethical Individualism and the Ancient Hebrew Concept of Collective Liability 185
3. Ethical Individualism and the Modern View of Substitution as a Universal Phenomenon in Personal and Socio-political Life 191
4. Pannenberg's Doctrine and the Phenomenon of Substitution 196
5. The *pro nobis* of Jesus' Death 202

Chapter IX:
The Cross as God's Passion — Further Questions and some Constructive Suggestions 207

1. The Rank of the Cross in the Christ Event 207
2. The Christ Event as Revelation 209
3. What is Love? 213
4. Christ's Suffering in Relation to God the Father's 216

Selected Bibliography 229

1. Works by Wolfhart Pannenberg 229
2. Other Literature 230

INTRODUCTION

Christian faith in Jesus Christ in whatever form has always been supremely involved with his death on the cross. An understanding of Jesus' passion and death in connection with his message, work, and resurrection from the dead is paramount to faith, and to work toward such understanding is a prime task of systematic theology.

Now the interpretation of Christ's death of the Reformers and of Protestant scholasticism has become uncertain with the entrance into the modern period. For the Reformers the *sensus literalis* of Scripture possessed *claritas et sufficientia*. Scripture was *sui ipsius interpres* because only a minor gap was felt to exist between a Scriptural statement, its historical truth, and its doctrinal truth. For the modern period these three aspects have much more fallen apart into three distinct entities: history, kerygma, and theological interpretation. Neither do the rational-speculative foundations of classical metaphysics for biblical theology any longer exist. The traditional supranaturalism and rational theism had been refuted through Kant's "Critique of Pure Reason". St. Anselm of Canterbury's doctrine of the atonement in "Cur Deus Homo?" faces the profound questions of all rationalists since the Socinians. Abelard's counter-doctrine, the refuge of many modern theologians, overcame the rigid legal cast and the quantitative measuring of guilt and grace and well answered the problem of appropriation of salvation. But the stumbling-block of the traditional, even biblical doctrine for the modern mind, that Jesus dies a vicarious penal death, is not removed here either.

Many neo-Protestant, post-Kantian efforts at constructing an understanding of the atonement do not entirely satisfy. Schleiermacher's doctrine depends on an inference of God's existence from his effects, as manifested in man's religious experience. Man's valuation of an event which as such is immanently causally determined (corresponding to Kant's *Ding an sich* and its phenomenon) becomes the ground of faith. But this makes faith a completely subjective "truth". Similar methods are used by W. Herrmann and R. Bultmann, particularly obviously in the latter's distinction between a fact and its *Bedeutsamkeit*. Dialectical theology abandoned all efforts to establish the truth of the Christian faith objectively, either through historical studies or metaphysically. Unlike the afore-mentioned theologians, Albrecht Ritschl verified theological statements not merely in experience but also historically. Yet he presupposed the historical facticity of the Gospel narratives, on the whole, and his position was undermined by the insight modern historical-critical research of the New Testament offered into the kerygmatic nature of the Gospels. Paul Tillich's theology wishes to meet the modern situation by steering beyond both a kerygma-theology and the theology of historical verification. He claims ontic reality for the objects of faith by virtue of his Logos-ontology. In consequence of his concept of symbol, however, no biblical and, with one exception, no theological statement is literally true.

Reflecting on a theology of atonement, two fundamental questions come to mind with regard to the cross: What does it mean? And how does it reveal its meaning? The latter question can also be put saying: How *can* it reveal this – or anything? Because here the hermeneutical question puts itself alongside the historical and theological one. Under these fundamental questions one might ask: *Must* or *can* cross and resurrection be historically established before they can become meaningful for us in accordance with the kerygma? Can historiography establish an event which goes beyond all known analogies? Is the biblical message about the meaning of Christ's death to be received without question – an information not to be understood, a mystery not to be verified – in blind faith? Or may we, and even must we, search for an interpretation which agrees with those criteria of truth which we use in other areas of life also: historical trustworthiness, reasonableness, compatibility with experience and the findings of the other sciences? Questions with regard to the death of Christ might include: Is the salvific understanding of his death inseparable or separable from its vicariousness and penal character? May we, and how can we, replace its understanding as an expiation of sin or propitation of God (satisfaction)? Of what does the salvific effect consist? And how is it to be appropriated or imputed? Is the atonement objective or subjective or both or beyond both? How is Christ's death to be understood with regard to himself (an act or a destiny) and how is it related to God (Does Jesus suffer in place of man or of God?)? Does his passion and death primarily accomplish an acquittal from guilt and punishment (cf. the Reformation's forensic interpretation of justification and of the *pro nobis*, also the concept of *justitia aliena*)? Or does it release a power of love which renews and changes the world? Or is it a paradigm to be imitated, showing the way of each Christian's passion and cross in Jesus' footsteps? May we abandon or may we uphold the understanding of the cross as judgment? Must our concept of God determine our interpretation of the cross or vice versa be determined by what the cross comes out to mean?

To engage in this study with reference to the thought of Wolfhart Pannenberg might be considered to be of particular interest for the following reasons. Pannenberg claims to construct his theology on the basis of what is historically and scientifically thinkable and thus strikes the mood of much contemporary demand. He defies the concept of faith of dialectical theology and revives Luther's and Melanchthon's notion of *fides informis* as *notitia historiae* which is the ground of *fides* as *fiducia*. Secondly, he attempts an impressive retention and reinterpretation of the vicarious, penal, and universally efficacious understanding of Christ's suffering, backed up by scientific reasoning.

The analysis and evaluation of Pannenberg's thought on the meaning of Jesus' death demonstrated the closely knit and carefully interwoven character of Pannenberg's theologizing so that a scrupulous look into the methodology and the presuppositions of this theology as a whole and an exposition of his christology and of his highly determinative concepts of God, being, the future, and prolepsis in particular proved indispensable. Consequently, a plan to bring Pannenberg's staurology into relief by juxtaposing it to other very contemporary efforts, such as the understanding of atonement in the process theology of Daniel Day Williams or in Frederick Herzog's theology of liberation, turned out to be too far and broad an aim and had to be abandoned within the scope of one dissertation.

The treatise begins with a short introduction to the setting of Pannenberg's staurology and a description of his methodology (chapter 1). In an exposition of Pannenberg's christology we follow the author as he applies his premises and criteria and establishes Jesus' divinity on grounds which – at the same time – do perfect justice to the authentic humanity of Jesus in his concrete historical life. Only on this basis his doctrine of the cross will become intelligible (chapters II–IV). Our curiosity as to the tenability of the author's premises and the motives of his procedure thus aroused, we proceed to analyze his determinative concepts (chapter V). Subsequently the examination is directed to Pannenberg's interpretation of the cross directly, first offering its exposition, then its critique (chapters VI–VIII). The treatise demonstrates Pannenberg's contention that Jesus died a vicarious penal death to be unacceptable on his own terms.

Chapter IX represents an effort to construct an interpretation of the cross by drawing out and further developing Pannenberg's own suggestions. The aim is to arrive at an understanding of the passion of Jesus that, unlike Pannenberg's, consistently applies his methodology. The result might be persuasive to contemporary sensitivities: The cross demonstrates the sheer love of the triune God as vulnerable *misericordia*, bearing the hurt and pain of his love as well as of the life of the creatures and as unifying the separate and distorted. This love is *Selbstverwirklichung Gottes und des Menschen* and warrants the eschatological consummation of God's redeeming work.

CHAPTER I

INTRODUCTION INTO PANNENBERG'S DOCTRINE OF THE ATONEMENT

1. The General Theological Setting of the Doctrine

Wolfhart Pannenberg develops his doctrine of the atonement in chapter 7 of his important study in christology, *Jesus — God and Man*. The chapter bears the title "The Meaning of Jesus' Vicarious Death on the Cross" and begins with the programmatic statement:

> Jesus' death on the cross is revealed in the light of his resurrection as the punishment suffered in our place for the blasphemous existence of humanity[1].

Pannenberg understands Jesus' active ministry to consist of his proclamation, in word and deed, of the imminent coming of the kingdom of God. He agrees with Johannes Weiss[2] that Jesus shared the apocalyptic view of the eschaton according to which the end of the world is expected in a temporally concrete and imminent future in which God will come to raise the dead and to exercise judgment and bring salvation and eternal life. Pannenberg sharply disagrees with R. Bultmann's severing of history and eschatology[3]. Bultmann dehistoricized the meaning of 'eschatological' when for him this word came to mean the ever present 'now' of the existential decision for or against God in the encounter with the kerygma, understood as summons to obedience. Pannenberg thinks,

> But the contrast between eschatology and history cannot be maintained either for the apocalyptic or for Jesus. Without the conviction of the temporal imminence of the transformation of the world with the coming of the kingdom of God, that openness

---

[1] Wolfhart Pannenberg, *Jesus-God and Man*, (Philadelphia: Westminister Press,⁵ 1974) p. 245. Future quotations from this work will be located by page-numbers in brackets behind the quotation. Henceforth abbreviated JGaM.
[2] Johannes Weiss, *Die Predigt Jesu vom Reiche Gottes* (Göttingen: Vandenhoeck & Ruprecht, 1892), p. 32.
[3] Rudolf Bultmann, *Theology of the New Testament*, vol. 1, (New York: Charles Scribner's Sons, 1951), p. 21.

toward the future which is so characteristic for Jesus' message would never have arisen. Cut loose from every reference to a temporally concrete future, the attitude of unworldly openess in the framework of a noneschatological understanding of the world could hardly endure, apart from the fact that it would mean something other than the conduct to which Jesus calls. (242)

For Pannenberg, Jesus' resurrection is a historical fact, established with historical-critical tools, and means that God confirmed Jesus' message and claim. For raising Jesus from the dead, God partially fulfilled the expectation of the apocalyptic and of Jesus in that he raised one, if not all from the dead; thus Pannenberg understands the resurrection as a prolepsis of the eschatological consummation which functions as confirmation of Jesus' message and works and of the messianic claim therein implied. This confirmation is not only a noetic one. From the human perspective Jesus' resurrection also establishes ontologically who Jesus was from the beginning: a man in essential unity with God.

> Jesus' resurrection is not only constitutive for our perception of his divinity, but it is ontologically constitutive for that divinity. Apart from the resurrection from the dead, Jesus would not be God, even though from the perspective of the resurrection, he is retrospectively one with God in his whole pre-Easter life. (224)

This conclusion is informed by Pannenberg's determination to construct his christology "from below", i e., from the historical realities of the life of the pre-Easter Jesus as it is recognizable through historical-critical research. Within this procedure the incarnation and divinity of Christ are not premises from which to start out but inferences at which one can only arrive on grounds of the evidence.

2. *The Biblical Understanding of Jesus' Death*

Given this background, Pannenberg considers Jesus' crucifixion and resurrection as Jesus' fate, not, like his ministry, something actively accomplished. "Both were 'sent' to Jesus as an occurrence to be suffered and accepted." (245) For the passion predictions must be judged as *vaticinia ex eventu*[4]. Now Pannenberg emphasizes that, contrary to Christ's resurrection, his crucifixion could *not* be understood by the Jews or the disciples within the horizon of understanding offered by the apocalyptic or any other dominant contemporary theology. This horizon made it possible to understand the resurrection and this quite independent of the crucifixion. The latter constituted no fulfillment of an expectation or a meaningful event either in the context of Jesus' proclamation or in that of the expected eschaton. On the contrary, it was an occurrence in need of interpretation, and it was ultimately interpreted in the light of Jesus' resurrection. The early church faced the question

> ... as to why Jesus had to go the way of suffering to the cross if God was subsequently to acknowledge in the resurrection the unheard-of claim with which Jesus appeared. Why did God permit Jesus' rejection by the Jews? Why did he not acknowledge Jesus earlier so unambiguously that Jesus would have been incontrovertibly shown to be God's authorized representative? Why must his path have led to the cross? (246)

Following F. Hahn[5], Pannenberg thinks that possibly the oldest tradition about Jesus' death interpreted it in correspondence to the rejection and murder of the prophets by the unrepenting people and that the core of this idea (cf. Mark 12:2ff.) may go back to Jesus himself "even though Jesus never understood himself as prophet in the strict sense." (247) Drawing on Acts 2:23 and 4:28, Pannenberg believes that with this the idea was connected that Jesus' rejection was foreordained by God's decree and that a divine "must" then was assumed to have stood over Jesus' passion (cf. Mark 8:31). To elucidate the necessity of Jesus' path to the cross the passion account was formulated under the influence of the *Weissagungsbeweis* (proof from prophecy) by the Palestinian community, and as regards the meaning of his cross, Pannenberg thinks that

> ... it seems that the notion that Jesus did not die for himself but for us had already taken on fundamental importance. Jesus'

---

[4] Pannenberg agrees with the reasons for this judgment as summarized by Willi Marxsen, *Anfangsprobleme der Christologie*, (Gütersloh: Gütersloher Verlagshaus Gerd Mohn, 1960), pp. 22 and 31 f.

[5] Ferdinand Hahn, *Christologische Hoheitstitel: Ihre Geschichte im frühen Christentum* (Forschungen zur Religion und Literatur des Alten und Neuen Testaments, 83; Göttingen: Vandenhoeck & Ruprecht, 1963), p. 49.

resurrection had proved that he though innocent had been rejected, given over to the Romans, and executed. Thus the meaning of his death could only be understood as an expression of service to humanity in the name of the love of God revealed in his message which determined his whole mission. It could only be understood as dying for us, for our sins. The Palestinian community understood Jesus' death in this sense as expiation – but not yet as expiatory *sacrifice* in the cultic sense. (247, italics by the author)

The exegetical basis for this understanding is the ransom-saying Mark 10:45 and the Last Supper tradition (cf. Luke 22:20, Mark 14:24) according to which Jesus' blood was shed "for us" or, respectively, "for many" which last expression possibly indicates a connection with Isa. 53:12[6]. But the plural γράφαι in 1. Cor. 15:3 rather points to more than a specific reference to Isa. 53:12. Paul's formula binds together two independent motifs: (1) the concept of the expiatory power of the suffering and death of prophets and martyrs current in Judaism, and (2) the fundamental idea of the old passion account that God foreordained and Scripture predicted the death of the Son of Man. The connection of these two motifs allowed the inclusion of (3) the motif of the expiatory suffering of the Servant of God which in Judaism played no role as a promise of vicarious expiation. The inclusion of this motif yielded the understanding of Jesus' death as of universal significance ("for many") and in this respect transcended any contemporary Jewish concept of expiation since it means the ultimate and final expiation, in no need of further supplementation.

Further concepts which the early church took from its Jewish tradition in order to understand Christ's death include: the concept of an expiatory sacrifice (cf. Romans 3:25 and Hebrews) which Pannenberg considers to be

---

[6] Pannenberg identifies here and in the following with the exegetical studies by F. Hahn, Ibid; Eduard Lohse, *Märtyrer und Gottesknecht: Untersuchung zur urchristlichen Verkündigung vom Sühnetod Jesu Christi* (Göttingen: Vandenhoeck & Ruprecht, 1955); Rudolf Bultmann, *The History of the Synoptic Tradition*, (Oxford: Basil Blackwell & Mott, Ltd., 1963); Joachim Jeremias, *The Parables of Jesus* (New York: Charles Scribner's Sons, 1963); Günter Bornkamm, "Herrenmahl und Kirche bei Paulus", *Studien zu Antike und Urchristentum: Gesammelte Aufsätze*, Band II (Beiträge zur evangelischen Theologie, 28; Munich: Chr. Kaiser Verlag, 1959); Dietrich Rössler, *Gesetz und Geschichte* (Neukirchen Krs. Moers: Verlag der Buchhandlung des Erziehungsvereins, 1960).

more metaphorical than the other motifs; the concept of the eschatological Passover Lamb; the concept of the covenant sacrifice which, as no expiation known to Judaism could accomplish, founds a new covenant and possibly at the same time possesses expiatory power.

Basic for Pannenberg's evaluation and interpretation of Paul's understanding of the cross is the study by E. Brandenburger, *Adam und Christus*[7]. Pannenberg says with respect to 1. Cor. 15:21f.,

> E. Brandenburger . . . argues convincingly that Paul "forces" the anthropos category "from the sphere of the suprahistorical-speculative into that of history" (p. 238), and, in the sense of an eschatological universalism of salvation (p. 244) in which the universality of the forgiveness of sins accomplished by the death of Christ (p. 237), presupposes a corresponding universality of the sin that humanity incurred through the first Adam, which therefore is not to be understood only as violation of the Mosaic law (pp. 203 ff.) As Brandenburger stresses, this historical-typological inversion of the doctrine of the first and the second man was possible only in the context and by means of the Jewish apocalyptic traditions (pp. 241, 246). We can add that in the figure of the apocalyptic Son of Man the understanding of the genuine reality of man had already been shifted into the eschatological future. This is true even though this original, symbolic meaning of the future of the Son of Man which appears in Daniel . . . may subsequently have been forgotten in favor of a rather "mythological" understanding of the Son of Man as an individual eschatological figure. Paul, then, with his doctrine of the "Second Adam", restored the original meaning of the idea of the Son of Man as the eschatological realization of the human in its heavenly destiny. But he also "fundamentally restructured" (p. 246) this apocalyptic eschatology by means of the archetypal language of the Adam speculation that was on the way to developing into Gnosticism. Apparently this had to happen because for Paul the eschatological destiny of man had already dawned in Jesus Christ, thus raising the question of participation in it. This question could

---

[7] Egon Brandenburger, *Adam und Christus: Exegetisch-religionsgeschichtliche* Untersuchung zu Röm. 5:12—21 (Neukirchen Krs. Moers, Verlag der Buchhandlung des Erziehungsvereins, 1962). Pages given in the above quotation refer to this work.

be answered by the archetypal aspect of the anthropos category. Thus Paul, in the light of the experience of the Christ event, transformed not only the Adam speculation about the first, prototypal man, which we find in Philo, but also the eschatological turn that had already been given to this speculation in apocalyptic. (200f., n. 13)

Pannenberg summarizes with a sentence which states what is a fundamental contention of his entire theological system: *"Paul thus shifted the locus of true humanity from the distant past to the future. For mythical orientation to a prototypal distant past, he substituted an eschatologically oriented concept of human history."* (200, italics mine) The Adam-Jesus speculation with its use of the anthropos category implies, of course, Paul's assertion of the universal significance of Jesus' suffering. Uniquely Pauline is the idea that the cross means the end of the law. "Jesus has taken upon himself on the cross the indicting power of the law, its curse, and thus removed it from us (Gal. 3:13) . . . Jesus Christ, by taking upon himself the curse of the law as an innocent person, has nullified completely the indicting power of the law." (249) So also in Col. 2:13f. Christ's death sets the law aside which in Eph. 2:14–16 opens the way to the mission to the Gentiles. Paul himself had taught so in Gal. 3:14; Rom. 11:11ff.

3. The Epistemological Criterion: Historicity

In a manner highly significant for his method, Pannenberg now raises the question,

How are all these assertions related to each other and to the event of Jesus' death on the cross? To what extent is Jesus' crucifixion to be understood with Paul as the consequence of the power of the law's curse against him? Can a relation be demonstrated between Jesus' death and the law that would permit or even demand that we adopt this concept of Paul's? (250)

Biblical statements for Pannenberg are not self-evident, i. e., they are not true on Paul's authority. Nor are they true just because they coincide with other Biblical statements (scriptura sui ipsius interpres). Neither does it suffice to point to the religious experience one might have of the present

Lordship of Jesus. "But in order to understand that present reality, we must once again start with the historical Jesus of Nazareth to assure that we do not speak unknowingly of something quite different under the name of Jesus." (365) Rather, theological statements about Jesus require for us a verification in Jesus' own history. Pannenberg approvingly quotes A. Ritschl's judgment, "If the conception of his present Lordship cannot be filled out with definite characteristics of his earthly ministry, it is either a worthless schema or an excuse for every possible enthusiasm[8]." What, then, historically was the relation of his way to the cross to the traditional law? Equally the attribution of such concepts as vicariousness and expiation to Jesus' death need such verification. The New Testament interpretations are meaningful for us

> ... only if Jesus' own path to the cross contains a vicarious element and if the common human situation of selfish entanglement in personal concerns designated with the term "sin" is thereby transformed and can be convincingly presented as having been transformed. (250)

That is to say: a theological interpretation, for Pannenberg, is valid and legitimate only if it meets the criterion of historicity (and, as will be shown later, the hermeneutical criterion of a contemporary *Wirklichkeitsverständnis*). It must have its basis in Jesus' own pre-Easter life and ministry. Contrary to E. Brunner's christology in his work *The Mediator*[9] or K. Barth[10] or H. Vogel[11] Pannenberg thinks a christology may, today, not be constructed from "above" but from "below". For three reasons Pannenberg rejects the construction from "above". First, such a christology presupposes what a contemporary christology has the task of showing: why we ascribe divinity to Jesus of Nazareth. "Instead of presupposing it, we must first inquire about how Jesus' appearance in history led to the recognition of his divinity." (34) Second, a christology which starts from the divinity of the Logos is chiefly concerned with the union of God and man in Jesus and consequently

---

[8] Albrecht Ritschl, *The Christian Doctrine of Justification and Reconciliation*, vol. iii (Edinburgh: T. & T. Clark, 1902), p. 406. (*JGaM*, p. 365)

[9] Emil Brunner, *The Mediator* (New York: The Macmillan Co., 1934)

[10] Karl Barth, *Church Dogmatics* (12 vols.; Edinburgh: T. & T. Clark, 1936–62), vol. iv/1, 59.

[11] Heinrich Vogel, *Gott in Christo: Ein Erkenntnisgang durch die Grundprobleme der Dogmatik* (Berlin: Lettner-Verlag, 1951).

disregards "the determinative significance inherent in the distinctive features of the real, historical man Jesus of Nazareth" (34), especially his interwovenness with the Judaism of his time which — most crucially so for Pannenberg's view! — is essential for an understanding of Jesus' life and message. Third, a christology which presupposes the incarnation is out of the question because "one would have to stand in the position of God himself in order to follow the way of God's Son into the world" (35).[12] This stand point cannot be ours. Why not? Because, as Pannenberg axiomatically declares, — and this is another premise of his theological position —

> ... *we always think from the context of a historically determined human situation.* We can never leap over this limitation. Therefore our starting point must lie in the question about the man Jesus; only in this way can we ask about his divinity. *How the divine Logos, the Second Person of the Trinity, would be thought of apart from the incarnation and thus apart from the man Jesus completely escapes our imagination.* (35, italics mine)

Pannenberg emphasizes that the present situation requires us to start from "below" and that it was not simply a mistake of the historically predominant incarnational christology to proceed from "above". He elaborates this later in this work. The Barthian Otto Weber[13] contends that one cannot ascend from a given "below" toward an "above" without holding this "above" to be at least potentially also given in the "below" and that, following Pannenberg's way, one would know beforehand what the believer knows exclusively through his encounter with Jesus Christ.

---

[12] Of course, it would appear quite easy for the believer to do this from the standpoint of his own understanding, without claiming God's standpoint. However, Pannenberg's concern is with the *wissenschaftliche Verifikation* of the content of faith as far as possible. This for him is the task of theology. Our time in which authorities other than the empirical data of history and the sciences do not count unless they argue on the basis of such data, requires all who carry on *wissenschaftliche Theologie* to demonstrate what revelation is by means of the evidence. This relationship of theology to the sciences is extensively dealt with in Pannenberg's most recent book, as yet untranslated, *Wissenschaftstheorie und Theologie* (Frankfurt am Main: Suhrkamp, 1973), especially part II, pp. 225–442.

[13] Otto Weber, *Grundlagen der Dogmatik* (vol. ii; Neukirchen Krs. Moers: Verlag der Buchhandlung des Erziehungsvereins, 1962), pp. 26 ff. and 34 ff.

Against this Pannenberg points out (a) that Weber conceives of the "below" as of a generality and not of the historic singularity of the man Jesus, (b) that an understanding of the word "God" and the reality thereby designated is presupposed by Jesus and the early church and "must in one way or another be likewise presupposed by us if we ask about Jesus" (!) (36), but (c) that – and this is the pivotal contention, it seems – "What is inherently new and contingent in a historical occurrence, and especially in Jesus' history, nevertheless radically qualifies all foreknowledge, even the foreknowledge about God that is unavoidably presupposed." (36) Pannenberg goes on to say,

> Precisely for this reason, God has "met" men in Jesus in a way that is not the case otherwise, and one also cannot adequately grasp such differences of historical particularity as merely a matter of degree. A general idea of God and the word "God" related to this idea express only the human quest for God's reality. The particular way in which God's reality, about which one really has only the question in the general concept of God and in the word "God" which is related to this, confronts men historically through Jesus can only come into view in the light of the historical particularity of Jesus himself. (36)

It is for this reason that Pannenberg insists that, starting with the historical man Jesus, the first task of christology is not to feature the saving significance of Jesus but his unity with God. *"Every statement about Jesus taken independently from his relationship to God could result only in a crass distortion of his historical reality."* (36, italics mine) Pannenberg is concerned with "a total characterization of his (Jesus') appearance", and then "the decisive point lies in his relationship to God, or more precisely, to the God of Israel." (36)[14]

---

[14] Pannenberg distinguishes between a general concept of God, implied in man's quest for his destiny (future, wholeness; cf. chapter V) and the God of Israel who is the referent of Jesus' particular historical God-consciousness. The latter, for P., qualifies all presupposed concepts of God. Generally speaking, the anthropological basis for God verifies the reasonableness of a general concept of God. If we consider the God of Jesus, i.e. the God of Israel modified by Jesus' proclamation and resurrection, as the answer to the open question of God's reality, as it is implied in the general concept of God, we can do so only on the basis of the proven historical reality of Jesus' unity with this God.

In this procedure Pannenberg identifies with attempts in this direction in the ancient church, middle ages, and Luther. He chides rationalism for having lost interest in Jesus' unity with God in the sense of the christological dogma. Schleiermacher's way of verifying Jesus' divinity on the basis of his God-consciousness (Gottesbewußtsein) alone is dissatisfactory. The first to go Pannenberg's way in the 19th century was Albrecht Ritschl, and generally in this direction went the christological work of Wilhelm Herrmann, Werner Elert, Paul Althaus, Emil Brunner, in his revised christology, Friedrich Gogarten, Gerhard Ebeling, and Carl Heinz Ratschow. Differing with their solutions as to how to substantiate Jesus' divinity, Pannenberg identifies with their direction and principle: *the divinity of Jesus needs substantiation, it is not self-explanatory.* One important shibboleth for a correct method of substantiation for Pannenberg is that *Jesus' divinity does not consist of his saving significance for us.* Rather his saving significance proceeds from his identity! The contention that the New Testament "pronouncements about Jesus' divinity or deity are not, in fact, pronouncements of his nature but seek to give expression to his significance"[15] Pannenberg deems to be fallacious. Here Christology is reduced to soteriology, to the quest for Jesus "existential *Bedeutsamkeit*". For Pannenberg – this is another decisive feature of his position – *Jesus' unity with God is ontic, not merely functional,* and

> The divinity of Jesus remains the *presupposition* of his saving significance for us and, conversely, the saving significance of his divinity is the reason why we take *interest* in the question of his divinity. (38, italics by the author)

Highly significantly and revealing for his position, Pannenberg says about the neo-Protestant concepts of Jesus' salvific significance,

> ... one notices the modesty of its soteriological interest. The neo-Protestant theologians are concerned only with making possible the humanness of life in earth. They are no longer concerned with the conquest of death and with the theme of resurrection, and they deal with the question of the forgiveness of sins only in the sense that the possibility for every individual's overcoming sin derives

---

[15] Rudolf Bultmann, "The Christological Confession of the World Council of Churches", *Essays: Philosophical and Theological* (London: SCM Press, Ltd., 1955), p. 280.

from Jesus. Precisely because overcoming death through a transcendent being is not an issue here at all, one also cannot speak of a vicarious penal suffering of Jesus through which sin is overcome at a level that is inaccessible to us. (45)

To be sure, the soteriological interest is the starting point causing us to ask about Jesus' identity. *But it may not determine our quest. The salient point of the relationship between soteriology and christology is the historical justification of soteriological statements on the basis of Jesus' life, message, and destiny as far as historically validated.* When the soteriological interest, how meager ever in compass, dominates, it triggers the danger that one projects upon Jesus' figure *human desires* for salvation, deification, "of human striving after similarity to God, of the human duty to bring satisfaction for sins committed, of the human experience of bondage in failure, in the knowledge of one's own guilt and, most clearly in neo-Protestantism, projections of the idea of perfect religiosity, of perfect morality, of pure personality, of radical trust . . . The distinction between a Christ *principle* and its application to the historical *person* Jesus from Alois Emanuel Biedermann to Paul Tillich also lies along this line." (47, italics by the author)[16] To the suggestion that not the historical Jesus but merely his significance as the offer of a new *Existenzverständnis* for us is at issue[17], Pannenberg counters:

> Jesus possesses significance "for us" only to the extent that this significance is inherent in himself, in his history, and in his person constituted by this history. Only when this can be shown may we be sure that we are not merely attaching our questions, wishes, and thoughts to his figure . . . Soteriology must follow from Christology, not vice versa. Otherwise, faith in salvation itself loses any real foundation. (48)

---

[16] Pannenberg quotes Tillich's statement "Christology is a function of soteriology", *Systematic Theology*, vol. ii (Chicago: The University of Chicago Press, 1957), p. 150.

[17] Pannenberg mentions that Luther's *pro-me*-principle may not be referred to in order to justify this procedure. He follows the significant verdict of Hans Joachim Iwand in his article, "Wider den Mißbrauch des pro me als methodisches Prinzip in der Theologie", *Theologische Literaturzeitung*, LXXIX (1954), pp. 453–456.

4. A Preliminary Statement on Pannenberg's Presuppositions of his Epistemological Criteria

But is this procedure an option? First, is it possible to *know* anything about the historical Jesus beyond the "that" of the Christevent? Has not form criticism disclosed the thoroughgoing kerygmatic character of the New Testament material sources? Second, is it permissible to speak of a soteriological meaning for us as inherent in such a history of Jesus? Finally, would not knowledge of such soteriological meaning inherent in the history of Jesus jeopardize the Christian faith as such, replacing faith as trust in the word of the kerygma by reliance on known facts? Has not early dialectical theology rightly emphasized that all we encounter is the kerygma as it is proclaimed to us as a summons and a call to a decision, and that to believe means to accept this call obediently without *Hinterfragung*, and that to ask for a historical or any other verification of the kerygma amounts to its rejection, amounts to sinful search for *securitas* and thusly to man's missing out on the purpose and meaning of his existence (seine Existenzverfehlung)? Pannenberg is aware that he squarely opposes the premises of the theology of the Word or *theologia crucis* as Ernst Käsemann, for example, exposited it in a recent article.[18] The three questions asked above touch upon three issues in theology on which Pannenberg takes a very pronounced stand. The second question refers to the *relationship of a historical fact and its meaning*. Pannenberg holds that the separation of a fact "in itself" from its meaning "for us" is a result of the reduction by positivistic historiography of historical facts to *bruta facta* and of the Kantian dualism of things-in-themselves and their appearance to us. Here the appearance becomes independent and the *Ding-an-sich* becomes inaccessible. Pannenberg criticizes this stance, following Hegel's critique of Kant, and proposes his fundamental thesis of *the unity of a fact and its meaning in the original context of the fact in its Traditionsgeschichte* (history of the transmission of traditions) in which it occurred.

> The past reality of Jesus did not consist of brute facts in the positivistic sense, to which arbitrary interpretations, one as good as another, could be added. Rather, meaning already belongs to the

---

[18] Ernst Käsemann, "Die Heilsbedeutung des Todes Jesu nach Paulus", *Zur Bedeutung des Todes Jesu*, ed. Fritz Vierung (Gütersloh: Gerd Mohn, 1967), pp. 11–34.

activity and fate of Jesus in the original context in the history of traditions within which it occurred, from the perspective of which all subsequent, explicit interpretations can be judged. Thus, Christological research finds in the historical reality of Jesus the criterion for the critical examination of the Christological tradition and also the various soteriological concerns that have determined Christological presentations. (49)

The first question posed above refers to the problem of the extent to which the New Testament sources are authentic. Pannenberg denies that the ambiguity of the historical witness to the pre-Easter ministry and the Easter appearances of Jesus of Nazareth is so complete that no trustworthy statements can be made. He goes along with the contentions of such New Testament scholars as represent the so-called new quest of the historical Jesus-school, started by E. Käsemann in 1953,[19] according to whom historical-critical research yields a certain amount of definite knowledge about Jesus. And the most decisive knowledge which Pannenberg establishes in this context is the knowledge of the historical factuality of Christ's resurrection, interpreted in the light of *Traditionsgeschichte*.

The third question posed above touches upon the issue of the *relationship between knowledge and faith*. Pannenberg sees it, on the basis of his understanding of Luther and Melanchthon and for other reasons, as the relationship between trustworthy historical knowledge and its acceptance, on the one hand *(notitia historiae and assensus)*, and faith as trust and dedication of life to that which is thusly established *(fiducia)*, on the other. For a detailed discussion *vide infra*, chapter V, pp. 101–104.

From this it must be concluded that for Pannenberg the search for historical justification of any soteriological statement on the basis of what can be known of Jesus' life, message, and destiny is not only a possible option but indeed the solely permissible path for christological construction. To sum up this point: this thrust of Pannenberg's position is motivated by his conviction that theological statements about Jesus' significance may under no circumstances be *mere assertions*. The gist of by and large all historical and contemporary christologies is that in Jesus the destiny of man in general was fulfilled. However, this *must remain a mere belief unless the universal significance of Jesus is substantiated as derived*

---

[19] Ernst Käsemann, "The Problem of the Historical Jesus", *Essays on New Testament Themes*, pp. 15–47.

from God. This is why christology needs to be constructed prior to soteriology.

5. *The Hermeneutical Criterion: the Contemporary Wirklichkeitsverständnis*

One might say, that for Pannenberg the epistemological presupposition of a theological sentence is that it is based on what is historically known. Now a theological interpretation must also meet a hermeneutical criterion in order to be acceptable, viz., it must be comprehensible to and compatible with the present day *Wirklichkeitsverständnis*. (The two criteria are, to some extent, inseparable since what is historically known is surely also a matter of our present *Wirklichkeitsverständnis*.)

In order to understand Pannenberg's further procedure in his discussion of the atonement it is necessary to elucidate this point. To do so, I turn to the significance of Jesus' resurrection from the dead. As was mentioned above, Pannenberg considers it to be possible to establish it as a historical fact. But what does its historical facticity imply? In itself, the fact that someone was raised from the dead conveys no theological meaning. But it no doubt requires an extension of the possibilities with which historiography has to reckon in its research. It would invalidate the principle that "what is dead does not rise" with which much modern historical scholarship has from the outset denied the possibility of establishing the resurrection of Jesus historically. Now Pannenberg does not consider the resurrection of Jesus as an event by itself but — just as all historical events! — this event must be understood in its context of tradition history. *The context in which Jesus' resurrection occurred is the apocalyptic expectation of the resurrection of the dead as an eschatological event.* This expectation was shared by apocalyptic Judaism, Jesus, the disciples, and the early church in general. In this context Jesus' resurrection means: God raised Jesus from the dead, which in turn means: God has confirmed Jesus' message of the imminent coming of God's kingdom and the significance which, according to Jesus' claim, man's encounter with Jesus possesses for his participation in God's kingdom (cf. Luke 12:8 which Pannenberg deems to be an authentic saying of Jesus).

> Only the traditional expectation of the end of history rooted in apocalyptic gave Paul the opportunity of designating the particular

event that he experienced, as Jesus' other disciples had experienced it previously, as an event belonging to the category of resurrection life. Therefore, Paul called the expectation of a resurrection of the dead the presupposition for the recognition of Jesus' resurrection: "If the dead are not raised, then Christ has not been raised" (I. Cor. 15:16). (81)

Or he can say, "the expectation of resurrection must already be presupposed as a truth . . . when one speaks about Jesus' resurrection." (81) So far, then, historiography and *Traditionsgeschichte* have established what Jesus' resurrection means and must mean for people who share the apocalyptic beliefs of late Judaism. However, if the expectation of the resurrection of the dead is a presupposition for envisioning and correctly understanding the resurrection of Jesus, then the question comes to mind: How can people attain to this expectation for whom it is no part of their traditional, inherited truth — as it is not for Gentile Christians or modern man?

Does perhaps the fact of Jesus' resurrection first give rise to this expectation in the minds of Gentile converts? Pannenberg argues Jesus' resurrection "can strengthen *ex post facto* the truth of the expectation, but cannot establish it for the first time". (81)

> Admittedly, the general concept of the resurrection cannot altogether be established from Jesus' resurrection alone. Were that the meaning of Paul's argument, one would have to notice critically that Paul wants to deduce more from the message of Jesus' resurrection for the truth of the general idea of resurrection than can be obtained from it. Such an argument would run in a circle. (81)

Neither, for Pannenberg, *is the expectation of the resurrection of the dead proved to be true simply by the fact that according to Israelite-Jewish faith the dead shall rise because God so promised*. This seems to be of utmost importance for an accurate understanding of Pannenberg's position. Pannenberg does *not* argue: *Because in the context of Traditionsgeschichte* Jesus' resurrection proves that God raised him and confirmed his claim to truth, this is proved to be the case *for us also*. Had he argued in this fashion Pannenberg would have shifted the demand for blind faith, which dialectical theology ties to the present proclamation of the kerygma, merely to the acceptance of the apocalyptic tradition! In other words, we would need a foregoing faith in the accuracy and general truth of the latter. But this is not Pannenberg's course. The historical factuality of the Jewish apocalyptic expectation is one thing, its truth another. That in Israel and late Judaism God is considered as one who acts in this fashion in history is one thing, the universal truth of this facet of Israelite religious history another. Consequently and logically the decisive issue reads, "*Can the apocalyptic conceptual world still be binding for us?*" (82, italics mine). One can say without exaggeration that for Pannenberg the Christian faith is no option if this is not the case.

For (a) only in such a context does Jesus' resurrection mean anything, and (b) *only if we can reasonably and persuasively establish the truth of this expectation also for the present day world can Jesus' resurrection and consequently his message become meaningful for us*. The contention under (a) presents Pannenberg's conclusion from his historical studies.

> At any rate the primitive Christian motivation for Faith in Jesus as the Christ of God, in his exaltation, in his identification with the Son of Man, is essentially bound to the apocalyptic expectation for the end of history to such an extent that one must say that *if the apocalyptic expectation should be totally excluded from the realm of possibility for us, then the early Christian faith in Christ is also excluded*; then, however, the continuity would be broken between that which might still remain as Christianity after such a reduction and Jesus himself, together with the primitive Christian proclamation through Paul's time. One must be clear about the fact that *when one discusses the truth of the apocalyptic expectation of a future judgment and a resurrection of the dead, one is dealing with the basis of the Christian faith*. Why the man Jesus can be the ultimate revelation of God, why in him and only in him God is supposed to have appeared, *remains incomprehensible apart from the horizon of the apocalyptic expectation*. (82f., italics mine)

For this reason the eschatologization or, rather, de-eschatologization of the kerygma in the theology of Rudolf Bultmann where "eschatological" becomes descriptive of the present existential moment of summons and obedient decision with no reference to a concrete, temporal future amounts, in Pannenberg's judgment, to an unacceptable de-historization and mythologization of christology.

> The basis of the knowledge of Jesus' significance remains bound to the original apocalyptic horizon of Jesus' history which at the same time has also been modified by this history. If this horizon is eliminated, the basis of faith is lost; then Christology becomes mythology and no longer has true continuity with Jesus himself and with the witness of the apostles. (83)

But can we share this horizon? Only if so (cf. contention b) is the Christian faith accessible to us. How does Pannenberg want to verify the viability of the expectation of the resurrection of the dead today?

> Whether or not the apocalyptic expectation of a resurrection of the dead can still have binding validity as truth today may be decided by *its relation to an understanding of man consistent with the approach and results of a way of thinking that is engaged with all presently accessible phenomena*. Does a meaningful relation exist here — perhaps even a relation that is *indispensable to a sober understanding of the human situation* — or not? (83, italics mine)

Even more stringently Pannenberg says with respect to the transformation of the Greek concept of the Logos as the divine world law on the basis of the perception of Jesus' installation as the eschatological pantokrator: "As in other areas, it must be shown whether the Christian transformation *can be subsequently justified by its opening up of the understanding of the whole of reality that we experience in common with all other men more profoundly than every philosophical point of departure.*" (394, italics mine) This then is the second criterion of a legitimate theological interpretation of any locus of doctrine: Does the interpretation agree with the sumtotal of accessible phenomena? Does it offer an even better understanding of all known reality than any other philosophical starting point?

This concern is expressed also in the context of Pannenberg's effort to establish the truth that Jesus, as the self-revelation of God, is divine and his mission and activity is universally valid. Here Pannenberg says,

> In fact, Jesus can be the ultimate revelation of the one God only if the true relation of men and of their world to God has been entirely brought to light by his actions and fate. *If essential elements of our experience of reality with its ultimate questions do not receive an answer from the figure of Jesus, then we live without Jesus and without the God revealed in him in those areas.* This would call into

question the universal divinity of the God of the Bible as he is revealed by Jesus as the Father. (235, italics mine)

How Pannenberg establishes the contemporary truth of the apocalyptic expectation of the resurrection of the dead will be discussed in a later chapter (*vide infra*, chapter V). Suffice it to say here that his arguments derive from modern anthropology and especially a phenomenology of hope. The following quotation may once more demonstrate Pannenberg's concern and concomitant method.

> ... the expectation of a resurrection from the dead need not appear meaningless from the presuppositions of modern thought, but rather it is to be established as a philosophically appropriate expression for human destiny. Thus, precisely today a continuity of our thought with the apocalyptic hope again has become possible at a decisive point, and with this also a continuity with the primitive Christian perception of the event of Jesus' resurrection. (88)

6. *The Application of the Epistemological Criterion to Jesus' Death*

We now return to Pannenberg's exposition of his understanding of the atonement. Again we hear his significant sentence,

> The typological relating of Jesus' death to expiatory sacrifice, covenant sacrifice, and the Passover mean something for us only if Jesus' own path to the cross contains a vicarious element and if the common human situation of selfish entanglement in personal concerns designated with the term "sin" is thereby transformed and can be convincingly presented as having been transformed. (250)

This statement points to both of the criteria discussed: An interpretation is truthful, and thus legitimate, if it coincides with the history of Jesus and if it is meaningful for the present day understanding of reality. With regard to the particular formulation of the above statement one might almost say, its truth must be empirically testable by the difference it makes to reality (here the reality of sin which Pannenberg, in accord with his theological criteria, interprets as "the common human situation of selfish entanglement in personal concerns", his rendering of the traditional *peccatum originale* and *actuale*). And both demands can be met. The concept of expiation, attached to Jesus in various ways in the tradition, is "most easily accessible for us today" (250) in terms of the image of the just man who suffers vicariously for his people. For this concept is not tied to the idea of a specifically *cultic* substitution and sacrifice which Pannenberg considers to possess a special problematic. To establish its validity, though, demands a basis in "the unique character of his (Jesus') own course" (250f.). What basis is there? Three things are pointed out:

(1) Jesus himself may have been familiar with the image mentioned above through the prophetic-apocalyptic theology of suffering. He may have stood in this tradition.[20]

(2) There are references to Jesus' innocence II Cor. 5:21; I Peter 2:21 ff.; 3:18. "However, it is not sufficient to convince us of the substitutionary and expiatory character of Jesus' death. It is clear that we cannot judge every subjectively innocent death as having the character of vicarious expiation." (251)

(3) Jesus' sinlessness has to be understood so as to include conflict with the law. For Paul asserts that Jesus was under the curse of the law. Consequently Pannenberg regards an investigation of Jesus' conflict with the law and its relation to his death necessary to arrive at reliable evidence for the question of a substitutionary expiatory significance of his death.

---

[20] Pannenberg bases this assumption on the study by Dietrich Rössler, *Gesetz und Geschichte* (Neukirchen Krs. Moers: Verlag der Buchhandlung des Erziehungsvereins, 1960), pp. 88 ff.

CHAPTER II

JESUS' DIVINITY ESTABLISHED

1. The Proleptic Character of Jesus' Pre-Easter Ministry

In order to better understand the procedure and results of this proposed investigation it seems advisable to first relate Pannenberg's view of Jesus' earthly life and resurrection and their significance for a demonstration of Jesus' divinity more fully. For Jesus' death is preceded by his earthly ministry and succeeded by his resurrection, and both shed light on his death. And Jesus' identity, as we saw, is of significance for the question of the salvific meaning of his life, work, and cross.

Jesus' divinity can be known, and it *must* be known if reliable soteriological conclusions are to be drawn from it. How is it known?

Even before New Testament scholarship renewed its interest in the continuity between the historical Jesus and the church's kerygma about Christ systematic theology had argued for the necessity of the legitimation of the kerygma through the pre-Easter Jesus.[1] Pannenberg agrees with the thesis of the majority of exegetical scholars that the christological titles were conferred on Jesus by the early church as a consequence of their faith, but that the claim which Jesus raised for his significance through his message and work preceded the faith of his disciples. As a historian, Rudolf Bultmann affirms that there is a christology implied in Jesus' claim[2] but, as a theologian, denies its importance. The kerygma needs no legitimation by a recourse to the historical Jesus, he says. But precisely the contrary assumption animates the new quest of Bultmann's pupils and others.

> Only if Jesus' proclamation decisively coincides with the proclamation about Jesus is it understandable, reasonable, and necessary that the Christian kerygma in the New Testament conceals the message of Jesus. From this perspective we are required,

---

[1] Pannenberg discusses the various positions of W. Elert, G. Bornkamm, P. Althaus, A. Ritschl, E. Brunner, F. Gogarten, C. H. Ratschow, H. Diem, R. Bultmann, E. Fuchs, H. Conzelmann, U. Wilckens, H. E. Tödt, H. Braun, F. Hahn, W. Marxsen, et al., pp. 53–66 of *Jesus-God and Man*.

[2] Rudolf Bultmann, *Theology of the New Testament*, vol. i, p. 43.

precisely as historians, to inquire behind Easter . . . By this means we shall learn whether he stands behind the word of his church or not, whether the Christian kerygma is a myth that can be detached from his word and from himself or whether it binds us historically and insolubly to him.[3]

While Käsemann sees Jesus' claim in his message, Ernst Fuchs concentrates on Jesus' conduct as the real context of his preaching. He points to Jesus' fellowship with sinners and people of disreputable professions and to the fact that Jesus anticipated the eschatological meal which, according to tradition, was a matter of the future and reserved for the righteous and celebrated it with them. These meals enact the message of Jesus' parables; in Jesus' conduct of love for sinners the kingdom of God was already present.[4] Pannenberg also quotes the church historian Hans von Campenhausen,

> With the forgiveness of sins Jesus not only set himself against the law that was valid, . . . but he directly assumed the place in which only God can stand according to Jewish faith and knowledge.[5]

Furthermore, the work of G. Bornkamm shows that Jesus' claim resulted from the *presence of the expected eschatological future* in Jesus' activity. Pannenberg approvingly quotes Bornkamm's statement, "To make the reality of God present, this is the essential mystery of Jesus."[6] Jesus' horizon is the horizon of apocalyptic. H. Conzelmann agrees that Jesus stands in the apocalyptic tradition and that the element of future in his message can not be denied. Contrary to Bornkamm, however, he argues that for Jesus this horizon plays no role. In Conzelmann's view, for Jesus

---

[3] Ernst Käsemann, "Probleme neutestamentlicher Arbeit in Deutschland", *Die Freiheit des Evangeliums und die Ordnung der Gesellschaft* (Munich: Chr. Kaiser Verlag, 1952), p. 151.

[4] Ernst Fuchs, *Das urchristliche Sakramentsverständnis* (Schriftenreihe der kirchlich-theologischen Sozietät i. Württemberg, 8; Bad Cannstatt: R. Müllerschön Verlag, 1958), pp. 37ff.

[5] H. v. Campenhausen, *Kirchliches Amt und geistliche Vollmacht in den ersten drei Jahrhunderten*.

[6] Günter Bornkamm, *Jesus of Nazareth* (New York: Harper & Row, Publ., Inc., 1960), p. 62.

God's presence is all in the present.[7] Here, Pannenberg judges, "Jesus' claim to be the presence of God is absolutized." (58) And: "As much as it is to be granted to Conzelmann that what is expected in the future in Jewish tradition has been 'anticipated' in Jesus' activity, the reduction of Jesus' temporal statements to an existential meaning of immediate encounter with the Kingdom of God must be judged as a deactivation of the tension between the 'already' and the 'not yet' in Jesus' message." (58) Pannenberg is persuaded by Bornkamm and Wilckens[8] and holds: The futuristic aspect may not be eliminated or interpreted away; the present is dominated by Jesus' claim to authority, his message that the kingdom of God is close at hand, and his call to a decision in his presence which is decisive for the future judgment of the Son of Man; the futurity of the end and the finality of the present decision are in tension with each other. This tension *"definitely leaves room for the question about the verification of Jesus' claim"* (58) and shows — this is one of the key concepts of Pannenberg's thought! — *the proleptic character of Jesus' claim.*

The claim is proleptic because it requires a substantiation, authorization, and legitimation which it does not possess at the time Jesus makes it but which it will receive only from the future. In other words, Jesus' claim is in need of God's *confirmation* and *verification*. An important piece of evidence for Pannenberg's contention is the saying Luke 12:8, "And I tell you, everyone who acknowledges me before men, the Son of man also will acknowledge before the angels of God." In a lengthy and thorough debate with the leading German New Testament scholars about the authenticity of this Jesus-saying, Pannenberg, mainly in agreement with R. Bultmann, G. Bornkamm, H. Braun, H. E. Tödt, and F. Hahn and against Ph. Vielhauer, E. Schweizer, E. Käsemann, and W. Marxsen, argues for the genuineness of this saying mainly because "All versions of the saying, with the exception of Matt. 10:32f., have in common that Jesus distinguishes the Son of Man from himself as a different figure. This constitutes the most important argument for the age of the saying: after Easter such a distinction

---

[7] P. refers to Conzelmann's article "Gegenwart und Zukunft in der synoptischen Tradition", *Zeitschrift f. Theol. u. Kirche*, LIV (1957), pp. 286ff. and "Jesus Christus", *Religion in Geschichte u. Gegenwart*, III, 3d ed., pp. 619ff.

[8] Ulrich Wilckens, "Das Offenbarungsverständnis in der Geschichte des Urchristentums", *Offenbarung als Geschichte* (Göttingen: Vandenhoeck & Ruprecht, 1961), pp. 42–90, esp. pp. 58ff.

between Jesus and the judge at the end of the age would no longer have been formulated." (59)

Salvation is proleptically – not consummationwise – present in Jesus, "namely as anticipation of the future verdict. This is the proleptic structure of Jesus' claim." (60) For its interpretation Pannenberg points to the corresponding relationship between the visions of an apocalyptic or God's prophetic word in the Old Testament, on the one hand, and history or, respectively, the future, on the other.

> The prophets received words that must be confirmed by their future fulfillment, and thereby must be shown to be Yahweh's words. The apocalyptic's view of history, which also grasped future events before they occurred, required confirmation by the actual course of the events themselves. (61)

Does this correspondence in structure between Jesus, apocalyptic visions, and Old Testament prophecy mean that Jesus was an apocalyptic? Pannenberg affirms profound differences between the two. He lists four differences all of which explain why Jesus did not use a pseudonym but presented his message in his own name.

(a) He is fully aware of bringing something new.

(b) Like John the Baptist he perhaps expects the end to be imminent, thus did not elaborately describe its coming but merely called to repentance.

(c) In him the eschatological salvation, even though in need of confirmation, *was present*.

(d) With him "the end is not only seen in advance, but it has happened in advance." (61) Pannenberg concludes that this explains why in Jesus' message the apocalyptic pictures of the eschatological drama are secondary and scarce. "Apocalyptic remains, nevertheless, the intellectual context of the Baptist's preaching of repentance as well as of the proleptic occurrence of God's rule through Jesus." (61)

For Pannenberg's construction the decisive point of identity between Jesus' claim and apocalyptic visions or prophetic predictions is the need of future confirmation. None of these is valid on its own account! *But of what does Jesus' confirmation consist?*

First of all, discussing the pericopes Mark 8:11f., Matt. 12:38–42; 16:1–4; Luke 11:16. 29–32; 12:54–56, Pannenberg concludes on account of Matt. 11:5f. and Luke 11:20 that Jesus' rejection of a sign of his authority did not mean that "Jesus had rejected any legitimation at all as a presupposition for recognizing his mission" (64) Jesus could point and did point to his mighty deeds as something confirming his authority. Still, these confirmed his claim only to a certain extent. Pannenberg distinguishes, "Jesus' deeds could point to the beginning of the time of salvation, but they could not show unambiguously whether Jesus personally was the one in whom salvation or judgment are ultimately decided." (64) Jesus' claim centered in the statement that a man's survival or judgment at the end of time would be decided on the basis of this man's attitude to Jesus in the present. Consequently a complete and univocal verification of Jesus' claim could transpire only in the future eschaton itself! In fact, Jesus himself could not offer this final seal – because it concerned the legitimation of his own person and because only God himself could bring about the end of history. Jesus expected this end to come in the near future. On this account ". . . it must have been of secondary significance for Jesus whether he himself would have to endure death before the end came. The truth of his proclamation did not need to depend on this." (66)

Our question, How is Jesus' divinity known? thus receives the answer: It is not known through Jesus' claim to authority. The latter is in need of verification. This, for Pannenberg, is not only a theological position but a historical fact. For Jesus himself thought so. Therefore his claim, and faith in it, are no adequate basis for a christology. To prevent christological statements from being only assertions to be believed and to found christology on known fact, something other than Jesus' claim must be the foundation. This other is its confirmation by God. But *how can Jesus' divinity be known if, in order to be known, it needs God's confirmation and this confirmation takes place only at the occurrence of the end of history?*

2. *The Resurrection of Jesus as God's Confirmation of Jesus' Identity*

It is in answer to this problem that *Jesus' resurrection* receives its full significance in Pannenberg's thought. Those confronted with Jesus' resurrection had to understand it as the beginning of the universal resurrection of the dead and thus the commencement of the eschatological drama promised partly by prophecy, and expected by the apocalyptic. Pannenberg is of course aware that promise and fulfillment or expectation and factual events did not entirely match since only Jesus himself was raised. He rightly says that for the second generation it was clear "that Jesus' resurrection was *not* yet this beginning but some special event which happened to Jesus alone" (66) and that the more the tension between the present and the yearning for the future consummation was lost, the less was the resurrection of Jesus interpreted in the horizon of the eschatological drama. Still, Pannenberg is persuaded that (1) the significance inherent in the resurrection is that the eschaton now begins, and (2) that the resurrection of Jesus originally had this significance for the first generation. "For Jesus' Jewish contemporaries, insofar as they shared the apocalyptic expectation, the occurrence of the resurrection did not first need to be interpreted, but for them it spoke meaningfully in itself: If such a thing had happened, one could no longer doubt what it meant." (67) Here a critical question comes to mind. *If this is the case how is it to be explained that not all Jews who shared the traditional apocalyptic hopes took Jesus' resurrection as such a signal?* Did his resurrection perhaps remain the private knowledge of a few? Or was the single resurrection of one man too different from the expected universal resurrection as to be able to be conceived as the start of the general resurrection? Or did Jesus' destiny on the cross perhaps forbid it for a pious Jew to view him as the divine messenger, Son of Man, Messiah, or the like? These questions will have to be clarified. They are crucial for Pannenberg's position, to be sure. To further follow Pannenberg's argument, he is certain that because of the context of *Traditionsgeschichte* in which Jesus rose from the dead his resurrection had the following significance: With it the end of the world has begun. If he rose God raised him. If God raised him he thereby confirmed Jesus' pre-Easter activity. In the light of the suffering of the righteous and the prophets Jesus' suffering and death did not necessarily put him in the wrong. Yet they constituted *no conclusive confirmation* of Jesus' identity and authority.[9] Jesus' resurrection suggested to the witnesses of Jesus' pre-Easter claim and message that *the Son of Man whose coming some of the apocalyptic tradition and Jesus expected and foretold "is none other than the man Jesus who will come again."* (68, italics mine) If Jesus' resurrection means the beginning of the end events and, if not for all men, still for Jesus and in Jesus the end has already occurred, *then the ultimate is already present in him*. And this – so Pannenberg extrapolates – means, "God himself, his glory, has made its

---

[9] Against Friedrich Mildenberger, "Auferstanden am dritten Tage nach den Schriften", *Evangelische Theologie*, XXIII (1963), pp. 265–280.

appearance in Jesus in a way that cannot be surpassed. Only because the end of the world is already present in Jesus' resurrection is God himself revealed in him." (69)

This, then, is the cornerstone of Pannenberg's christology. Here it is known who Jesus was and is. In Hellenistic terminology and conceptuality it means that in Jesus God himself has appeared in the world. "God himself — or God's revelatory figure, the Logos, the Son — has been among us as a man in the figure of Jesus." (69) When the Palestinian tradition was translated into the Syrian sphere eschatology became epiphany. For Hellenistic thinking revelation means epiphany, and this concept of revelation prepared the later doctrines of the incarnation and of the true divinity of Jesus.

We note that Pannenberg made three pivotal decisions in order to arrive at this interpretation of the significance of Jesus' resurrection. (1) He thinks it is cogent to assume that Jesus' resurrection signifies the in-breaking of the future eschaton, the ultimate consummation of history, even though it is *only its beginning*, even though what is awaited occurs only in the instance of *one man*. Pannenberg does not simply put up with this gap but interprets it positively as evidence for his thesis that the fulfillment never merely meets the expectation but always also transcends and changes and reforges the expectation. (2) He extrapolates the appearance of God himself in the person of Jesus from the fact that God raised him and that in this event Jesus' message of the coming kingdom is confirmed and the end has partly begun. (3) He postulates that God's appearance in Jesus cannot be surpassed in order to gain a basis for his contention that God revealed himself in Jesus. For his concept of God's self-revelation which will be discussed later on includes the idea of completeness, ultimacy, and unsurpassability. The later discussion will show that this postulate will appear to be in tension with, if not contradiction to, Pannenberg's thought that *all* events, except for the universal consummation of the future, are proleptic and consequently preliminary and that what a thing really is will be revealed only in the future, and that this — as Pannenberg *expressis verbis* said — is true also of God himself.[10]

Of course, it must not be forgotten that the resurrection by itself cannot establish the truth of the apocalyptic expectations or of anything Jesus'

---

[10] We will consider the *mode* of God's presence in Jesus and the character of Jesus' unity with God in chapter III.

resurrection signifies in the context of these expectations. For Pannenberg, Jesus' resurrection has this significance only for people who by tradition or other means, today especially anthropology and philosophy, *share* this expectation! When we speak of the knowledge about Jesus' identity which his resurrection provides this must be kept in mind. It is no unpremised knowledge. However, for Pannenberg, the premises themselves for us today are available in the realm of knowledge. Therefore one can speak of knowledge without reservation.

3. The Resurrection of Jesus as Abrogation of the Law

We now return to Pannenberg's discussion of the significance of Jesus' resurrection. In the following point for the first time a facet of this significance is named which rises from the particular kind of Jesus' death, viz., his death as the crucified and rejected one. *"The transition to the Gentile mission is motivated by the eschatological resurrection of Jesus as resurrection of the crucified One."* (70, para.e) Pointing out the biblical and historical facts, Pannenberg agrees with Joachim Jeremias[11] that the dominant conception in post-exilic Judaism "regarded the Gentiles simply as godless and ... hoped for the time of God's vengeance on Israel's oppressors and their final annihilation at the arrival of the Messianic Kingdom" (70), that a minority, though, held fast to the promises of some psalms, II Isa., Ezekiel, and the tradition of the election of David and Zion that *ultimately all nations* will serve Yahweh and his messiah, and that Jesus expected God to include the Gentiles into his people by an eschatological act of power at the end of time. The *mission* to the Gentiles, however, did not arise from Jesus' message but from and after his resurrection, so Pannenberg argues against Jeremias and F. Hahn.[12] For Jesus' resurrection was understood as his elevation to Lordship in heaven, and this news had to be proclaimed everywhere. And Paul – and this is the salient point here – had interpreted Jesus as the end of the law, viewing his crucifixion as the curse of the law and his resurrection as abrogation of the law as a way to salvation by God himself (*vide supra* p. 10).

---

[11] Joachim Jeremias, *Jesus' Promise to the Nations* (Studies in Biblical Theology, 24; Alec R. Allenson, Inc., 1958), p. 41.
[12] Ferdinand Hahn, *Mission in the New Testament* (London: SCM Press, Ltd., 1965), pp. 40ff.

> Thus, even though the transition to the Gentile mission does not represent a direct consequence of the significance inherent in Jesus' resurrection by itself, it was inevitable as soon as Jesus' resurrection was understood in its connection with the crucifixion as the expression of his rejection by Israel (cf. Rom. 11:11ff. and Acts 13:45). (72)

Finally, the significance inherent in Jesus' resurrection as discussed coined the words which the early church transmitted as the words of the risen Christ. These words are an explication of this significance. "Paul's gospel . . . is the exegesis of the appearance of the resurrected Jesus that he experienced." (73)

For Pannenberg's theology this is an important clue and attains to principal significance. Event and word in the resurrection appearances form a unity. The resurrection or, respectively, the appearances of the risen are no brute facts without significance, or else with certainty the origin of faith would not be understandable from these events. The resurrection of one man means nothing in itself. "But that event had its own meaning within its sphere in the history of traditions: the beginning of the end, the confirmation and exaltation of Jesus by God himself, the ultimate demonstration of the divinity of Israel's God as the one God of all men. Only thus can Jesus' resurrection be the basis of faith without being supplemented by an external interpretation added to it." (73).

These considerations are of principal importance because they are the ground for Pannenberg's conviction that *the historical events in their traditionsgeschichtlichem Zusammenhang speak for themselves and are in no need of supplementation by a word revealed apart from that Zusammenhang that discloses their meaning*, whether at that time or in the present, when a man is called to faith in Jesu Christ. In this sense salvation is knowable. How this knowledge is related to faith and what faith, then, can mean, will have to be investigated later. Contrary to the resurrection of Jesus his crucifixion, on account of the absence of a univocal crucifixion tradition in Israelite-Jewish history, was obscure and uncanny and had to be interpreted. We had begun following Pannenberg's effort of tracing and evaluating these interpretations (*vide supra* p. 22f.) and will resume this task. Before doing so we should note what conception of resurrection of the dead Pannenberg advocates in order to understand his thinking.

4. What Does the Conception Resurrection of the Dead Mean?

The following can perhaps characterize Pannenberg's position:

(a) When the early Christian witnesses use the expression "resurrection from the dead" they do not mean just a random miracle but "a very particular reality expected by postexilic Judaism in connection with the end of history" (74)

(b) "To speak about the resurrection of the dead is not comparable to speaking about any random circumstance that can be identified empirically at any time." (74) It is a metaphor. An image of a thiswordly occurrence, viz., the waking and rising from sleep, is used to express, as a parable, a destiny which itself is yet completely unknown. The intended reality is essentially different from the mode of language used to express it. We cannot know this reality as we know objects scientifically or experience life now, this side of death. However, "metaphorical" for Pannenberg does not mean void of a reality which to a definite degree coincides with what the image of the metaphor conveys. *To be sure, the intended reality is essentially different from the mode of language used, but at the same time this and no other metaphor conveys however much of the new reality is to be comprehended in the old reality of the present.* Pannenberg therefore does not speak of the concept of resurrection as of an *Interpretament*, as W. Marxsen does. An *Interpretament* is a random image or metaphor used *ad libitum* to convey the meaning of something. For Marxsen[13] primitive Christianity expressed its belief that Jesus' relevance continued after his crucifixion by the use of the familiar apocalyptic concept of resurrection: he is alive, his cause continues. Pannenberg rather speaks of an *absolute metaphor*.[14] The *tertium*, i. e. the element of truth in the parable of waking from sleep, is that what was dead will live. This will need further explication.

(c) The early church did not mean – as the literal reading of the expression resurrection implies – a revivification of the corpse. "For Paul, resurrection means the new life of a new body, not the return of life into a dead but not yet decayed fleshly body." (75) The new body is not fleshly but spiritual (cf. I Cor. 15:35-56). Pannenberg calls the Pauline relationship

---

[13] Willi Marxsen, *Die Auferstehung Jesu als historisches und theologisches Problem* (Stuttgart: W. Kohlhammer Verlag, 1964), pp. 21 ff.

[14] W. Pannenberg, "Analogie und Doxologie", *Grundfragen systematischer Theologie*, (Göttingen: Vandenhoeck & Ruprecht, 1967), p. 200, n. 35.

between the physical and the spiritual body a "radical transformation". Nothing will remain unchanged, no substantial or structural continuity will connect the new with the old existence. *Still it is a transformation of and an occurrence to the physical body* and, Pannenberg argues with W. G. Kümmel against Bultmann,[15] ". . . *there is a historical continuity in the sense of continuous transition in the consummation of the transformation itself.* The expression 'historical continuity' here means only that connection between the beginning and the end point which resides in the process of transformation itself, regardless of how radically this process may be conceived." (76, italics mine)

For Pannenberg, speaking about Jesus' resurrection rests on a *Rückschluß* (inference, induction) from the appearances of Jesus to his life.

> Der Rückschluß geht aus von den *Erscheinungen* des lebendigen Herrn. Das bedeutet aber nicht, wie Willi Marxsen behauptet hat, man könne diesen Rückschluß beliebig durch andere 'Interpretamente' der Erscheinungen ersetzen. *Vielmehr hat der Rückschluß eine innere Notwendigkeit:* Wenn Jesus (nachdem er tot war) jetzt lebt, dann ist er – bevor er als Lebendiger zum erstenmal gesehen worden ist – entweder wiederbelebt oder aber (wenn die Art seines jetzigen Lebens das ausschließt und sein Tod zweifelsfrei feststeht) zu einem anderen "Leben" verwandelt worden.[16] (italics 4th line mine)

The kind of this life is unknown and as yet unknowable. Therefore "life" here is a metaphor. But it is an irreplaceable metaphor because the resurrection is ". . . ein Jesus, und zwar den *toten* Jesus, betreffendes Ereignis – ein Ereignis, das jedenfalls bedeutet, daß Jesus danach nicht mehr tot war."[17] Pannenberg thusly more specifically qualifies the term "metaphor" when used for the resurrection of Jesus or the universal resurrection. An "absolute" metaphor is one "that can no longer be displaced and outbid by concepts in the strict sense of that term." What is expressed through such absolute metaphors will be known only in "the

---

[15] W. G. Kümmel, in Lietzmann, *An die Korinther I/II*, p. 195, against Bultmann, *Theology of the New Testament*, vol. i, p. 198.

[16] W. Pannenberg, "Dogmatische Erwägungen zur Auferstehung Jesu", *Kerygma u. Dogma*, 14. Jg., 1968, 2. Quartalsheft, p. 111.

[17] *Ibid.* p. 113.

What Does the Conception Resurrection of the Dead Mean? 35

future expected and hoped for by men . . . . because only in that final future can God be known by us as he has revealed himself."[18] And Pannenberg qualifies "metaphorical" still in a second fashion. To overcome the merely metaphorical sense of "life" in connection with the concept resurrection of the dead or resurrection life Pannenberg intimates an extension and transcending of the familiar meaning-content (Bezeichnungssinn) of "life" and the forming of a new conception.

> Wäre es nicht möglich, einen Begriff des "Lebens" zu bilden, innerhalb dessen unser organisches und . . . todverfallenes Leben *nur einen speziellen Fall darstellt?* Ja, hat nicht sogar Paulus einen solchen Begriff von Leben bzw. σῶμα besessen? Ein solcher Lebensbegriff *wäre zwar nicht durchweg empirisch kontrollierbar,* er wäre vielleicht auch durch Ausweitung eines engeren Begriffes von Leben und insofern durch einen Übertragungsvorgang entstanden, *aber seine Gegenstandsintention, sein Bezeichnungssinn wäre nicht mehr metaphorisch.* (Italics mine)[19]

(d) Paul understands Jesus' resurrection as shown under c. His statements about his encounter with the risen Jesus, the only direct report of a man who had seen the resurrected one in the New Testament, leave no doubt that Paul conceived of the risen one as "a reality of an entirely different sort." (77)

> This leads to the conclusion that one must sharply distinguish the resurrection of the dead in the Christian hope for the future from those resuscitations of corpses which are otherwise reported occasionally in ancient literature as especially marvelous miracles, even from the resuscitations accomplished by Jesus himself . . . Quite apart from the question of the credibility of such more or less late and legendary traditions, it is certain in any case that these narratives themselves have in mind an event of a different kind from that reported by the witnesses to Jesus' resurrection and that of the primitive Christian hope for the future. (77)

(e) However, Paul's understanding of resurrection does not simply rest on his encounter with the risen Jesus but is informed by the hope for the

---

[18] W. Pannenberg, "Analogy and Doxology", *Basic Questions in Theology*, vol. i, (Philadelphia: Fortress Press, 1970) p. 236, n.
[19] W. Pannenberg, "Dogmatische Erwägungen zur Auferstehung Jesu", p. 113

future in postexilic Judaism which was derived from apocalyptic. Here different forms of traditions embodied different concepts of resurrection. For Paul, resurrection will *happen to the believers and as such possesses saving character!* This is true also of Jesus' thought. Pannenberg finds the understanding of future resurrection as the content of salvation in Isa. 26:7ff. Enoch 22, the later Pharisaic party except for Hillel and Shammai, Syr. Baruch 30:1-5, Ps. Sal. 3:12. Pannenberg observes that the question what kind of transformation the transition from the old life to the new would entail became acute only in the first century A. D., e. g., in Syr. Bar. 50f. But contrary to the distinction one finds there between resurrection and transformation, Paul takes both *as a single event.* So also Jesus, Mark 12:25. Consequently — and this is important for Pannenberg's thesis —

> . . . the idea that a transformation is connected with the resurrection of the dead . . . is in no way a specifically primitive Christian or even Pauline understanding in contrast to the "orthodox" Jewish resurrection faith. It is a false generalization . . . that orthodox Jewish faith expected a mere resuscitation. Precisely with regard to the concept of transformation, primitive Christianity and especially Paul thought traditionally; and that Paul identifies resurrection and transformation, in distinction from Syr. Baruch, derives meaningfully from his opinion that the resurrection would be given to the believers only, while Baruch had expected a double resurrection to salvation and judgment. (80f.)

Both, then, the connection of transformation with resurrection and the qualitative difference between the resurrection life as imperishable and the present life as perishable has Jewish parallels. It is thus established:

> Only the traditional expectation of the end of history rooted in apocalyptic gave Paul the opportunity of designating the particular event that he experienced, as Jesus' other disciples had experienced it previously, as an event belonging to the category of resurrection life. (81) (*Vide supra* page 19)

Now one might raise the question: if the apocalyptic tradition, shared by Jesus, Paul, probably all the disciples, and the early Palestinian church, in such a way as described prefigurates and in advance defines the conception "resurrection from the dead" and if at any rate the understanding of Jesus' resurrection presupposes the expectation of the resurrection, is it not probable that the disciples, as e.g. Marxsen thinks, merely ascribed resurrection to Jesus in order to interpret their faith in his lasting relevance with a tool which they had at their disposal? Everything Pannenberg said about the significance of Jesus' resurrection, its place and function, *premises its historicity*! The latter needs to be established.

5. *The Evidence for the Historicity of Jesus' Resurrection*

How does Pannenberg establish the historicity of Jesus' resurrection? We limit the exposition of his treatment of "Jesus' Resurrection as a Historical Problem" (88 ff.) to a brief description of procedure, highlighting the results and key tenets. The Biblical Easter traditions form two complexes: one centers on the appearances of the risen Lord, the other on the empty tomb. Pannenberg examines them consecutively.

A. The Appearances

The Gospel reports of Jesus' appearances are strongly legendary and "one can scarcely find a historical kernel of their own in them." (89) Pannenberg concentrates on Paul's statements I Cor. 15: 1–11.

(a) Paul intends to give proof of the facticity of the resurrection by naming witnesses.

(b) The opinion (of, e.g., Hans Grass[20]) that Paul is not disinterested in his historical inquiry and thus does not offer what can be estimated as historical proof in the modern sense is faulty. *There is no inquiry without a pre-understanding and interest* although "such an interest certainly cannot be permitted to prejudice the results." (89)

(c) Paul writes close to the events themselves and uses formulations coined even previously; ". . . the assumption that appearances of the resurrected Lord were really experienced by a number of members of the primitive Christian community and not perhaps freely invented in the course of later legendary development has good historical foundation." (91)

---

[20] Hans Grass, Ostergeschehen und Osterberichte (3d ed.; Göttingen: Vandenhoeck & Ruprecht, 1964), p. 96, n.l.

(d) The thesis that parallels in the history of religions are responsible for the emergence of the early Christian message of Christ's resurrection is unconvincing. Pannenberg adduces the judgments of J. Leipoldt,

> One cannot doubt that the disciples were convinced that they had seen the resurrected Lord. Otherwise the origin of the community in Jerusalem and with it of the church becomes an enigma.[21]

and of G. Kittel according to whom "hardly the slightest traces" of cults of dying and rising gods can be found in the Palestine of the first century A.D. This means that we have to reckon with appearances actually experienced by the disciples. But of what kind were those experiences? Paul presupposes I Cor. 15 that the appearance imparted to him and to the other apostles were of the same kind. Pannenberg accepts this as a premise and takes Paul's descriptions Gal. 1:12 and 16f. as normative for the accounts in Acts. Except for the light phenomenon, all elements of the appearance visible there may also be presupposed for all other appearances of Jesus. The decisive fact is that "all witnesses recognized Jesus of Nazareth in the appearances". (93) That this reality experienced in the appearance of the risen Jesus could be comprehended "as an encounter with one who had been raised from the dead, can only be explained from the presupposition of a particular form of the apocalyptic expectation of the resurrection of the dead." (93) Or else it would remain completely alien.

As to the mode of the experiences the apostles had, Pannenberg follows H. Grass'[22] suggestion that we have to do here with a *vision* since not everyone present saw the risen Lord. This is characteristic of a vision. From his extensive study of the texts and the critical literature by Grass, Althaus, Wilckens, E. Hirsch, von Harnack, et al., Pannenberg concludes:

(a) ". . . the term 'vision' can only express something about the subjective mode of experience, not something about the reality of an event experienced in this form" (95). (b) Vision must be distinguished from illusion or hallucination which is subjective both in its mode of experience and its content. (c) Grass' assertion according to which the event "had no neutral witnesses nor any who were only halfway involved"[23] is a mere

---

[21] Johannes Leipoldt, "Zu den Auferstehungsgeschichten", *Theologische* Literaturzeitung, LXXIII (1948), p. 737, and Gerhard Kittel, *Deutsche Theologie*, IV (1937), p. 159.
[22] Hans Grass, *Ostergeschehen und Osterberichte*, p. 229.
[23] *Ibid.*, p. 222.

The Evidence for the Historicity of Jesus' Resurrection 39

postulate. (d) The vision with which we have to do here has its parallel not in the psychiatric concept of vision where the word connotes a psychological event without corresponding extrasubjective reality ("Only if the corresponding psychiatric point of contact can be inferred from the texts could this understanding of vision be used" 95). (e) The objective reality of the vision experience might be assumed on the basis of some scientific evidence emerging from recent studies of the phenomena of prophetic intuition (precognition), clairvoyance, and telepathy in the field of parapsychology. Pannenberg calls attention to the work of Joseph Banks Rhine, *New World of the Mind*.[24] (f) From David Friedrich Strauss to date all attempts to explain the visions of the risen Jesus in terms of mental and historical presuppositions on the side of the disciples, *while denying the reality of the content of the vision,* have failed. Pannenberg judges,

> The Easter appearances are not to be explained from the Easter faith of the disciples; rather, conversely, the Easter faith of the disciples is to be explained from the experiences. (96)

For there was no historical or psychological possibility for the disciples to create the Easter appearances out of their mental or historical situation. Christ's death almost annihilated their faith in him. So little sense did it make. The tradition of the death of the righteous, prophets, and martyrs offered no *Interpretament* because this tradition *did not include the rising of an individual.* Neither does the apocalyptic tradition offer evidence for the assumption that the disciples produced the Easter appearances. Pannenberg here relies on the ". . . findings in the history of traditions, in this case the improbability of the assumption that people who came from the Jewish tradition would have conceived of the beginning of the events connected with the end of history for Jesus alone *without compelling reasons.*" He goes on to say,

> The primitive Christian news about the eschatological resurrection of Jesus — with a temporal interval separating it from the universal resurrection of the dead — is, considered from the point of view of the history of religions, something new, precisely also in the framework of the apocalyptic tradition. Primitive Christianity required a long time to learn that with Jesus' resurrection the end had not yet begun in general . . . One observes how the Easter message as an

---

[24] 2d ed.; William Sloane Associates, Inc., 1953.

4 Neie: Pannenberg

account of an event that happened to Jesus alone only gradually took shape in the horizon of apocalyptic tradition. *Something like this did not arise as the mental reaction to Jesus' catastrophe.* (96, italics mine)

Thus the evidence does not favor a subjective vision hypothesis but an objective one. *However, can a historian ever detect and prove more than a subjective, psychological phenomenon* with regard to something like "resurrection from the dead"? Can a historian establish something that has no analogy in every day life experience like the reality of the life of someone who died? Can a historian say more than that at this time in Israel certain persons believed in the resurrection of Jesus, because an "event" like resurrection, since it has no analogy, does not in principle come under his scrutiny? But Pannenberg thinks the historian is obligated to "reconstruct the historical correlation of the events that has led to the emergence of primitive Christianity." (97) He names the crucial issue when he says, "Certainly the possibilities that he can consider in this will depend upon the understanding of reality that he brings with him to the task." (97) If his understanding of reality categorically affirms: the dead do not rise, the decision has been made beforehand that Jesus also has not risen.

> If, on the other hand, an element of truth is to be granted to the apocalyptic expectation with regard to the hope of resurrection, then the historian must also consider this possibility for the reconstruction of the course of events as long as no special circumstances in the tradition suggest another explanation. We have seen that the latter is not the case. Therefore the possibility exists . . . of speaking not only of visions of Jesus' disciples but also of appearances of the resurrected Jesus. (98)

As one will have observed, Pannenberg's assumptions are (1) that an element of truth is to be granted to the apocalyptic expectation on account of the fact that systematic anthropology, especially a phenomenology of hope oblige us to include such truth in our *Wirklichkeitsverständnis*, and that (2) no other explanations are satisfactory. *In this sense, then, it is possible to call Jesus' resurrection a historical fact:*

> If the emergence of primitive Christianity, which, apart from other traditions, is also traced back by Paul to appearances of the resurrected Jesus, can be understood in spite of all critical examination of the tradition only if one examines it in the light of the eschatological

hope for the resurrection from the dead, then that which is so designated is a historical event, even if we do not know anything more particular about it. Then an event that is expressible only in the language of the eschatological expectation is to be asserted as a historical occurrence.

Equally telling for an understanding of Pannenberg's position is his succeeding discussion of further arguments against the possibility of establishing the resurrection as a historical event. (A) Does the assumption of the resurrection of a dead person to imperishable life violate the *laws of nature?* Taking the presuppositions of modern physics, not all laws of nature are known, and, as far as we know, individual events are *not completely* determined by those laws.

> Conformity to law embraces only one aspect of what happens. From another perspective, everything that happens is contingent. Therefore, natural science expresses the general validity of the laws of nature but must at the same time declare its own inability to make definitive judgments about the possibility or impossibility of an individual event, regardless of how certainly it is able, at least in principle, to measure the probability of an event's occurrence. (98)

The historian, not the scientist, is the arbiter.

(B) Can eyes which belong to the old aeon behold the reality which belongs to the new? It is self-evident that this is not the case, many contend. Because of its importance for Pannenberg's position we must quote his replique at length:

> There is something quite correct about this argument. Because the life of the risen Lord involves the reality of a new creation, the resurrected Lord is in fact not perceptible as one object among others in this world; therefore he could only be experienced and designated by an extraordinary mode of experience, the vision, and only in metaphorical language. In this way, however, he made himself known in the midst of our reality at a very definite time, and to men who are particularly designated. Consequently, these events are to be affirmed or denied also as historical events . . . If we would forego the concept of a historical event here then it is no longer possible at all to affirm that the resurrection . . . really happened . . . *There is no justification for affirming Jesus' resurrection as an event that*

really happened, if it is not to be affirmed as a historical event as such. Whether or not a particular event happened 2000 years ago *is not made certain by faith but only by historical research*, to the extent that certainty can be attained at all about questions of this kind. (99, italics mine)

The quoted paragraph once more epitomizes three affirmations which centrally belong to Pannenberg's theological position. (1) He grants his critics that the risen one is not perceptible as one object among others in this world. Nor is he an object of every day empirical evidence. Such evidence requires analogies in the old aeon. (2) But realities of the new aeon are not non-perceivable on this account. Because they belong to the new aeon they are perceivable only through extraordinary modes of experience and expressible only through metaphorical language. Such experience allows a *Rückschluss* to the new reality which is experienced (*vide supra* p. 34). Historiography must be open for such operation − if all paths of explanation within the framework of the *Wirklichkeitsverständnis* of the old aeon offer no satisfactory solution and if a religious tradition exists which is able to make sense of the phenomenon by an anthropological consideration. For Pannenberg, as was noted, "metaphorical" or "symbolical" neither means unreal nor nonhistorical. The new life after death for him lies in the future, is bound to a spiritual body, and in a definite sense is continuous with the present life (*vide supra* p. 34). (3) Neither faith in the new reality nor an intuitive perception of past events, as Paul Althaus teaches, offers certainty. One might fall prey to an illusion! Pannenberg rejects Künneth's opinion that the certainty of faith (based on what?) as "unconditional certainty also involves the perception of historical facts,"[25] and declares, "The only method of achieving at least approximate certainty with regard to the events of a past time is historical research." (99)

This task of historical research is carefully delineated, naming both the limitation and the positive chance and obligation of the historian, when Pannenberg writes,

> Was . . . historisch über das Ereignis der Auferstehung Jesu gesagt werden kann, ist also, daß Jesus − der gestorben war − „lebt", ohne daß sich jedoch sagen ließe, was das Wort „Leben" hier genau

---

[25] Walter Künneth, *Glauben an Jesus? Die Begegnung der Christologie mit der modernen Existenz* (Hamburg: F. Wittig, 1962), p. 285.

bedeutet, über die Feststellung hinaus, daß Jesus nicht tot geblieben ist. . . . Diese Feststellung bedeutet nicht etwa ein negatives Ergebnis der historischen Frage nach der Auferstehung Jesu. Es wäre ein Kurzschluß, nun auf die Behauptung zurückzufallen, der Historiker könne eben doch nichts zu dieser Frage sagen, oder gar, der Historiker kenne a priori kein derartiges Ereignis, müsse es also in Abrede stellen. Vielmehr hat der Historiker − unter den genannten Voraussetzungen − etwas sehr Positives and theologisch sehr Wichtiges zu sagen: Daß ein Ereignis stattgefunden habe, dessen nähere Beschaffenheit sich seinem Urteil entzieht. Dabei handelt es sich auch keineswegs nur um ein abstraktes „Daß"; denn es ist ein Jesus, und zwar den *toten* Jesus, betreffendes Ereignis − ein Ereignis, das jedenfalls bedeutet, daß Jesus danach nicht mehr tot war. *Mit einer derart kritisch begrenzten, trotz ihrer negativen Form durch die konkrete Bestimmtheit dieser Negation eminent positiven Aussage hütet die Historie das Mysterium der Auferstehung Jesu.* Das wäre dagegen nicht der Fall bei einer abstrakten Unzuständigkeitserklärung des Historikers. Eine solche würde die Auferstehung Jesu um ihren Geschehenscharakter bringen, sie zu einem bloßen Theologumenon machen.[26] (Italics 15th line by the author)

B. The Empty Tomb

With regard to the question of the historicity of Jesus' empty tomb Pannenberg thinks that the above conclusion regarding the appearances is independent of its results. Still it has significance for the final conclusion concerning the resurrection. The empty tomb is of no great importance for Paul's theology because here Christ's resurrection and the future destiny of the believers in their relation to one another is the decisive concern. The empty tomb belongs to the singularity of Jesus' fate because Jesus had died only two days prior to his resurrection.

Contrariwise it was of greatest importance for the primitive community in Jerusalem. "How could Jesus' disciples in Jerusalem have proclaimed his resurrection if they could be constantly refuted merely by viewing the grave in which his body was interred?" (100) Pannenberg agrees with P. Althaus'

---

[26] W. Pannenberg, "Dogmatische Erwägungen zur Auferstehung Jesu", pp. 112f.

judgment that the resurrection kerygma "could not have been maintained in Jerusalem for a single day, for a single hour, if the emptiness of the tomb had not been established as a fact for all concerned."[27] The Jewish authorities shared the conviction that the grave was empty and explained this with the charge that the disciples had stolen the body. The textual traditions can counter this argument which rests upon general historical considerations only "if the existing text virtually forced one to make the opposite judgment" (102). Pannenberg criticizes Grass' judgment that the textual basis for the historicity of the empty tomb is not "unconditionally conclusive" and charges him with a theological bias, according to the famous principle *Nicht sein kann, was nicht sein darf*. Because it would render the resurrection provable which *may not* be the case because it is not God's will, there *cannot* exist conclusive evidence for its historicity. As to the dependence of the tradition of the empty grave upon the tradition of the appearances Pannenberg concludes that the two traditions came into existence independent of one another. This has the following significance:

> If the appearance tradition and the grave tradition came into existence independently then by their mutually complementing each other they let the assertion of the reality of Jesus' resurrection, in the sense explained above, appear as historically very probable, and that always means in historical inquiry that it is to be presupposed until contrary evidence appears. (105)

6. *The Proleptic Character of God's Confirmation in Jesus' Resurrection*

As was pointed out before, Jesus' resurrection must be established historically if it is to be considered as an event that has happened, and only if so, can it mean what it does in fact mean in the context of the Israelite-Jewish apocalyptic expectation of the resurrection of the dead. Without this context of *Traditionsgeschichte* the resurrection of Jesus, even if it were possible to establish it apart from the apocalyptic expectation, would not speak meaningfully. On the other hand, without the established historicity of the resurrection, the claim who Jesus was and that God confirmed his message, is inconsequential and irrelevant — at least void of evidence. For it

---

[27] Paul Althaus, *Die Wahrheit des kirchlichen Osterglaubens: Einspruch gegen E. Hirsch* (Gütersloh: C. Bertelsmann, 1940), pp. 22f.

would have to rest on Jesus' proclamation and crucifixion alone which by themselves possess no cogency. Thus the apocalyptic context and the resurrection of Jesus condition each other. But *they form no quilibrium*, it appears. *The greater weight is given to the apocalyptic expectation of the resurrection of Jesus condition each other. But they form no equilibrium*, it appearances of the risen Jesus to the disciples or the news of the empty grave were incomprehensible and unintelligible. The argument for the historicity of the resurrection depends upon whether the thought that a dead person will rise is conceivable. It was conceivable for the disciples on account of their tradition. It is conceivable for the historian today on the basis of a systematic anthropology. *However, the resurrection of Jesus requires the apocalyptic tradition once more as its premise, viz., to understand its meaning.* Only within this tradition does Jesus' resurrection mean the beginning of the end time, as the fulfillment of the promise of the universal resurrection of the dead in one instance, and thusly the confirmation of Jesus' proclamation and claim. A problem which we touched upon on p. 28f. above is the fact that the fulfillment does not simply agree but also disagrees with the expectation – the *universal* resurrection did not take place. Does not Pannenberg make light of this gap? Can Jesus' resurrection really mean the beginning of the eschatological time and the confirmation of Jesus' claim when obviously the end time did not begin, as we must say at a much later time? Our situation is different from the earliest community which understood Jesus' resurrection and return for judgment as directly connected in time.

> However, it no longer presses itself upon us so irresistibly that the resurrected Jesus is the eschatological judge. If we did not have the witness of the primitive Christianity, we would hardly arrive by ourselves at the idea that the One who was crucified almost 2000 years ago had introduced the end of the world through his resurrection from the dead. (107)

We face the question whether "we are still able to hold on to the tension that binds this past event with the end of the world which has not yet arrived." (107) It is a paramount tenet of Pannenberg's position that we are! He states it in this way,

> The relation of the Christ event to the end of the world in the sense of an anthropologically interpreted apocalyptic expectation is not

> bound to the length of the interval between both events. It is bound only to the material analogy of what has already happened in and with Jesus and that for which the apocalyptic expectation hopes from the ultimate future. In this we presuppose that this expectation can be justified as true in its fundamental elements, even if from a different horizon of interpretation than that of apocalyptic itself. (107)

The connection between promise and fulfillment centers on its material content, not its timing. The material content is the resurrection of the dead, Jesus' and the universal one. How much time elapses between the two is irrelevant. *Not irrelevant is the general basis for an expectation of the end of the world in the sense of concrete temporal future.*

> Only in connection with the end of the world that still remains to come can what happened in Jesus . . . possess and retain the character of revelation for us also. The question continually arises anew whether what had been evidently true at that time in the past still holds good as truth in the present also. There is no answer to this question that can be formulated in a single sentence; it is answered at any particular time by theology as a whole, and not only by theology, but also by the way in which the faith of Christians, which is grounded upon the truth known in the past, stands the test today in the decisions of life. (107)

Here Pannenberg introduces a *second concept of prolepsis*. Proleptic character, first, pertains to Jesus' claim because at the time of its raising it lacked substantiation and evidence. It needed confirmation. Jesus' resurrection is this confirmation from God if viewed in the context of its *Traditionsgeschichte*. Second, precisely this confirmation contains a proleptic element also. For Christianity, *then and now*, the fulfillment, because it was merely begun and not consummated, "has become promise once again". "The ultimate divine confirmation of Jesus will take place only in the occurrence of his return." (108) The delay of the Parousia, consequently, postpones the time of the ultimate fulfillment but does not waive its validity. In his discussion of the work of Christ Pannenberg names the gift of Jesus' proclamation. He calls it his message of the nearness of God's Lordship. His nearness means that human beings are opened up "for God's future through which man's destiny to openness toward the future — even in his relationships to the world — is realized."

This opening up, Pannenberg says, is "independent of *particular* apocalyptic deadlines." (226, italics by the author) It seems, however, that, in Pannenberg's thought, the fact of its independence of a *particular* date of its consummation not only is not detrimental to Christ's work but in deed is a necessary element within this work. For not only is it true that "What man is destined to be was revealed in the light of the message about the nearness of God's Lordship regardless of the date of its arrival." (226) The delay in fact seems to constitute a *conditio sine qua non* of the kind of human existence to which Jesus calls if it is true that

> Man as man is always something more than and extending beyond his present situation; his destiny is not fulfilled in any given framework of his life. God's reality is not only the ultimate source and guarantee of a present form of life, but points beyond every presently given or possible security and fulfillment of existence. (226)

However, as certainly as this kind of existence is possible — so it seems — only because the eschaton has not yet occurred and its date is unknown, equally certainly is this openness "in no way independent of the expectations of the end in general. If the future expectation of a transformation of our world and of the resurrection of the dead should collapse, then the openness for the future of human existence would also lose its decisive impulse." (227)

CHAPTER III

JESUS' DIVINITY DEFINED AND PANNENBERG'S CONCEPT OF REVELATION

In our investigation into Pannenberg's teachings about Christ's death on the cross we have accepted his principle that we first have to establish Jesus' identity, i. e. his divinity, before we can establish a soteriology upon this ground. We presuppose that the death on the cross has salvific meaning and belongs among the soteriological considerations. Therefore we have attempted to analyze Pannenberg's train of thought leading to the construction of Jesus' divinity. The latter's resurrection played a major, even the decisive part in this christological task, although, as was intimated, it also is of saving significance and it, to be sure, is worth a later consideration to what degree Jesus' resurrection in and by itself possesses salvific meaning, i. e. without the cross! *Does it perhaps promise and accomplish salvation quite without a special salvific function of Jesus' death?* This requires an answer since in the apocalyptic tradition salvation does not presuppose the death of the Son of Man prior to his coming for judgment and salvation and since Jesus, standing in this tradition, knows of no special function of his death either. As was pointed out, Pannenberg's clue to the salvific meaning of Jesus' death is that Jesus died as the rejected one and that he constitutes the end of the law. This serves as a key to Pannenberg's doctrine of the atonement.

But Pannenberg's christology needs further definition and clarification. Who was the one who is going to be crucified? What is the mode of his divinity? What is the mode of God's presence in him? What kind of unity obtains between God and Jesus?

1. The Concept of Revelational Presence

For Pannenberg, Jesus' divinity is inferred from his unity with God. The key to the clarification of Jesus' unity with God is to be found in "... the revelatory character of the Christ event, originally understood within the horizon of eschatology, and translated into Hellenistic categories as the epiphany of God in Jesus . . ." (115) For Pannenberg, the question of Jesus' unity with God must be extended to the question of God's presence in Jesus because Jesus' relation to God *can be ascertained* — this is decisive! — only in connection with the question "*of how God appears to other men through Jesus.*" (115f.)

> Jesus' relation to other men is the sphere in which the question of his relation to God arises, namely, insofar as he alone exercises God's authority toward the rest of humanity. Thus, from the very beginning the question of Jesus' unity with God involves the presence of God *for us* in Jesus. We must inquire about the way in which God is present to us, to the whole of humanity, in Jesus. Otherwise, the question of Jesus' unity with God cannot be posed at all if this unity is supposed to be found in God's revelation. (116, italics by the author).

Reviewing the history of christological thought, Pannenberg distinguishes five different conceptions of God's presence in Jesus which roughly center on the following:

(1) Jesus is connected with God through the Spirit. This motif is usually connected with an adoptionist view; Jesus' unity with God is functional here (e. g. Ignatius, Tertullian).

(2) Substantial presence. God is fully present in Jesus; Jesus is a divine person (e. g. the Alexandrian doctrine of incarnation).

(3) Mediator christology. These christologies have "no interest at all in the immediate presence of God himself in Jesus — neither accidentally nor substantially — but are simply interested in Jesus' mid-position between God and man." (123) The pre-existent heavenly being incarnate in Jesus is not God but a being subordinate to God and higher than man (e. g. Arianism, Logos christology).

(4) God's presence as mere appearance. There is present in Jesus an epiphany of God or of a divine being whose essence however is not identical with the essence of the man Jesus. This is represented in the Gnostic christology, all forms of docetism, the modalism of Sabellius which somehow continues in Schleiermacher, and christological formulas as symbols or ciphers for a presence of God in Jesus as one finds it today in Paul Tillich and Fritz Buri. "For Tillich, Jesus thus is not himself God but only a symbol for the perception of God." (126)

(5) Revelational presence. Under this concept Pannenberg defines his own christological understanding. *This concept combines God's presence as appearance with the idea of his substantial presence,* i. e., of an essential identity of Jesus with God in the revelatory event. This is to be understood "from the perspective of the functional unity of Jesus with God, which stood in the foreground in the history of the transmission of the christological titles in primitive Christianity, to the extent that Jesus' relation to God was explicitly reflected upon at all at that time." (127)

For Pannenberg, appearance and essence of God in the revelatory event belong together. Why? It is implied and expressed by the *concept of revelation as self-revelation.* In agreement with the predominant understanding of contemporary systematic theology[1] Pannenberg teaches that "revelation is not the communication of some 'truths' by supernatural means, by inspiration, for example, but it is essentially God's 'self-disclosure', as Karl Barth says." (127) Pannenberg traces the use of the word revelation with this connotation from German idealism, especially Hegel, to Philipp Marheineke and Wilhelm Herrmann.

> This innovation can be classed as a legacy of German idealism. The Enlightenment destroyed the old concept of revelation that belonged to 17th century orthodox dogmatics, namely the identification of revelation and the inspiration of Holy Scripture, the understanding of revelation as the transmission of supernatural and hidden truths. The assertion of such a revelation was suspected of fostering an obscurantism that would avoid the light of scientific reason. From the beginning of the 19th century, there was the suspicion that supernaturalism is superstition, and the concept of revelation could only be rescued by means of reducing its content to God's self-revelation. This reduction amounts to a definition excluding everything purely miraculous. . . . The strictly defined concept of revelation as self-revelation of the absolute appears to have been first introduced by Hegel, for with him it became clear for the first time that the full self-manifestation of God can only be a unique one. Hegel expressly reserved the designation "a revealed and revealing religion" for Christianity, not because it contains truths that have been trans-

---

[1] Pannenberg cites K. Barth, E. Brunner, P. Althaus, H. Vogel. O. Weber, H. van Oyen, W. Temple, Herbert Henry Farmer, H. R. Niebuhr, D. W. Richardson. Barth's cited statement: *Church Dogmatics,* I/I, pp. 362 ff.

mitted by supernatural means, but because, in distinction from all other religions, it rests on full disclosure of the nature of the absolute as spirit. Self-revelation is thus so strictly understood that it is no longer permissable to think of a medium of revelation that is distinct from God himself.[2]

If God reveals *himself* this revelation (1) is solely one, it is unique. It must be complete, unsurpassable, non-supplementable, non-correctable. "If God is already totally revealed in the special decisiveness of the Christ event, then he cannot in consistency be 'also' revealed in other events, situations, and persons."[3] If God reveals himself, then in this revelation (2) not only the revealer and what is revealed but also the revealer and the medium of revelation are essentially identical. "Karl Barth recognized this before any of the theologians of his day by stressing the unity of God with Christ in the context of his concept of revelation. The unity of Jesus with God is a unity-in-revelation and as such implies a unity of essence. The unity Jesus has with God in revelation must therefore be the root of christological statements about the divinity of Jesus Christ."[4]

This concept also implies (3) that revelation must not hide but actually reveal what it is supposed to reveal.

> In Barth . . . this fundamental insight is partly endangered by the assertion that the "form" of revelation also implies a veiling . . . The conception of a God who by nature has a veiled form of manifestation (the veiling is not just against those who misunderstand) runs contary to the unity of revelation as self-revelation: It could yield just as many divine manifestations as veiled forms. . . . Only if the form of revelation reveals God and – rightly understood – does not veil him, only then is Barth's thesis of the unity of revelation tenable.[5]

As reason for this inconsistency in Barth Pannenberg names Barth's own recourse to the Calvinistic axiom "finitum non capax infiniti", Barth's supernatural understanding of revelation, and the motifs of *theologia crucis* and crisis in his Commentary on Romans.

---

[2] Wolfhart Pannenberg, ed. *Revelation as History*, (New York: The Macmillan Company, 1968), pp. 4f. (Henceforth quoted *RaH*)
[3] *Ibid.*, p. 6.
[4] *Ibid.*, p. 7.
[5] *Ibid.*, pp. 7f.

Now although the vocabulary in the Old and New Testament translated by "reveal" or "revelation" does not have this meaning but connotes the making known of various informations through different media, both still speak of God's self-revelation. Pannenberg follows the studies of the divine *Erweiswort* (word of demonstration) by Walter Zimmerli.[6] Such words imply the understanding that the purpose of God's activity in history is to give knowledge of Yahweh. *In the course of Israel's reflection, to an ever greater extent all events came to be perceived as a single historical unity, a universal history.* This realization came along with the transition from polytheism to monotheism. And the more this view of history prevailed, the more also did it become prominent that *complete* knowledge of Yahweh could not be attainable while history was still in progress but *only at the end of all historical occurrences.*

> Yahweh would complete the entire course of world events, world history, in order that man might thereby know his divinity. Only at the end of history is he ultimately revealed from his deeds as the one God who accomplishes everything. (128)

From here derives the apocalyptic expectation of God's complete revelation at the end of time. This event was conceived as the future appearance of God's כָּבֹד (glory) which is his essence.

Obviously on the basis of these facts Pannenberg arrives at his particular interpretation of the resurrection of Jesus. When and where does a self-revelation of God occur? Ultimately only at the end of history! If this is true, in a very definite sense God has not yet revealed himself. However, by raising Jesus from the dead, God has anticipated the end time. In Jesus' resurrection the end time occurred proleptically in a single instance of one of the occurrences which are promised and therefore expected to happen universally at the end of history. To this degree, then, God, in Jesus' resurrection, revealed himself proleptically. And since his resurrection implies the confirmation of his message and work, the Christ event of Jesus' message, work, and destiny constitute God's self-revelation. Therefore both are true: God has and has not yet revealed himself. His self-revelation in Christ must be considered complete, unsurpassable, in no need of correction or supplementation. For what needs alteration cannot

---

[6] Walter Zimmerli, *Erkenntnis Gottes nach dem Buche Ezechiel* (Zurich: Zwingli-Verlag, 1954) et al. Cf. *JGaM*, p. 128, n. 30.

have been a self-revelation of God who essentially is the same yesterday, today, and in eternity. On the other hand, only the future, i. e., the end of history, will finally reveal and thus constitute what something is or was. It might be helpful to apply the concepts of extension and unfolding to this thought of Pannenberg's. God's self-revelation in Jesus is final and reliable, still it is only its beginning. It will be *extended* – not *altered* – and *unfolded*, not *surpassed*.[7]

This concept of revelation allows the establishing of Jesus' divinity. If appearance and essence must coincide in order to result in a *self*-revelation, the Christ event reveals God himself, which in Hellenistic language means that Jesus' essence is one with God's. "If this were not so, then the human event of Jesus' life would veil the God who is active therein and thus exclude his full revelation." (129) "Jesus belongs to the definition of God and thus to his divinity, his essence." (130)

It became evident why any theological talk about God's self-revelation in Jesus Christ is indissolubly tied to the resurrection, understood as the inbreaking of the eschaton. Pannenberg sums this point up,

> We do not first know who God is and then also something about Jesus, but only in connection with Jesus do we know that the ground of all reality about whom every man inquires, openly or concealed, consciously or unconsciously, is in its real essence identical with the God of Israel. We know this . . . because the end that stands before us and all things has already happened in Jesus as an event produced by Israel's God. The destiny of all that is has already been fulfilled in him. (130)

One should note, as we did before, that this is *no unpremised knowledge* of which Pannenberg here speaks. It is dependent on Pannenberg's reasoning as discussed in chapters I and II. We discovered an *ultimate*

---

[7] The fact that for P. God's self-revelation in Jesus is proleptic and, regarding the ultimate and total self-revelation at the eschaton, preliminary is reminiscent of Barth's idea of God's veiling within his self-revelation. One might indeed say that P. often seems to talk himself around to something he has previously seemed to reject. I owe this observation to Prof. Durwood Foster. My juxtaposition of extending and unfolding versus altering and surpassing is an attempt to accept the tension between the ultimate and the preliminary of God's self-revelation at the eschaton and in Jesus and reconcile this tension with the idea of prolepsis which implies and emphasizes the identity of the two.

presupposition of the train of thought which leads to the acceptance of the Old Testament God and his word in prophecy and apocalyptic and to the interpretation of the Christ event within this *Traditionsgeschichte*. This presupposition consists of an anthropologically established understanding of reality. For this a concept of God as the source and power of all of history and a concept of man's openness to the future, from whence fulfillment, salvation, and new life are expected, are constitutive! This presupposition will require closer attention in due time.

2. The Concept of Retroactive Ontological Enforcement

To clarify the transition from the concept of God's self-revelation to the divinity of Christ Pannenberg points out that this concept only claims the "identity of God with the event that reveals him." (130) But exactly in what way is God the event or in the event? What, again, is the mode of his presence in Jesus' life? We remember that the concept revelational presence combines the functional and essential sense of identity. Traditionally speaking, God does not only act through but *"was* in Christ". This combination forces the question,

> If Jesus is God's revelation through a particular event in his life, then did he only become one with God after this event or was he one with God from the very beginning? (133)

Pannenberg proposes the following answer. As is to be expected he argues that the primitive church understood Jesus' resurrection as the decisive point in the history of his relation to God. All christological titles ascribed to Jesus are an exegesis of the resurrection. The two-stage-christology of Romans 1:3f. most sharply expresses this significance of the resurrection, calling the pre-Easter Jesus "Son of David" and the risen one "Son of God". But this christology is not adoptionist in the sense that Jesus' exaltation to the "Son of God" implies that he was someone else before his resurrection. Following F. Hahn[8], Pannenberg is persuaded that

> As Son of David, Jesus at the same time had already been designated for the future reception of the honor of the divine Sonship. (135)

---

[8] Ferdinand Hahn, *Christologische Hoheitstitel. Ihre Geschichte im frühen Christentum* (Göttingen: Vandenhoeck & Ruprecht, 1963), pp. 259ff. and 262ff. on Mark 10:46-52 and 12:35-37.

This christology speaks of two functions only, not of two natures. The idea that Jesus was given divinity only as a consequence of his resurrection is untenable. Why? Because the resurrection means, among other things, God's confirmation of Jesus' pre-Easter claim. Now a confirmation is not a statement or an act which proclaims something to be true from the moment of its proclamation but is one which *confirms* a truth that prevailed prior to the statement itself. "Jesus did not simply become something that he previously had not been . . ." (135) Not Jesus' identity is the new thing which the resurrection brings about, but its manifestation. It gives Jesus' pre-Easter ministry the authentication and legitimation which, as proleptic, it did not possess at its time.

Having made this point clear and persuasive, Pannenberg now advances the surprising idea that "Jesus' essence is *established retroavtively* from the perspective of the end of his life, from his resurrection, *not only for our knowledge but in its being*". (136, italics mine) This seems to contradict what was said above that the resurrection functions as a confirmation of something which existed previously but, by its proclamation, was manifested and made known. And it seems to introduce an unfamiliar usage of the word confirmaton; it comes to mean not only to confirm or reaffirm an existing matter but to *retroactively enforce* something which was not valid or in force prior to the enforcement. This is envisageable, e. g., in the case of a law which retroactively declares a person to be employed and eligible for a salary. In this fashion an employee is so to speak "created" retroactively. However, he was no such thing prior to the act of enforcement of this law. Now Pannenberg contends that this is applicable to Jesus' identity as being in essential unity with God. That he was such we not only know since Easter, *it is true only since Easter*. But because Easter enforces this truth retroactively, it is true also prior to Easter! For common thought it would be easier to consider Easter as the establishment of Jesus' identity for our knowledge only (conventional meaning of confirmation). One tends to think: *either* Jesus was essentially divine prior to Easter but we know it only through Easter; *or* Jesus was not divine before, and at Easter his divinity was established ontologically. Pannenberg, however, insists that "it (Jesus' divine Sonship) had only been on the stage from the very beginning because Jesus has been raised from the dead." (137) Pannenberg wants to have it both ways. It is true since Easter that it was true all along. Thus *he understands "confirmation" unconventionally to mean retroactive enforcement and applies it to being*. His basis for this procedure is his ontology.

5 Neie: Pannenberg

For Greek thought which also determines our common sense essences are established once for all; essences transcend time. The essences of things are determined in a primordial past and persist in the succession of time and change. Pannenberg, on the contrary, extrapolates an *ontology of the future* from the Israelite-Jewish apocalyptic, validated by contemporary anthropological insights. According to it,

> ... the future is open in the sense that it will bring unpredictably new things that nothing can resist as absolutely unchangeable — for such thought only the future decides what something is. It is still to be shown what will become of man and of the world's situation in the future. (136)

It is not something unique about Jesus, then, but of universal ontological relevance that "the future decides (not merely makes known) what something is." (136) Pannenberg's ontology will soon be looked into more closely. For the moment, *what does this ontological stance accomplish for the christological problem?* It solves the otherwise insoluble tension between the essential identity of God and Jesus (or else it were no self-revelation) which requires that Jesus was and is God's Son from the beginning, and the fact that Jesus' resurrection is the decisive christological event. Pannenberg's position rejects both that Jesus became God through the resurrection and that Jesus became God through his baptism or his birth from a virgin. On the one hand, Pannenberg retains the traditional dogma of the incarnation and pre-existence.

> From the idea of revelation we attain access to the understanding of the old concept of Jesus' pre-existence. At least this concept appears as a meaningful *expression* for a material concern that we, too, must retain, namely, for Jesus' full and complete affiliation with the eternal God. (150, italics by the author)

On the other hand, he upholds the historical fact of the constitutive christological significance of the resurrection. Both are simultaneously possible only with the assumption of the retroactive ontic enforcement of Jesus' essential unity with God, taking place in the resurrection. Pannenberg sums up,

> Viewed from the confirmation of Jesus' claim by his resurrection, the inner logic of the matter dictates that Jesus was always one with

God, not just after a certain date in his life. And in view of God's eternity, the revelatory character of Jesus' resurrection means that God was always one with Jesus, even before his earthly birth. Jesus is from all eternity the representative of God in the creation. Were it otherwise, Jesus would not be in person the one revelation of the eternal God. We can no longer think of God in his eternal deity without Jesus. That is, indeed, the meaning of Jesus' resurrection. (153)

Historically the transformation of the original faith in Jesus as the one exalted through his resurrection to Jesus as the pre-existent divine being who descended from heaven accomplished a remolding of the message into a form understandable and attractive to Hellenistic thought. Here Pannenberg advances the important idea that such transformation may not be downgraded as an infiltration of alien ideas into the genuine Christian corpus of ideas. He says,

> In the history of ideas absolutely nothing is clarified and understood by the phrase: this or that has "influenced" something or other. The history of ideas is not a chemistry of concepts that have been arbitrarily stirred together and are then neatly separated again by the modern historian. In order for an "influence" of alien concepts to be absorbed, a situation must have previously emerged within which these concepts could be greeted as an aid for the expression of a problem already present. This preceding situation that first made an "influence" possible must be ferreted out if one wants to understand the change of a concept in the course of history. (153)

Applied to the christological problem,

> "the resurrected Lord's essential unity with God leads to the idea of pre-existence through its own instrinsic logic ... That the inner problematic of the Christ event pressed for an explication that simultaneously met the sense of truth and the desire for salvation in its environment reveals not the weakness but the strength of the primitive Christian message and constitutes its missionary power." (153f.)

3. The Unity of the Man Jesus With God

Adamantly faithful to his method, Pannenberg now asks,

> But can these concepts be anything more to us today than mythical pictures? In the age of technology can we seriously speak of the descent and ascent of a heavenly divine being? (154)

Pannenberg proceeds from the sentence thus far established, "If God has revealed himself in Jesus, then Jesus' community with God, his Sonship, belongs to eternity." (154) This basic fact, however, while it affirms Jesus' indivisibility with God, does *not* necessarily imply "the distinction between Jesus' community with God as something eternal and his temporal and transitory human person." (154) *This* distinction is, in the concept of pre-existence, extended to a conceptual separation of "Jesus' community with God as a special *being*, the pre-existent Son of God, and his temporal appearance" (154), the earthly human corporeal appearance of Jesus. This distinction is to be refuted because *it conceptually divides what in Jesus' existence belong together.* What together constitutes Jesus' concrete life is divided into two separate beings. This is the mythical element in the incarnation theory. Also the subsequent reunification of the two, necessitated by the assumed separation, is mythical. In Jesus' activity and fate no such distinction is envisageable, no such separation needs overcoming. Mythical thinking, Pannenberg defines, "separates the essence of reality as a special, prototypal essence from the appearance in order to reunite the two through a dramatic process especially conceived for the purpose." (155) Pannenberg himself, too, distinguishes the eternal Son of God from the man Jesus but *only as two different aspects of Jesus Christ.* He, too, considers the conjunction of the two elements a christological task. But the two aspects look at a single concrete life. Still, in the *ductus* of an incarnational christology this distinction must be upheld as also the idea of a movement from God to man.

Pannenberg validates this from his concept of revelation which includes one unique direct self-revelation of God and indirect self-revelations which obtain at all times. This requires further exposition later on. At any rate, the Christ event is, as we saw, the prolepsis of the direct self-revelation of God while the *ultimate* direct self-revelation is to occur at the end of history. In history up to the Christ event and thereafter God indirectly reveals himself through the historical connection of any particular epoch with the history of Jesus of Nazareth. For this reason, no other event and no other man either before or after Jesus is united with God's essence in the same way as the Christ event. That unity of the divine essence with the man Jesus . . . did not exist before Jesus appeared. To that extent one must say that in Jesus, God himself has come out of his otherness into our world, into human form, and in such a way that the Father-Son-relation that — as we know in retrospect — always belonged to God's essence now acquired corporeal form. (156)[9]

In this fashion the concept incarnation is verifiable today through the concept of revelation. It is founded on history and is derived from the Old Testament and apocalyptic theology of history. Under the influence of the Hellenistic categories, especially the Logos christology of the second century, the essential connection of christology with the Old Testament was imperiled.

To the extent that the concept of the incarnation cuts itself loose from the Old Testament and Jewish theology of history, it becomes a mere myth, a myth of a divine being descending from heaven and ascending again. The process in the history of traditions that led to the development of the idea of incarnation is here obscured and remains unintelligible. Then it easily appears that there is a rift between the incarnational Christology and the historical Jesus. (157)

But within the Old Testament horizon and that of universal history of apocalyptic thought the incarnational affirmations are not mythological but functional, i.e., they are expressions of the truth gained "from the perspective of God's eschatological revelation in Jesus." (157) They "are justified only as the expression, but certainly the indispensable expression, of God's eschatological revelation in the destiny of Jesus of Nazareth." (157) Such affirmations border on what is unsayable, and *paradoxical* statements emerge such as, e.g., the contention that Jesus both was and was not the divine Son prior to his resurrection. Namely, the resurrection makes it known (i.e., it was true before) and establishes it ontologically (i.e., it was not true before it was established). These paradoxa emerge from

---

[9] This wording seems to make the point in terms of retrospective knowledge, not retrospective ontological enforcement.

the prolepsis of the eschaton in Jesus' life, and this concept itself is paradoxical!

> Thus to speak of the end of everything that happens as having already happened in Jesus is contrary to the apparent literal sense. Nevertheless, this way of speaking can be *justified*, and *only then is it meaningful*. (157, italics mine)

By paradox he does not mean a contradiction which thought cannot overcome.

> The assumption of such a contradiction misunderstands the nature of thought, which transcends a contradiction in the act of establishing that the contradiction exists. (157)

The justification for the concept of prolepsis of the eschaton and its inherent paradox is the historical fact of the resurrection of Jesus and its significance within its *Traditionsgeschichte*. History as fact plus inherent meaning compels us to make such statements. Otherwise they were mythical and merely assertive. To be true, an incarnational doctrine is consequently tied to the Old Testament, the apocalyptic expectation, and the earthly life of Jeans. Pannenberg sums up saying,

> Only so long as the perception of Jesus' resurrection remains precedent to the concept of incarnation is the Biblical meaning of the idea of God preserved in Christology and only so long does Christology also remain related to the Biblical understanding of man and of the world as history. (158)

Now Pannenberg puts the question, Who is the subject of the incarnation, the eternal Son or God's essence in general?

4. *Jesus' and the Father's Divinity*

God's self-revelation in Jesus, to say it again, implies that Jesus' person is inseparable from God's essence. Now Jesus called God "Father" and thus distinguished the Father from himself. This might have motivated the early church to confer the title Son upon Jesus. These two facts, viz., the essential God-Jesus-unity and the Father-Son-distinction, *entail the conclusion that the distinction between the Son and the Father also belongs to*

God's divinity. Thus Pannenberg develops the cogency for trinitarian thinking from his concept of self-revelation or revelational identity, respectively. He says,

> The relation of Jesus as Son to the Father may be summarized with primitive Christianity as "obedience". It is therefore a relation proper to the essence of God himself. God is not only "Father", but as the God who is revealed through Jesus' resurrection he is in his eternal essence also "Son". Thereby the expressions "Father" and "Son" are to be strictly applied to the relation to God of the historical man Jesus of Nazareth. Here the word "Father" means the God of Jesus, who was the God of the Old Testament, to whom Jesus directed his prayers and from whose hands he accepted his fate. The word "Son" here does not designate, as it does in other places in the New Testament, Jesus' place of honor in contrast to humanity and the cosmos, but primarily his relation to the Father, a relation of obedience and "mission" (Rom. 8:3; Gal. 4:4; John 3:17, *passim*; I John 4:9), but also of trust. The latter term may well be taken as a more appropriate expression for that which Jesus' addressing God as Father implied in his own understanding. (159)

Pannenberg adds,

> We have been speaking of "Father" and "Son" in a figurative sense. Likewise, to speak of a contrast between Father and Son within the Godhead has a figurative, symbolic sense. It is justified only in the fact that Jesus' relation to the God of Israel as his "Father" belongs to the essence of this God himself, just as does the person of Jesus of Nazareth, insofar as he is revealed in Jesus. (159)

Modalism was and is wrong since deity of Jesus does not mean undifferentiated identity with the divine nature "as if in Jesus God the Father himself had appeared in human form and had suffered on the cross." (160) The classical Logos christology made Jesus' unity with the Father and his simultaneous differentiation from him comprehensible and it preserved monotheism since the Logos is different from the Father not in essence but in number.

> . . . it made the divinity present in Jesus familiar to Hellenistic society as a power that was decisive for its conception of the world.

> The Logos theory succeeded impressively in explaining the role of the pre-existent Son of God in mediating creation . . . The universal significance of God's revelation in Jesus is the natural consequence when the Logos, the foundation of the world's being, has appeared in his fullness in Jesus. (164)

As to the weaknesses of this theory, Pannenberg points out (1) the subordinate rank of the Logos as a person who proceeds from the Father in time, viz., in the beginning of creation, (2) the severing of the Son's divinity from the historical revelation, Jesus of Nazareth,[10] (3) the philosophical imprint which the Greek concept of God, mediated through the Logos theory, gave to the Christian concept of God. The Biblical God is not the immutable, simple, ultimate ground of the phenomenal reality but *"the free origin of the contingent events of the world whose interrelations are also contingent and constitute no eternal order but a history moving forward from event to event."* (165) A renewal of the patristic Logos doctrine today for Pannenberg is "hardly possible – and in any case meaningless." (166) Today's scientific perception of the world does not include a Logos figure who mediates between a transcendent God and the world which robs this doctrine of its presupposition. A renewal of the Logos christology in a sense different from that of the Apologists we find in the christologies of E. Brunner's *The Mediator* and K. Barth where Christ is the divine Word, understood not as prototypal world law but as "address" – which understanding goes back to Ignatius' concept of the Word through which God broke his silence.[11] Pannenberg deems this to be of no help, and his reason for this is very characteristic. He grants that

> Jesus' resurrection means that God has claimed as his own the promise of salvation made by the pre-Easter Jesus and thus recognized Jesus' word in a definite sense as his own word. Nevertheless it is still only a figurative expression when the event of God's

---

[10] Pannenberg comments, "One is often astounded at the way these theologians know how to say everything about Jesus' divinity without reference to the historical Jesus. This results from their taking a point of departure primarily from a philosophical theme in order to develop the concept of the Logos as a middle being between God and the world, with rather superficial appeals to New Testament assertions about Christ as the Son of God, the image of God, the Mediator of creation, and the Logos." (165)

[11] Ignatius, Magn. 8:2.

revelation in Jesus' fate is designated as God's "Word", an expression that — in order to be true — presupposes a substantiation outside itself for the fact that God is revealed in the person of Jesus. (167)

Such substantiation is not inherent in the concept of the "Word", it does not possess the ontological significance of an independent hypostasis beside the Father. Rather than this Word concept, God's self-revelation is the starting point for christology today because only the perception of Jesus as God's self-revelation can substantiate Jesus' essential unity with God and the differentiation between the Father and the Son within the essence of God himself which obtains in spite of this unity.

5. The Relation of Divinity and Humanity in Jesus

Jesus' resurrection, viewed in the context of its *Traditionsgeschichte*, yields the concept of God's self-revelation in Jesus. God's self-revelation, on account of its retroactive and confirmatory power, establishes the revelatory identity, which is essential identity, of Jesus with God and thus Jesus' divinity. Equally evident is Jesus' authentic humanity in his concrete activity and fate which Pannenberg develops in part II of *Jesus-God and Man*. But how can the authentic humanity and the divinity of Jesus exist together? To this classical question Pannenberg answers, "Jesus' unity with God is not to be conceived as a unification of two substances, but as this man Jesus is God." (283) He rejects the doctrine of two natures or substances in Jesus. He accepts its critique by F. Schleiermacher[12] that "two beings complete in themselves cannot together form a single whole." (287)

> In distinction from the formula *vere deus, vere homo,* the effort to conceive the unification of originally independently existing divine and human natures into a single individual in whom both natures nonetheless remain distinct leads inevitably to an impasse from which there is no escape. (287)

---

[12] Friedrich Schleiermacher, *The Christian Faith* (2 vols.; Harper Torchbooks, The Cloister Library; Harper & Row, Publishers, Inc., 1963), § 96, 1.

In a lengthy discussion of Nestorianism, Monophysitism, the problems inherent in the doctrine of the *communicatio idiomatum*, and the *kenosis* theory, Pannenberg shows that impasse and sums up,

> If divinity and humanity as two substances are supposed to be united in the individuality of Jesus, then either the two will be mixed to form a third or the individuality, Jesus' concrete living unity, will be ruptured. (287)

But he also criticizes von Harnack's and Gogarten's solutions according to which the community between God and Jesus was not physical but ethical.[13] Their concepts are one-sided like Ritschl's critique of the patristic christology; they exclude the general ontological problematic in their treatment. He agrees with Althaus that one has to insure oneself "against the moralistic leveling and dissolution" of the incarnation.[14] As we will see, however, Pannenberg's position is Ritschlian — with the no doubt fundamental difference that essential divinity is retroactively ascribed to the otherwise authentically human Jesus, thus overcoming Ritschl's one-sidedness.

From his critical analysis of the traditional christological types and solutions the following observations of Pannenberg's should be outlined; they express his own position.

(1) The dilemma of the Alexandrian and Antiochene christologies is insoluble because they depart from the incarnation instead of "seeking the basis of the confession to Jesus' divinity in the historical particularity of his human activity itself." (292) Here it always remained unclear how God and man could be one in the concrete person of Jesus.

(2) The dilemma of the diothelitic theory which became dogma becomes obvious precisely in its condemnation of monothelitism "because the basis for affirming Jesus' divinity lies precisely in his unity of will with the Father in the execution of his mission". (294) One's point of departure must be *the voluntary relation of Jesus to the Father*.

(3) In Scholasticism, which payed attention to the human individuality of Jesus, Duns Scotus comes closest to an adequate solution because he began not with the incarnation but the concept of person in general. For Duns, Jesus actualized his personal existence in dedication to God. The

---

[13] Friedrich Gogarten, *Die Verkündigung Jesu Christi*, p. 500.
[14] Paul Althaus, *Die christliche Wahrheit*, p. 447.

divine person "became the element of his existence which was constitutive for his person." (296) However, here Jesus does not dedicate himself to the Father but the human will of Jesus dedicates itself to the divine will of the Logos so that the doctrine remains within the pattern of disjunction christology.

(4) The theory of the *communicatio idiomatum* either destroys the authenticity of Jesus' humanity or results in a merely superficial linking of the two natures without ultimate reality.

(5) Barth's christology starts from the incarnation. It replaces the *communicatio idiomatum* by a *communicatio gratiarum* and thereby wishes to express the "complete determination of Christ's human nature by God's grace."[15]

> The enhypostasis of the human nature of Jesus Christ in the Logos is, according to Barth, "the essence and root of the whole of the divine grace given to him" (p. 100). What does that mean? If without reference to this event there is still a separate condition of the divine and the human natures taken by themselves, this formula moves along the lines of the disjunction Christology. Barth's language of "event", corresponding to the category of the "moment" and similar formulations in his commentary on Romans, must in fact be understood so punctualistically in the Prolegomena to the *Church Dogmatics*. If, however, as now seems to be the case, the meaning of "event" is identical with "the life of Jesus Christ" and thus includes a continuous temporal duration (p. 110), then it is not clear where the difference between Barth's position and the unification Christology of the orthodox Lutheran *communicatio idiomatum* according to the genus maiestaticum lies. Barth's emphasis upon the "dynamic" character of the divine-human unity in Christ does not overcome the dilemma of the orthodox doctrine of the communication of attributes; it avoids it. (302f.)

(6) Althaus' and Weber's designation of the divine-human unity as paradoxical[16] solves nothing because the mystery can best be respected by a perpetual attempt to better understand it which attitude is characteristic of patristic theology. "To retreat from the problems inescapably bound up

---

[15] Karl Barth, *Church Dogmatics*, IV/2, pp. 91-115.
[16] Paul Althaus, *op cit.*, pp. 448f. and O. Weber, *op. cit.*, vol. ii, p. 136.

with a particular approach with the explanation that it has to do with a mystery means the abandonment of the effort given to theology to understand critically its own statements." (303 f.)[17]

(7) With certain reservations Pannenberg expresses his appreciation for the approach of the 19th century theologian I. A. Dorner who envisions a process of continuous growth for the incarnation "in that God as the Logos continually grasps and appropriates each new aspect that emerges from true human development, just as conversely the growing real receptivity of the humanity consciously and voluntarily unites with ever new aspects of the Logos."[18] But this hardly matches with what Pannenberg said about the decisiveness of the resurrection.

(8) The kenotic christologies limit the fatal consequences of the realistic *communicatio idiomatum* as named under 4, and achieve a place for the concrete human life of Jesus. A Christ who possesses but merely renounces or hides his glory is, however, incompatible with the historical reality of Jesus of Nazareth. In the 19th century the kenosis doctrine was renewed with the difference that here not the God-man, not the incarnate Logos, but the divine Logos himself was the subject of kenosis.

> Thereby connection was made with the most widely held exegesis of Phil. 2:7 in the patristic church. But now the self-emptying of the Logos was no longer understood in the merely moral sense of a humble bending down to humanity, imparting to it unification with God. Rather, a physical self-limitation of the Logos in his divinity was conceived. It was supposed that this idea would harmonize the old Christological dogma with the modern, historical picture of the life of Jesus in his mere humanity. (310)

But this doctrine impairs the permanence of the deity of the Logos.[19] "The *vere homo* is achieved only proportionately to subtractions from the vere

---

[17] Pannenberg comments on Weber's critique of the Antiochene theologians that they could not think in paradoxes, "People who are prepared to refuse to continue thinking at specific points are hardly gifted in that particular art. Had the only issue been the 'paradox', patristic christology could have been satisfied with the formulas of Ignatius and saved itself the intellectual wear and tear of the following centuries." (304)

[18] Isaak August Dorner, *A System of Christian Doctrine* (Edinburgh: T. & T. Clark, 1890), vol. ii/I, § 104, p. 328.

[19] Pannenberg takes up Althaus' judgment that relinquishment of the "relative"

deus" (311), which also jeopardizes the trinity, viz., God's immutability no matter whether this is understood as static or in the historical sense of faithfulness to himself (the latter being Pannenberg's position; cf. section on his doctrine of God, infra chapter V, pp. 110ff.)

> Is not the Son, who had given up his relative divine attributes in the flesh, excluded from the Trinity for this period, since during his humiliation he was apparently not equally God with the Father and the Spirit? A self-limitation of the divinity at the incarnation results in a transformation in the Trinity. (311)

(9) K. Barth's doctrine[20] that God compromisingly sought community with sinful man without ceasing to be God and without self-contradiction is countered by Pannenberg,

> To say of God, "He chooses condescension. He chooses humiliation, humbleness, obedience" does not show it is thinkable that "the one true God" now "is identical with the existence of the humiliated, humble, obedient man Jesus of Nazareth" (p. 217). On what basis does theology accept responsibility for such assertions? How can the presence of the one true God in Jesus of Nazareth be expressed in such a way that this man at the same time remains understandable in his humanity and one with God in the totality of his existence. The humble course of the life of this man is surely not as such that of God. (313)

Because Barth constructs his christology "from above" he cannot help distinguishing between God and man in Jesus or asking how both can be united.

> For Barth the unity in Christ seems to consist only in the 'deed', in the 'history', in the 'event' of that humble condescension which takes on and determines the humanity of Jesus and thereby humanity in general. It is surely understandable that by the act of God's condescension he respects man's particularity and elects him to community with himself. It is also understandable that Jesus as the

---

divine attributes results in a "relative de-deification" of Christ. Cf. Paul Althaus, *RGG,* III (3d ed.), 1245, art. "Kenosis".

[20] Karl Barth, *Church Dogmatics,* IV/1, pp. 172ff. The page number within the quotation refers to this work of Barth's.

humble man to a certain extent participates in God's own act of humility. But is such functional community personal unity? (314)

Pannenberg's assessment of Karl Rahner's[21] concept of kenosis is highly significant because he considers it to be superior to all usage of that term in contemporary theology. This is due to "the conceptual clarity of his dialectic of self-differentiation." (318) Rahner apparently uses Hegel's dialectic of this concept, viz., to be identical with itself in the other, and says that God as creator constitutes the differentiation to himself by retaining the other as his, and to have the other as his own he constitutes it in its authentic reality. Thus God remains himself in the other and still becomes something; through this he empties himself, he gives himself away. But Rahner infers God's unity with the other in the figure of the man in the act of the incarnation from God's being with himself in the other and has thus circumvented the abyss between God and the creature which the incarnation must bridge. His dialectic of self-differentiation aids an understanding of the incarnation so far as *it makes it intelligible how God can be one with himself in the other*. But how can he be one with something different like a man who is creaturely reality, no longer *absolutely* God's reality? Rahner's concept best serves to explain the inner-trinitarian self-differentiation of God. The incarnation cannot find a satisfactory explanation via this concept. Rahner's other important concept of man's openness to God stands convergent but unrelated to this thought. But the incarnation must involve a connection of these two aspects.

Because all contemporary kenosis theories have denied God's renunciation of his divine attributes, kenosis lost the radicality of self-relinquishment, and this is true of Rahner's version also. But only via such self-relinquishment could the kenosis-theologians of the 19th century arrive at the historically concrete existence of Jesus, really different from God. Their theology grasped the width of the gap which the incarnation shall bridge. This is its merit. But Jesus' historical existence means self-relinquishment of the Logos. And then the two cannot be one.

If God's self-humiliation to unity with a man is conceived only as manifestation of the divine glory and not as sacrifice of essential

---

[21] Karl Rahner, LThK, V (1960), 956, art. "Jesus Christus", and "Zur Theologie der Menschwerdung", *Schriften zur Theologie*, 1960, vol. iv, pp. 135-155.

elements of the divine being, this expression does not help make the full humanity of Jesus in the incarnation intelligible; for then Jesus would remain an almighty, omniscient, omnipresent man, even though he humbly hides his glory. Or he remains a dual being with two faces in which divine majesty and human lowliness live and work parallel to one another, but without living unity. A human consciousness of Jesus is unthinkable in proportion to the degree that a living unity is affirmed. (318f.)

What conditions for an adequate understanding of the incarnation has this investigation pointed to? How is Jesus' unity with God as the incarnation of God compatible with the general concept of God, i.e., the God of Israel and of Jesus? The first condition is "that God in all his eternal identity is still to be understood as a God who is alive in himself, who can become something and precisely in so doing remain true to himself and the same." (320) God is changed in his inner being by making and shaping of another being, but his identity is not changed thereby. This is possible *if the presence of eternity includes in itself and unites what is separated in the succession of temporal events.* Then a becoming in God as is implied by the act of incarnation which is a new work of God would not infringe upon God's divine eternity. However, incarnation means no general becoming but God's uniting with something other than himself! The second condition then is Rahner's dialectic of self-differentiation as a pre-supposition, no more, no less, to God's unity with something other than himself. The third condition is that what comes into view as novelty from time to time in the divine life has been true in God eternally. The "intention" of the incarnation had been decreed from all eternity. However, as Pannenberg drives home significantly, true to his method, "the truth of such an assertion is dependent upon the temporal actuality of that thing (incarnation) . . . What is true in God's eternity is decided with retroactive validity only from the perspective of what occurs temporally with the import of the ultimate. Thus, Jesus' unity with God – and thus the truth of the incarnation – is also decided only retroactively from the perspective of Jesus' resurrection for the whole of Jesus' human existence, on the one hand, . . . and thus also for God's eternity, on the other." (321) As a critical examination of the tradition shows, Jesus' unity with God was not only hidden to other men prior to his resurrection, but also to Jesus himself because it had not yet been ultimately decided. Pannenberg says,

One would speak differently only by depriving the event of the resurrection of its contingency, of its elements of newness, by means of some sort of theological or physical determinism, or if one wants to deny the significance of Jesus' resurrection in general for the question of Jesus' unity with God. (321 f.)

This position preserves the contingency and novelty which the resurrection historically possessed and adequately attributes meaning to it for the construction of a christology. The most valuable yield of this procedure is the fact that Pannenberg's thesis of the retroactive enforcement of Jesus' unity with God from the resurrection explains (a) the *concealed* character of this unity in Jesus' pre-Easter life and work and thus provides a space for the authentic humanity of this life and (b) accomplishes a compatibility of the idea of this unity existing from the beginning with the idea of the genuine humanity of Jesus' activity. This substantially solves the christological problem. Pannenberg paraphrases his incarnation concept and says,

> ... out of his eternity, God has, through the resurrection of Jesus which was always present to his eternity, entered into a unity with this one man which was at first hidden. This unity illuminated Jesus' life in advance, but its basis and reality were revealed only by his resurrection. (322)

Two things should be noted in connection with this formulation. (1) "Revealed" here must mean both "it became known" and "it was retroactively instated". Only the latter concept allows the inference that this unity "illuminated Jesus' life in advance". Only if this unity is somehow extant during Jesus' pre-Easter ministry can it illuminate it in advance, i. e., before it was wholly and principally (even though not yet ultimately, which will transpire at the end of time only) illuminated at Easter. Once again the concepts "to establish ontologically" and confirmation understood as retroactive enforcement are tied to Pannenberg's ontology from the future. Within Greek thinking one can retroactively enforce the validity but not the being of something. Here being is determined in the primordial past; the movement from potentiality to actuality flows from the past into the present into the future. For Pannenberg it flows from the future into the present and, retroactively, into the past. (2) The quoted formulation surprises perhaps in that is speaks both of a hiddenness and of an illuminating

The Relation of Divinity and Humanity in Jesus 71

function of this unity in Jesus' pre-Easter ministry. There seem to exist two intentions in Pannenberg's train of thought whose correlation might require clarification. On the one hand, Jesus' unity with God is esthablished by the resurrection of Jesus. This provides the basis and (by retroactive enforcement) the reality of what Pannenberg calls the *revelatory* and *essential* unity of God and man in Jesus. In this sense the binding unity between the eternal being of God and the totality of Jesus' person follows *structurally* from the revelatory unity. This emphasis coincides with what Pannenberg says about the hidden character of this unity in Jesus' pre-Easter life. The pre-Easter life is ambiguous. The basis for this unity does not lie in Jesus' humanity.

But then, on the other hand, this unity *illuminates* the life and ministry of Jesus! In what sense? And what function do this statement and its demonstration have? What is Pannenberg's motive and intention in such a contention? He downright declares that, being effective in advance, this unity "thus *really constitutes* the *unity of his earthly life*"! (322, italics mine) Apparently the incarnation, inferred from the revelatory and essential God-Jesus-unity, must, in Pannenberg's thought, not remain an inference but must be substantiated on the basis of the facts in the historical particularity of the man Jesus. And only if there is evidence *that there is a unity of Jesus' earthly life* is this concept of incarnation wholly and finally conclusive! Apparently not only the resurrection as event and its significance require historical verification but equally its achievement in terms of retroactive enforcement. This appears to be quite in line with Pannenberg's epistemological principle. One merely has questions with regard to the compatibility of the *hidden* with the *effective* character of the unity in the pre-Easter life of Jesus. At any rate, this emphasis is as important here as the first.

> The unity of Jesus with God . . . can be found only in the historical particularity of the man Jesus, his message, and his fate. This is not to say that the basis of this unity resides in Jesus' humanity. Of course, the incarnational doctrine is quite right in affirming that the initiative in the event of the incarnation can be sought only on the side of God. However, we can perceive this unity only from the perspective of Jesus' historical reality. (322f.)
>
> . . . we spoke of the revelatory unity of Jesus with God . . . There however we could not yet consider the internal uniqueness of this

unity. We dealt only with the structure of revelation as the route toward the knowledge that, because of the revelation, the God revealed in it cannot be separated from Jesus through whom he is revealed, without contradicting the concept of revelation. (324)

Pannenberg calls the inference of the essential unity from the resurrection *structural* or *negative*. The last quotation speaks of the "internal uniqueness of this unity" (324). Perhaps one may say, the revelatory unity is *structurally* an essential one. *What is it materially and positively?*

CHAPTER IV

JESUS' IDENTITY AS THE SON OF GOD

1. Jesus' Personal Community With the Father and its Function

It is Pannenberg's thesis that materially and positively the unity connecting Jesus with God is a unity of person; it has *personal character*. To substantiate this thesis Pannenberg focusses on the *humanity* of Jesus. The question how the essential unity illuminates or affects Jesus' life and ministry is coterminous with the question, "what Jesus' divinity means for his human existence. How does it express itself in his human life?" (325) Pannenberg epitomizes his aim, "We are now concerned to characterize, not the divinity of Jesus, but its relation to his particular human being" (325), and his thesis reads, "Only his personal community with the Father demonstrates that Jesus is the Son of God" (324).[1]

Pannenberg turns to Jesus' *self-consciousness* because "self-consciousness is an inescapable condition of personality." (325) If both Jesus' unity with God and his authentic human existence as a person are to be taken seriously, this unity must constitute the *unity of Jesus' earthly life*. And if it does so, this must be reflected in Jesus' self-consciousness. In other words, Jesus' essential unity with God *must be a personal unity* if it includes the whole of his concrete human life. And this "cannot take place entirely outside Jesus' pre-Easter life and consciousness", or else "one could not properly speak of a unity of his whole existence with God." (326) This is so because of Pannenberg's concept of the transcending openness of a human life which, esthablished on anthropological findings, constitutes man's self-distance, self-reflexion, and more or less complete self-knowledge and self-

---

[1] This is the translation in *JGaM* of Pannenberg's sentence, "Erst die Personge-meinschaft mit dem Vater erweist Jesus als Sohn Gottes", *Grundzüge der Christologie*, p. 335. The translation is misleading since "erst" unlike "only" does not connote exclusiveness but the "final, last, and in this sense ultimately conclusive" element among several. "Demonstrates" is an accurate rendering of "erweist". "Erweisen" (to demonstrate, to show conclusively) like "beweisen" (to prove) have to do with the foundation of the knowledge of truth, not the foundation of truth itself (Erkenntnisgrund vs. Seinsgrund). The sentence could be rendered, First his personal community ... conclusively shows ... God.

contradiction. Self-contradiction appears as life in contradiction to the human destiny[2] and as lack of identity with one's self. Had Jesus lived in self-contradiction, i. e., had he not been related to his unity with God in his self-consciousness, he would not have been self-identical and to this extent not one with God. *"The presupposition* (his unity with God) *would then be proved to be false."* (326, italics mine).[3] This is methodologically significant. In effect it says: *unless a self-awareness of this unity of Jesus with God is empirically evident the christological conclusion drawn from the resurrection collapses.* This proof for such a self-awareness is part of the ultimate historical validation of christology. It is not the basis and reality of its truth — this rather must be said to be the future ultimate revelation of everything or its anticipation, viz., the resurrection as proleptic ontological establishment of the God-man unity. But for our perception and discovery the historical actuality of the concrete existence of Jesus is the evidence from which to depart. Pannenberg's statements quoted on pages 69 and 70 above which gave rise to our suggestion on p. 71 now receive confirmation.

2. *Jesus' Indirect Identity with the Son of God*

Now Pannenberg concurs with the representatives of the more critical New Testament research. Jesus applied none of the christological titles to himself. His awareness of a special oneness with God expresses itself, as H. Conzelmann puts it, "only indirectly".[4] There is Jesus' claim to speak and act on God's authority. What sort of self-consciousness is implied in this activity, as far as ascertainable?

This question concerns (a) the type of self-knowledge Jesus had (Supernatural knowledge, given by God, or natural knowledge, gained by reflexion?), and (b) its extent in the sense whether it was complete from the beginning, or in a process of growth toward completion or some state of incompleteness. Of decisive importance is Pannenberg's anthropological contention that man's "authentic selfhood about which he inquires in the

---

[2] Destiny in the sense of God's *Bestimmung*, i.e., the divinely determined, chosen, or appointed goal for man.

[3] Pannenberg approvingly quotes Rahner who says substantially the same thing. (326) Pannenberg's anthropological tenets, so fundamental for the grounding of his system, will be thematized later.

[4] Hans Conzelmann, *RGG*, III (3d ed.), p. 632

openness of his existence is not yet ultimately decided but always still open to decision" (330). This rules out all theories which assume a definitive knowledge of Jesus that he is God. For any such closed knowledge would waive the structure of openness.

Pannenberg pays close attention to an article by Rahner[5] which in his judgment carries the discussion a significant step forward. Rahner's theory tries to solve the problem of consciousness. He claims that (1) the unification of the Logos with the human nature does not minimize it but, quite the opposite, leads to its highest possible realization, and (2) that general human consciousness is not identical with objective knowledge so that self-consciousness does not necessarily mean objective self-knowledge. Man has an *"a priori,* nonobjective knowledge about oneself as a fundamental given of the spiritual subject in which it is by itself and simultaneously aware of its transcendental reference to the totality of possible objects of knowledge and freedom."[6] This fundamental, given, non-objective self-"knowledge" is immediate, unthematic, unreflective, and directed to God. It is *universally human.* Jesus, the hypostatic union, is "to be understood as the most radical actualization of human spirit generally".[7] Over against this consciousness the objectively reflective coming to oneself yields knowledge and is a second step. It is, generally and thus also in the case of Jesus, a personal intellectual history of self-interpretation.

With respect to this hypothesis Pannenberg raises two critical questions. (1) Can the immediately given ever be conscious *without the mediation of an objective content of consciousness?* (2) Is not the history of self-interpretation *always interwoven with the individual's social milieu?* For Jesus this milieu was the Israelite religious tradition, and Jesus' (as any man's) clarification of this fundamental given is inseparable from and requires his appropriation of and dialogue with the contents of the traditions of his environment! Against Rahner, Pannenberg will not attribute only an *a posteriori* and insignificant role to his environment and the concepts of self-interpretation it provided for Jesus. Pannenberg obviously contests Rahner's hypothesis because he is persuaded that history is *Traditionsgeschichte,* and meaning is part of fact. Therefore those elements of Israel's

---

[5] Karl Rahner, "Dogmatic Reflections on the Knowledge and Self-consciousness of Christ", *Theological Investigations,* vol. v, pp. 193–215.

[6] *Ibid.,* pp. 200f.

[7] *Ibid.,* p. 235

religious tradition which helped Jesus to clarify his fundamental given openness to God are dogmatically significant and are not interchangeable and replaceable ciphers to be relinquished to the life of Jesus research. The relevant traditional conceptual milieu for Jesus includes especially the Israelite concepts of God, salvation, and eschatology. It is certain "that Jesus' self-consciousness was decisively stamped by his message of the nearness of God and his Kingdom." (332) This is a *basic datum* in Jesus' self-consciousness in its relation to God. Two further opinions distinguish Pannenberg's position from Rahner's:

(1) Pannenberg's radically historical approach is concerned first with the relation of Jesus' consciousness not to the Logos but to the Father. Only the latter is a concrete historical reality of the pre-Easter life of Jesus, a direct datum.

(2) What became known in the process of clarification of what was immediately conscious is not something which Jesus "in the ground of his existence" "always knew about himself"[8]. Why not? Because *man's self-knowledge is always open to a yet unfulfilled, unrealized future*. Pannenberg concludes,

> Thus even Jesus' nonobjective, fundamentally given immediacy to God as it is to be presupposed as the background of his historical activity is not only to be conceived as historically conditioned through objectified traditional material but also as directed toward a still incomplete future. (332)

Jesus' self-consciousness, then, is characterized by a *limited* self-knowledge with regard both to his relation to God and to his future, and precisely this constitutes the condition under which his dedication to God, to the God of the eschatological future, could and did reach perfection. For only under such circumstances could his dedication be one of ultimate and highest *trust*. *"This lack of knowledge is actually the condition of Jesus' unity with God."* (334, italics mine)

Therefore Jesus' sonship is dialectic, and one has to speak of an *indirect* identy of Jesus with the Son of God. In his self-consciousness Jesus did not identify with the Logos but with the Father. He knew himself "functionally to be one with God's will in preactualizing the future full reality of the Kingdom of God and thus to be one with God himself, namely, in the

---

[8] *Ibid.*, p. 241

function of his message and his entire activity determined by his message which made up his public existence." (334) This "identity", however, included Jesus' awareness of an infinite distinction between himself and God and his subordination to God. Jesus' conciousness of his mission was compatible with this. Only through Easter the church understood Jesus' mission and death as perfect dedication and sacrifice to the Father and she expressed this understanding when she spoke of the unique unity between the two and when she called Jesus the "Son". Direct is Jesus' relation to the Father; his relation to the eternal Son is indirect, to be arrived at, as Pannenberg says, by way of a *detour,* viz., by way of his relation to the Father.

The personal community with the Father is demonstrable in Jesus' behavior and his fate on the cross. Historically, Jesus' mission, i. e., his proclamation, determined his activity and led to his death. And his resurrection confirmed these and thus demonstrated that all of Jesus' activity was dedication actually to God and not a phantom and that his death, suffered on account of this dedication, was an integral part of his mission and of God's will for Jesus.[9] But *Jesus himself up to his death* could not yet realize what was comprehensible only after Easter. For him his fate on the cross appeared to be unintelligible darkness and failure of his mission. Yet he endured it in dedication to his mission and thus in dedication to God. Here, on the cross, *his dedication became self-sacrifice.* For his mission and proclamation as such offered no *Verstehenshorizont* and thus no self-assurance or self-certainty to Jesus dying on the cross. Only after Easter his fate appeared to be "an act of God to him and through him." (355)

3. *The Concept of Dedication to God and the Final Step Toward Jesus' Identity as Son of God*

Jesus' essential unity with God, developed from the concept of God's *self-revelation,* if it is not a fiction, had to constitute the unity of his earthly life and consequently had to be a personal unity. As was shown, only this *unio personalis* can lead to cognition of Jesus' identity as the Son of God. Unless this *unio personalis* is historically perceptible in Jesus' self-

---

[9] For how the resurrection demonstrates this cf. chapter VI, *infra.*

consciousness it may not be asserted. Pannenberg's train of argument showed that indeed there is evidence for this personal unity. The *unio personalis* turned out to consist internally and materially of Jesus' unconditional dedication to the Father.[10]

We may anticipate here that Pannenberg manages to gain a meaningful understanding of the atonement *inter alia* from his concept of Jesus' dedication which is similar to Ritschl's concept of Jesus' *Berufsgehorsam*. This dedication was put to its greatest task when — as we saw — the mission to which it was directed apparently failed. Continuing steadfastly inspite of failure, his dedication became self-sacrifice. Thus Pannenberg gains a historical foundation for a sacrificial interpretation of the cross, as will be discussed later. On account of this "senselessness" of his death (compared to his activity!), motivated by sheer dedication without understanding, Jesus gained nothing for himself. At Easter

> Jesus is not confirmed by the resurrection in something which he might have been by himself, but precisely in his having reserved nothing for himself in his human existence, in having lived entirely from God and for the men who must be called into the Kingdom — both in his mission and his unheard-of claim, but precisely also in his fate on the cross, which seemed to exclude him from all community with the God of Israel and with men. (335)

This total self-giving is Jesus'. However, when Jesus' identity with the Son of God and thus the incarnation of God are established, Pannenberg, on the basis of this self-giving, will have gained a persuasive historical ground for the view that the Son of God and in so far God emptied himself and died on the cross, which can be highly significant for an interpretation of the cross. (To what extent Pannenberg takes recourse to his line of argument will be seen later.) But first this identity needs to be established conclusively. Again, his resurrection legitimized Jesus' mission and claim as from God, his zeal as dedication to God, his work as obedience to God, his death as sacrifice to God. Now because Jesus' resurrection is the prolepsis

---

[10] This is not to say that such *unio personalis* may be assumed to exist wherever there is a comparable dedication, e. g., Jeremiah. For the historical datum, verifying the ontological decision from the Resurrection, is indispensably in need of its confirmation through God's direct self-revelation which gives rise to the structural oneness of Jesus with God. Only when both is given, as in the case of the Christ event, can P. speak of *unio personalis* of a dedicated martyr with God.

of God's ultimate direct self-revelation (ultimately revealing the divinity of Israel's God at the end of history), it follows that through the resurrection

> he is the revealer of God's divinity to the extent that he is confirmed in the resurrection as the one who had been wholly and completely dedicated to God, as he also is henceforth. Just as the one completely obedient to the Father, he is the revealer of God's divinity and thus himself belongs inseparably to the essence of God. Thus he is the Son. (336)

Now Jesus' resurrection, in its *traditionsgeschichtlichem* context, no doubt proleptically establishes the divinity of the God of Israel. One might ask: why should, for Jesus, essential identity follow from dedication? Does Pannenberg not, like Ritschl, infer Jesus' divinity from his *Berufsgehorsam* to and oneness of ethical willing with God? Admittedly, he does not, as W. Herrmann, infer it from the psychological and ethical facts of Jesus' inner life which, on the whole, is unknowable. But does he not proceed like Ritschl?

In fact he does not. To make it quite clear, we must distinguish between the question of the relationship between dedication and essential oneness with the one to whom I dedicate myself, on the one hand, and the *other* question of the true identity of the one to whom Jesus dedicated himself and thus was essentially one with. The latter is only decided by the *resurrection*. This distinguishes Pannenberg univocally from Ritschl. But the former is worked out by recourse to the idea that I come to share the essence of one to whom I am totally dedicated. Why? Personal community is at the same time essential community because (1) to exist in dedication is the essence of a person. Pannenberg draws on Hegel's statement that it is "the character of the person . . . to supersede its isolation, its separatedness" through dedication. "In friendship and love I give up my abstract personality and win thereby concrete personality. The truth of personality is just this, to win it through this submerging, being submerged in the other."[11] and (2)

> To be submerged in the "Thou" means at the same time, however, participation in his being. Thus the divinity of Jesus as Son is mediated, established through his dedication to the Father. In the

---

[11] Georg Wilhelm Friedrich Hegel, *Lectures on the Philosophy of Religion*, (Humanities Press, Inc., 1962), vol. iii, pp. 24f.

execution of this dedication, Jesus is the Son. Thus he shows himself identical with the correlate Son already implied in the understanding of God as the Father, the Son whose characteristic it is not to exist on the basis of his own resources but wholly from the Father. The mutual dedication of Father and Son to one another which constitutes the Trinitarian unity of God also establishes thereby first of all the true divinity of the Son. (336)

But personal distinctiveness is not abolished by personal community with and dedication to the other. Pannenberg can say, "An 'essence' common to both emerges in the course of their interaction." (344)

Such is the detour of the path to the essential oneness of this man Jesus of Nazareth with the Son of God. The path departed from the man Jesus' community with his God, the Father, the God of Israel, and arrived at his being the Son of God. The incarnation is structurally (externally) established through the resurrection (God's self-revelation, confirmation). Materially (internally) it is established through the perception of Jesus' self-dedication to the Father (unio personalis) which via the inherent meaning of dedication gives rise to essential oneness. Jesus' being as man is indirectly identical with the divine Sonship.

4. *The Mutual Dependence of the Noetical and the Ontological Foundation of Jesus' Identity as Son of God*

In the final analysis of Pannenberg's statements Jesus' pre-Easter consciousness, i.e., his dedication, proves nothing by and in itself. Neither does the resurrection. Jesus' self-consciousness and dedication lead to cognition of his identity but requires as a "co-supposition" his resurrection. Jesus' resurrection leads to cognition of his identity but requires as a "co-supposition" his self-consciousness and dedication. Both confirm and require each other. Both are mutually dependent upon one another. Ontologically the resurrection is first, the self-consciousness of Jesus in his pre-Easter ministry is its result. Noetically Jesus' community with the Father is first, the resurrection its confirmation. But to some extent, as was discernable from Pannenberg's formulations under way, *both* have at times ontological, at other times noetical significance.

Thus Jesus' identity with the eternal Son of God is dialectical: the understanding of this man . . . leads to the confession of his eternal divinity. Conversely, anything said about an eternal Son of God can be sufficiently established only by recourse to the particularity of this man, to his unity with God. The synthesis of this dialectic, the unity of God and man in Christ, emerges fully only in the history of his existence. (343)[12]

The detour achieves that the identity of Jesus with the divine Son is historically thinkable; it demonstrably checks with the full humanity of Jesus' earthly existence. For Pannenberg the concept of the Son is not a symbolic correlate to that of the Fatherhood of God but describes an ontic reality. Ontologically it is established from the end, yet effective and illuminating and consequently perceptible from hindsight, and temporally by anticipation or from before the event. Pannenberg sums up,

Thus the perception of Jesus' eternal Sonship as dialectically identical with his humanity is based noetically upon the particularity of just this human being in his relation to the divine Father; ontologically,

---

[12] The mutual dependence of the noetical and ontological foundation of Jesus' identity as the Son of God escaped Klappert in his analysis of P.'s christology. He says, "Das Geschick Jesu als Prolepse des Endes der Universalgeschichte und damit als vollkommener Spiegel der 'Herrlichkeit Gottes' ist wesensidentisch mit Gott und impliziert damit die ontische Begründung der Gottheit Jesu. Die Gottheit Jesu ist damit nichts anderes als das Derivat des (weil Prolepse der *Universalgeschichte*) *wesensidentischen Geschicks Jesu mit Gott.* D. h. die Gottheit Jesu ist ein Prädikat der Wesensidentität des Auferweckungsgeschicks Jesu mit der Gottheit Gottes, *wobei der Gedanke der ontischen Begründung der Gottheit Jesu durch das mit Gott wesensidentische Geschick Jesu die teleologische Identität der Universalgeschichte mit dem Wesen Gottes zur Voraussetzung hat.* Das Christusgeschehen ist – weil Geschichtsprolepse – offenbarungs- und wesensidentisch mit Gott und als solches die Begründung der Gottheit Jesu. Das vere deus Jesu ist also nach P. lediglich ein Prädikat des mit der Gottheit Gottes wesensidentischen Geschicks Jesu. 'Christus' ist ein Prädikat des Christus'geschehens'." (Berthold Klappert, *Die Auferweckung des Gekreuzigten, Der Ansatz der Christologie Karl Barths im Zusammenhang der Christologie der Gegenwart* (Neukirchen-Vluyn: Neukirchener Verlag des Erziehungsvereins, 1971, p. 56, Italics Klappert's). Jesus' divinity is not only a *Derivat* of the *wesensidentischen Geschick Jesu mit Gott* because Jesus' divinity is equally dependent on his genuine humanity as the *Erkenntnisgrund* of all ontological statements.

the relation is inverted, for the divine Sonship designates the ontological root in which Jesus' human existence, connected with the Father and nevertheless distinguished from him, has the ground of its unity and of its meaning. (337)

By comparison, Pannenberg, unlike Ritschl, has paramount ontological interests. For both the historical *Berufstreue* of Jesus is fundamental for christology. But Pannenberg establishes Jesus' essential oneness with the Son by way of the Hegelian understanding of dedication and, above all, by his anthropology and his ontology from the future, as was shown.[13]

---

[13] Pannenberg's distinction of the human and the divine aspect of this one historical existence of Jesus of Nazareth as much as his treating Jesus' divinity from an ontological and a noetical viewpoint seems similar to Albrecht Ritschl's fundamental method of distinguishing between the religious (dogmatic) and the ethical *Betrachtungsweise*, as Rolf Schäfer explained it convincingly (*Ritschl, Grundlinien eines fast verschollenen dogmatischen Systems,* 1968). But the resemblance is, apart from the strong historical interest of both men, only formal. The methodological difference, as I see it, is this: For both theologians the material of dogmatics is the faith of the community as expressed in Scripture and tradition, especially the New Testament. Equally both consider the person of Jesus of Nazareth as the center of revelation. Ritschl's two foci are justification and "the universal moral Kingdom of God" (*The Christian Doctrine of Justification and Reconciliation,* vol. iii, 1900, para. 2) Pannenberg has two foci also: Jesus' pre-Easter mission and his resurrection. More strongly than in Ritschl for him *both* of these are tied to the Kingdom of God which, to be sure, is very differently understood. And finally both want to be *wissenschaftliche* theologians and have two criteria of validation the first of which they have in common: the historical life of Jesus is the epistemological filter for christological statements. "Wo eine wissenschaftliche Behandlung der Objekte des christlichen Glaubens in Aussicht genommen wird, kann man nicht in mechanischer Weise die Urkunde der Offenbarung als Lehrgesetz verwenden, sondern man muß vom Mittelpunkt der Offenbarung aus den Inhalt derselben organisch entwickeln. . . . Ritschl (schreitet) zu der Erklärung fort, daß die Person Christi in der Dogmatik als Erkenntnisgrund für die Abgrenzung jeder Lehre in Betracht gezogen werden müsse, daß der Offenbarungswert Christi der Erkenntnisgrund für alle Aufgaben der Theologie sei." (Gustav Ecke, *Die theologische Schule A. Ritschls und die ev. Kirche in der Gegenwart,* vol. i, 1897, p. 134) Cf. also Pannenberg's quotation of Ritschl on p. 11 above. For Pannenberg the historical life of Jesus includes his resurrection, however. Both are to be verified *historically*. And history includes eminently the *Traditionsgeschichte* in which Jesus stands. The fundamental opposition of these two

His construction allows one to uphold the gist of the post-Chalcedonian *enhypostasis*-doctrine according to which the whole of Jesus' human existence is ontologically dependent on the Logos and at the same time to hold that the actual event of the unification of God and man takes place "in the temporal course of Jesus' existence" (338) and that "Jesus' unity with God is mediated through his human dedication to the Father" (339). This stance preserves Jesus' full humanity and does justice to the texts. Pannenberg favors the *enhypostasis*-formula only as an ontological judgment in the sense of a summary statement that looks at the whole *a posteriori*. Contrary to the patristic *enhypostasis* idea, for Pannenberg *Jesus as man is the Son*. He is not dependent in his existence upon the Logos but upon the Father and *precisely in this dependence on the Father and in his dedication to him he is the Son*.

> ... as this man, Jesus is the Son of God and thus himself God. Consequently he is not to be thought of as a synthesis of the divine and the human ... Nor does something new, a third thing, result from a mixture of the two. Nor is his humanity absorbed in divinity so that it disappears. Precisely *in* his particular humanity Jesus is the Son of God. (342, italics by the author)

The divine Sonship constitutes the particularity of the man Jesus and – "above all the converse is true" (!) (342) – the uniqueness of Jesus' humanity established (Pannenberg does not continue: his divine Sonship, but) the confession of Jesus as the Son of God. Two characteristic ideas of Pannenberg's help to explain this contention more precisely.

---

theologies lies in the second criterion of validation, the hermeneutical! For Ritschl it is his "ethical view": Scientific theology has "the task of verifying everything which is cognizable as belonging to the gracious operations of God upon the Christian *by the corresponding religious and moral acts which are called forth by revelation*". (para. 3) Each act of God here involves "an analysis of the corresponding voluntary activities in which man appropriates the operations of God. ... For apart from voluntary activity ... we have no means of understanding objective dogmas as religious truths." (para.6). In short, here experience (Frömmigkeit) and history verify. Revelation is independent of philosophical and *wisssenschaftliche* verification. Insofar Ritschl is *Offenbarungstheologe*. For Pannenberg the historical data are acceptable and relevant only if compatible with the phenomena in the whole of known reality, anthropology having the key position here. History and reason verify. (Italics mine)

(1) The particularity of the man Jesus, again, is centrally his dedication to the Father. Now that his dedication is such that it penetrates, envelopes, and surpasses all other elements and characteristics of his life, Pannenberg does not conclude from his historical evidence for Jesus' self-consciousness but from the fact that God confirmed him. In the light of the resurrection his dedication to his mission and message is proved to have been the all-encompassing content of his striving. Because he was raised he was one with God; because he was one with God, his dedication was total. This distinguishes Pannenberg's from positions like Ritschl's. Jesus' historical place within the apocalyptic expectation, his striving, and its confirmation – *these together* constitute his uniqueness and the uniqueness of his dedication. No one else can, merely on account of his perfect dedication to God, be said to be the Son of God.

(2) The second point is so subtle that we have to follow Pannenberg's formulations almost slavishly. Traditionally the doctrine of the trinity has to do with a plurality of persons who participate in a single nature; christology with a unification of two natures in a single person. In christology the common nature of the trinitarian persons confronts the realm of human life as a single reality, and the one person with whom christology deals is also the person of whom statements about the trinity are true. Participation of several individuals in a common nature is conceivable, but a synthesis of separate natures to form a single person is – as Schleiermacher insisted – impossible. It would destroy the *Personeinheit*. This judgment is true also when one distinguishes individuality from *Personalität* and understands the latter as concrete existence and concrete existence as personal relation. Personal differentiation (Verschiedenheit) is possible inspite of a common essence, but personal particularity (Besonderheit) presupposes a unity of essence or, as Pannenberg significantly adds, "at least the essence must be integrated into unity by the person himself." (344) As Pannenberg said when he explained how dedication gives rise to essential unity, personal community results in a share in the essence of the other. This does not, however, waive personal distinctiveness. The latter continues. In fact, as Maximus Confessor according to Pannenberg realized,[14] "increasing differentiation (and above all increasing consciousness of such differentiation) is a condition for increasingly intensive community and unity" (348), and this holds true of all personal

---

[14] J. P. Migne, *Patrologiae cursus completus, series Graeca*, 91, 97 A.

community. In the course of their interaction, their give-and-take of receiving and acting, the events of active or passive experiences, an "essence" common to both emerges.[15] Any personal community includes such integration. The ineradicable difference between God and man in Jesus Christ was integrated into a whole through Jesus' personal communication with the Father. However, this was not so integrated in Jesus' own, individual *Lebenseinheit*. Rather,

> ... the particular elements of human life in Jesus' existence were integrated in this way to a whole by his person, that the integrating person realized itself precisely thereby as the person of the Son belonging eternally to the divinity of God. (344)

With the reservation that the degree of complexity of the matter permits no adequately concrete description, Pannenberg says,

> ... the existence of Jesus is integrated into the person of the eternal Son of God precisely through the history of his earthly way in its reference to the Father. In this sense, the person of Jesus is the locus in which God's essence (in which Jesus participates as a person of the Trinity) and the essence of man, integrated through just this person, is united, as is apparent from Jesus' resurrection. (344)

5. Some Consequences for Theological Anthropology

A discussion of Pannenberg's anthropology was postponed to a later stage of this treatise. Within its structure the general phenomenon of *man's openness in relation to the world*, a finding of modern behavioral anthropology, is of fundamental importance. Pannenberg thinks that, if radicalized, it means openness to God. This concept possesses pivotal significance for Pannenberg's doctrine of God, his ontology from the future, and his way of rendering the apocalyptic expectation of the resurrection of the dead essentially true and relevant for our contemporary thinking. We encountered this concept several times in Pannenberg's deliberations. For his christology, this concept proved to be decisive also. For Christ's dedication to God which constitutes his personal identity with

---

[15] Pannenberg does not mean a substance or nature by essence.

the Son is an expression of this openness in its radical form. We remember that because of the open-ended character of this openness to the future (the future of the God who acts and creates novelty and is "incomplete" at any moment of time prior to his ultimate self-revelation which alone will determine what a thing, or a person, is and was) Christ *could not* have definitively known that he was God before he was raised from the dead. Now because man, like Jesus, is characterized by openness to God, Jesus, in his *unio personalis* with the Father, is the fulfillment of the human destiny.[16] The truth of this concept of openness is the presupposition without which the dogma of Chalcedon were meaningless today. This concept allows it to ascertain and argue the identity of Jesus as the Son without taking away anything from the genuine human reality of Jesus. Jesus' *Personalität* was, as we saw, achieved by a process of integration through personal community. On *this* account Jesus fulfilled the universal human Bestimmung and his life rises to paradigmatical stature and validity. ". . . all human existence is designed to be personalized by its dependence upon God, to be integrated into a person through its relation to God the Father in such a way that men are constituted as persons by the Fatherly God in confrontation with him." (345) "Sonship" is man's *Bestimmung* "even though it became historical reality only in Jesus' activity and fate." (345) Pannenberg points to Paul's concept of sonship to express the universal role of Jesus' personality. Jesus is the new man who brings man's *Bestimmung* to a fulfillment which is superior to the first creation. As such he is the Son of God. He shares his sonship with us.

> Thus Christians share Jesus's divine personality as Son *through* Jesus, and this distinguishes them at the same time from Jesus himself. Through him they share his relation of dedication to the Father. (346)

What does it mean, to share Jesus' sonship? It means to share Jesus' relation of dedication to the Father. This relation, we remember, is characterized by Jesus' integrating the divine essence into unity with himself. Natural man is lacking in self-identity; he is disintegrated, he lives out of tune with his *Bestimmung* and reality. "Through the Spirit of Sonship the Son of God wants to become the person-building, existence-integrating power in all men." (346) Thereby sonship is an abstraction from the totality of the

---

[16] "Destiny" here as frequently is the translation of *Bestimmung*. Cf. note 2, page 97 above.

events in which, actively or passively, Jesus' unity with God's essence is achieved or enhanced; it happened within all on-going events which related Jesus to God and to the world. Thus Pannenberg spoke of Jesus' indirect, mediated, dialectic Sonship. The Christian's participation in Jesus' sonship is of the same nature as regards content, but *different in structure*. For Jesus' eschatological message and its retroactive legitimation constitute his *essential oneness* with the Father. Jesus participates in God's essence in that his behavior demonstrably was that of sonship corresponding to God's Fatherhood. This can be true of any Christian. But he *also was the Son*. The key role in this distinction is played by the eschatological message of Jesus and its confirmation without which his dedication or self-sacrifice remain ambiguous and *vice versa*. These — vide p. 83 f.! — define the uniqueness and unrepeatability of Jesus' claim, its meaning, and its fulfillment, i.e., of the mode of his unity with the Son of God. Contrary to this,

> Christians become sons of God only to the extent that they participate in Jesus' Sonship. They achieve a share in Jesus' Sonship only in proportion to the degree of their community with this one man who as a man is the Son of God. (347)

Of both, Jesus and the Christians, it is true that community with and participation in God's essence are mediated through personal community with the Father. But Jesus' community is distinguished first by a different degree-apparently his dedication is perfect, the Christians' imperfect. Second, our community with the Father is *structurally* different; it depends on our community with the Son. The uniqueness of Jesus' eschatological mission makes all the difference here. On its account the personal differentiation of Christians from the Father remains. In our individual existence we remain essentially different from the Father. The Christian shares in God's glory not in his particular individuality but in and through his community with Christ.

> The openness to God that belongs to the structure of human existence as such (even when in fact it is lived in contradiction to God) and that finds its fulfillment only when human existence is personally integrated in dependence upon God, is *fulfilled in Jesus* by the divine confirmation . . . . It is fulfilled *in all other men* only through their historically mediated relation to and community with Jesus of Nazareth. (348, italics mine)

7 Neie: Pannenberg

CHAPTER V

ANALYSIS OF THE DETERMINATIVE CONCEPTS OF PANNENBERG'S THEOLOGY AS A WHOLE

In our previous discussion of Pannenberg's christology we briefly described or merely referred to a number of basic concepts in Pannenberg's thought while postponing their elucidation to a later time. Such elucidation and analysis should be our task now. An understanding of the use Pannenberg makes of anthropology and of New Testament studies and how he derives from those his concepts of history as revelation and of ontology from the future and his notion of God — all this is needed to firmly ground his christology which in turn is the necessary background for his teachings on Christ's passion and death.

1. Three Motives of Pannenberg's Theology

Three motives underlie Pannenberg's theological efforts and, together with a number of important impulses from others, go into the making of the determinative concepts of his theology. The first motive to be perceived is Pannenberg's deep conviction of the *historicalness* (Geschichtlichkeit) of man, society, culture, the world. There is no primordial past in which is determined once and for all what reality is. History is a process in which change takes place and novelty emerges. Ideas come and go, interpretations of reality undergo corrections based on new, better insight. Maturer views are given rise to by new and different situations. Any present view can be superseded and surpassed. All we know and perceive or hold to be correct now is preliminary. The true view of reality is not to be found in the mythical light of a primordial past but in each new present, i. e., in the future. It is still open what man will be; it is his task to identify and seek his destiny, and his views must always be ready to be relinquished. Concepts are historically conditioned.

The approach of sociology must also be superseded to make room for a more comprehensive science that would pursue the concrete change in the life of individuals and of groups of men. That is historical science. Presupposing all other anthropological investigations, it arrives at the closest approximation to concrete human life .... historical science is the crown of all anthropological sciences. It embraces all the others and describes the concrete, always diverse, individual actualization of human existence.[1]

We always think in the context of a historically determined human situation. This explains why it is only in more modern theology that "the entire problem of the concept of revelation and especially of the connection between Revealer and what is revealed in God's self-revelation has been thought through ..." (131). In earlier periods the existence of God was self-evident. It was secured through the philosophical arguments for his existence. But the Enlightenment and Kant destroyed the old theistic construction.

For this reason, the problem of revelation has become the fundamental question in modern theology, that is, the only possible basis for speaking about God himself ... Thus for contemporary theology the central significance of the concept of revelation is closely related to *its specific situation in the history of ideas. However, certain Biblical facts only come to view at all from the perspective of this historically conditioned way of putting the question.*" (131, italics mine).

As is evident from this remark, Pannenberg does not hold a reconstruction of a contemporary natural theology to be a viable option. More accurately, Pannenberg believes that the criticisms against the traditional ideas of God as *ens summum* and transcendent person are cogent (a) in so far as they deny the possibility of affirming such God on a speculative metaphysical basis, (b) in so far as they refute the finitization of God as a being alongside other beings in the present world. The impact of this critique "certainly does bear upon the finite and anthropomorphic character of concepts of God."[2]

---

[1] Wolfhart Pannenberg, *What is Man? Contemporary Anthropology in Theological Perspective* (Philadelphia: Fortress Press, 1970), p. 138 (henceforth quoted WiM)

[2] Wolfhart Pannenberg, "The God of Hope", *Basic Questions in Theology* vol. ii, (Philadelphia: Fortress Press,² 1972), p. 235 (henceforth quoted BQiT)

> A God conceived as a thing at hand, even as a thingified person . . . is no longer credible. One may ask however wether such a characterization does full justice to the intention of the traditional philosophical-theological doctrines of God in the transcending, self-critical movement of their reflections upon the inadequacy of their own statements. Wathever the case may be, an absolute in the mode of being present at hand *(Vorhandenheit)* is no longer thinkable. For everything that already exists, all beings, can be fundamentally called into question and superseded.[3]

A further reason for Pannenberg to reject the old God of theism is his idea that such a God precludes the human freedom to transcend every present situation. "A being presently at hand, and equipped with omnipotence, would destroy such freedom by virtue of his overwhelming might."[4] With Paul Tillich, then, Pannenberg contends that God cannot be *a* being *among others* today; on the other hand, he believes that we must think of God as an independent being ("ein selbständig Seiendes") and as personal – for reasons which will be given shortly. For the impersonal ground of the depth of being itself cannot be plausibly said to be God; the depth of being appears to be uncanny and absurd.

> . . . the word "God" is just as difficult to combine with the dark abyss of an empty transcendence as it is with the life-force in the depths of reality. Other grounds for speaking about God are needed if one is to justify the claim that there is some relationship between him and the supporting depth of being or the absurd groundlessness of existence.[5]

In our historically conditioned present, then, neither a reconstruction of theism nor the application of the concept of God in connection with the reinstatement of the older metaphysical tradition, prior to its procreation of theistic concepts, will do. Nor can the existence of God and the validity of any theology be *posited authoritatively*. Pannenberg is convinced that we have moved *out of the authoritarian age of thinking* – no peremptory air may be assumed for theology. No teachings are *eo ipso* entitled to claim obedience and acceptance on the mere authority of the church, or Scripture,

---

[3] *Ibid.*, p. 241
[4] *Ibid.*, pp. 242f.
[5] *Ibid.*, p. 236

nor upon that of the "Word" of God (Kerygma theology). Therefore Pannenberg reacts negatively to the characterization of faith as obedience as common in Bultmann and his school. How, then, is theology to be founded? This question leads to another motive behind and in Pannenberg's works, that of *the unity of truth*.

Truth is one, is undivided, and theological statements may not limit their claim to truth to a special sector of reality. Such limited statements which lay no claim to correspondence with the whole of reality are ultimately irrelevant.

> Since the Enlightenment, the question of the truth of their faith has been put to Christians with constantly increasing poignancy. It is the question of its power to encompass all reality – even that of modern science, the technological control of nature, and the forms of individual life – and to claim them all as evidence for the content of the Christian message. The question about the truth of the Christian message has to do with whether it can still disclose to us today the unity of the reality in which we live, as it once did in the ancient world, which was the basis for the victory of Christianity in the ancient *oikumene* surrounding the Mediterranean Sea. Thus the question regarding the truth of the Christian faith is not concerned with a particular truth of one kind or another but with truth itself, which in essence can only be one. It asks whether the Christian faith still contains the truth that gathers together everything experienced as real. For this reason, the question . . . cannot be answered by the mere assertion that Jesus Christ is the truth, but only with regard to the whole of the reality which we experience. Only in this way is the unity of truth . . . guaranteed. If the Christian proclamation should abandon the consideration of the totality of reality experienced by its hearers, then it would neglect "Christian solidarity with the godless", and could no longer raise a well-founded claim to be speaking about *the* absolute truth. As a result, the Christian proclamation would gradually become fit for display in a museum.[6]

Therefore theology must be not only rational in structure but also reasonable in content in that it focusses on *all* available phenomena and is

---

[6] Wolfhart Pannenberg, "What is Truth?", *BQiT,* vol. ii, p. 1f.

compatible with them. The concept of God of theology must reflect the totality of meaning which historical man experiences.

> ... my thought does not start with the future as do other approaches of eschatological theology. In some sense this is the case with Jürgen Moltmann. But I start with a concern for wholeness of meaning, an inner-phenomenological structure of historical experience. Everything I say about the end and eschatology is an extrapolation from this.[7]

A theological God-concept must be able to account for the experience of historicalness, contingency, freedom, and responsibility of human existence. It must make better sense of it than any other point of departure and interpretation. Therefore theology must be rational and verifiable. And the God we worship must be one who demonstrates the truth of himself ("Selbsterweis seiner Wahrheit") by offering us an understanding of the reality in which we live that agrees with this reality itself.

> Israel's experience of reality as history means that the reality in which we live becomes perceptible as it really is only when it is seen in terms of the God of the Bible. But if reality becomes visible as it is in relation to the Biblical God and only in relation to him, this constitutes the self-demonstration of the truth of this God.[8]

This motive of Pannenberg's includes the conviction that the clue to the understanding of the whole of reality *can be received only from a particular experience of reality*, i.e., from a particular point of view. We must experience a definite occasion that produces a perspective which offers this view on the whole of reality. For this reason *truth is revealed*, is given, and is not arrived at by rational reflection and man's own resources. Pannenberg is no rationalist.[9] But once this perspective is given it is open to

---

[7] "A Theological Conversation With Wolfhart Pannenberg", *Dialog*, vol. xi, Autumn 1972, p. 287.

[8] *WiM*, p. 146

[9] Wolfhart Pannenberg, "The Question of God", *BQiT*, vol. ii, p. 207, says, "This (verifiability of the Christian proclamation) need not involve a court of appeal *prior* to the biblical revelation of God before which the latter would have to legitimate itself. Such a court of appeal would in fact be incompatible with the majesty of the divine revelation (!). Christian speech about God can be verified only in such a way that it is the revelation of God itself which discloses that

investigations as to all-encompassing truth and consequent trustworthiness. For God is the origin of my own and of all reality. Thus Pannenberg says,

> ... Subjectivity must presuppose God as the origin and unity of everything real. Only such a God, who embraces everything, can be the truth itself. For this reason, every representation of God is to be tested as to whether it permits understanding reality as a whole and thereby satisfies the unity of truth.[10]

And,

> *That it alone founds the unity of truth means . . . the demonstration of the truth of the Christian message itself.*[11]

A *third* of Pannenberg's *motives* to be noted is *his concept of meaning as future fulfillment*. The contention that there is but one truth derives not only from the fact that modern man views reality in this fashion at the present stage of the historical process of thought so that no concept of God will do unless it is the referent of *all* of reality, as Pannenberg intimates again when he says,

> The quest for the ultimate unity which integrates and thus unifies everything is the question reaching for God, as that question has been asked since the beginning of Greek philosophy. For us, too, the way in which we must test any concept of God is by asking whether it can account for the unity of all reality. If an idea of God fails that test, it does not comprehend the power dominating everything and is, therefore, not a true concept of God.[12]

This unity of all reality is not merely a viewpoint, a way of envisioning reality. But, as Pannenberg's formulation betrays, it is a power which works toward and effects unity where there is disunity, discord, and schism. The unity integrates and unifies. A notion of God which will do must not only account for all of reality but identify God as striving toward unity. More unity means enhancement of life. The underlying concept of

---

about man and his world in relation to which its truth is proved. In this way Christian speech about God would be more than mere assertion."

[10] "What is Truth?", p. 27.

[11] *Ibid.*, p. 26 (italics by the author)

[12] Wolfhart Pannenberg, *Theology and the Kingdom of God* (Philadelphia: Westminster Press, 1969), p. 60 (Henceforth quoted ThaKoG)

meaning is *fulfillment*. Meaning for Pannenberg lastly and ultimately means fulfillment, restoration, repair, integration, union, wholeness, completion of everything. Unity of the world, already perceptible as the goal of the world from the particular perspective granted by the experience of the whole through a particular occasion, is to be expected from the future. "Therefore the unity of all things should not be understood in terms of an eternal cosmos but as something to be achieved by a process of reconciling previous schisms and contradictions. Reconciliation is a constitutive aspect of creation."[13] "The coming of God to his sovereignty over the world is his gift to the world, unifying its scattered events."[14] To be meaningful thus is to be directed toward fulfillment, and when Pannenberg, as we will see, attributes power and creativity to God then not only is it love which motivates and qualifies this power and creativity but it is "successful" love, love which gets what it desires, reaches what it strives for, attains to its goal: *fulfillment, nothing less*. Life has meaning because it is headed for fulfillment in the sense of completion and consummation. The corresponding notion of God has power and creativity as its form and omnipotent love as its content.

2. Important Systematic Influences[15]

A. Georg Wilhelm Friedrich Hegel

Pannenberg's determinative theological concepts reflect some strong systematic influences which can be named. *Hegel* introduced the concept of revelation in the strict sense of God's self-revelation (see above p. 50). This

---

[13] *Ibid.*

[14] *Ibid.*, pp. 59f.

[15] In this section no attempt is made to trace and list the theological and philosophical influences upon P. exhaustively. A study of the origins of P.'s thought, such as M. Douglas Meeks wrote it for Jürgen Moltmann's (*Origins of the Theology of Hope*, Philadelphia: Fortress Press, 1974), would have to cover P.'s teachers, the colleagues of the *Arbeitskreis* at Heidelberg, the dialogue with Moltmann during the years at Wuppertal, and the other literary *Anstöße* which were received and utilized by P. after the principal thought structure was forged and published which happened in 1960 when P., R. Rendtorff, Wilckens, and T. Rendtorff presented their view (in print: *Offenbarung als Geschichte*, Beiheft 1, Kerygma und Dogma,

concept, as Pannenberg states,[16] was mediated to him through his teachers Karl Barth and Heinrich Vogel, and Barth pays tribute for it to the Hegelian Philipp Marheineke. But Pannenberg refers directly to Hegel when he explains his concept of *revelation as universal history* (Universalgeschichte). Hegel completed the conception of *Universalgeschichte* as indirect self-revelation of God systematically.

This conception originates with the view-point of the Israelite-apocalyptic-early Christian *Traditionsgeschichte* that

> ... the fundamental proof for the divinity of Yahweh exists in his acts in history. Instead of a direct self-revelation of God, the facts at this point indicate a conception of indirect self-revelation as a reflex of his activity in history. The totality of his speech and activity, the history brought about by God, shows who he is in an indirect way.[17]

Göttingen: Vandenhoeck & Ruprecht, 1961). For the history of P's thought cf. Richard John Neuhaus, "Wolfhart Pannenberg: Profile of a Theologian", in Wolfhart Pannenberg, *Theology and the Kingdom of God* (Philadelphia: Westminster Press, 1969), pp. 9–50, especially pp. 15ff; E. Frank Tupper, *The Theology of Wolfhart Pannenberg* (Philadelphia: Westminster Press, 1973), especially pp. 21 ff.; James M. Robinson, "Revelation as Word and as History", in *New Frontiers in Theology*, vol. iii: Theology as History, ed. by James M. Robinson and John B. Cobb, Jr. (New York: Harper & Row, 1967), pp. 1–100, especially pp. 3–32 *et passim*; and Meeks (op. cit.) in whose book there are passages on P. Within the scope of my theme I limit myself to comments on three thinkers from whom P. acknowledges (directly or indirectly) to have received *Anstöße*; of course, P. acknowledges his indebtedness to many more authors, e.g. Dilthey and Troeltsch. I also have to forego the difficile subject to what extent Moltmann, when at Wuppertal, influenced Pannenberg, if at all, and whether Moltmann related ideas of E. Bloch to P. It seems to me that P.'s novel concepts as published in *OaG* had been worked out during the Heidelberg years together with the *Arbeitskreis*, that is, prior to his coming to Wuppertal in 1958, and that this work formed the basis for the manuscripts of his anthropology and christology on which he wrote while at Wuppertal. Hence I agree with Meeks when he says, "If we were to designate a *primum movens* of the new eschatological thought, first in the person of Pannenberg and then Moltmann, it would be the new understanding of the biblical views of revelation and history arrived at by Gerhard von Rad." (*op. cit.*, p. 68)

[16] *RaH*, pp. 5ff.
[17] *Ibid.*, p. 13

Pannenberg distinguishes between a direct and an indirect communication. A direct one communicates what shall be communicated. In the case of an indirect one, the content discloses its real and intended meaning only if viewed from a different perspective. A direct revelation, then, has God as its content in an unmediated way. Not so an indirect one.

> Every activity and act of God can indirectly express something about God. It can say that God is the one who does this or that. Here the event in question does not have the same aspect as it would if one merely stood under the impact of its content. Not only is the content perceived for its own value; it is also seen that the event defined in this way has God as its originator.[18]

Now Pannenberg concludes significantly,

> If we wish to understand the indirect self-communication that resides in every individual act of God as revelation, then there are as many revelations as there are divine acts and occurrences in nature and history. But this would not match with revelation in the strict sense of God's self-revelation. Instead, then, we have to conceive *of the totality of the acts of God – which means, since God is one, the totality of all events – as of God's self-revelation.*[19]

There were two ways to proceed from here, according to Pannenberg. One can understand the whole of reality as a cosmos of unchangeable conditions. In this way Greek philosophy and traditional natural theology approach the problem of God. The alternative was the option of German Idealism.

> In contrast, when the totality of reality in its temporal development is thought of as history and as the self-communication of God, then we find ourselves on the road which German idealism has taken since the time of Lessing and Herder.[20]

---

[18] *Ibid.*, p. 15

[19] *Ibid.*, p. 16 (translation and italics mine)

[20] *Ibid.*; for this Pannenberg takes recourse mainly to the following studies: D. W. Lütgert, *Die Religion des deutschen Idealismus und ihr Ende*, vol. i., 1923, pp. 153–183; E. Fülling, *Geschichte als Offenbarung*, 1956; W. Schulz, *Die Vollendung des deutschen Idealismus in der Spätphilosophie Schellings*, 1955, pp. 259–270.

The unity of truth can only be thought of as a *history* of truth. Truth itself has a history, and its nature is the process of this history.

> Historical change itself must be thought of as the essence of truth if its unity is still to be maintained without narrow-mindedly substituting a particular perspective for the whole of truth. To date, Hegel's system should be regarded as the most significant attempt at a solution of this problem. . . . truth is not to be found already existing somewhere as a finished product, but is instead thought of as a history, a process. "The truth is the whole." That which makes this whole into a whole can become visible only at the end.[21]

According to Pannenberg, Hegel's view is biblical in that (1) truth is in process and (2) only the end will show the unity of the process which – on the way – seems full of contradictions. A fundamental weakness in Hegel's construction, though, is the fact that in order to think the unity of history he had to consider his own standpoint as the end of history! This meant theologically that Hegel lost the open future, the eschatology. In his doctrine of the Spirit of the church eschatology is radically transformed into the present ("radikal vergegenwärtigt"). Thus he missed the goal of his effort: if future truth is necessarily precluded from his system, not all truth is embraced within the stages of this dialectical system and consequently the unity of truth and the concomitant concept of God are not achieved. Pannenberg is persuaded that this flaw accounts for the other weakness so frequently objected to, *viz.*, that Hegel did not take the contingency of the events seriously enough and in its stead made the logic of the notion (Begriff) the lord of reality. In these points Pannenberg strives to correct Hegel. For him, as for the biblical point of view, the contingency of the events of history and the consummation of history are taken radically seriously which entails that *the future remains open*.

> What really accounts for the fact that in primitive Christianity, despite the ultimacy of the revelation of God that appeared in Jesus, the future still remained open, so that the truth of God was not participated in by means of the concept (*Begriff*) in the last analysis, but rather – beyond all conceptualizing (*Begreifen*) and being driven by the process of conceptualization itself – by faith alone, by trust

---

[21] "What is truth?", p. 21.

in the coming God? The answer lies in the proleptic character of the Christ event.[22]

This character is the tool with which to refute Strauss' objection how a particular event, the destiny of Jesus, can have absolute importance as revelation of God if the totality of history only is God's revelation.

Of course, Pannenberg's solution of Hegel's aporia of truth rests on the presupposition with which we already are familiar, *viz.*, that the apocalyptic hope for the resurrection can be true for us (the anthropological evidence!) and that Jesus' resurrection can be established as a fact (the historical evidence!).

B. Ernst Bloch

Pannenberg's futuristic ontology, extrapolated from the Israelite, apocalyptic, and early Christian understanding of truth and corroborated by modern anthropology (see below, pp. 101 ff. and 104 ff.), received systematic support through Ernst Bloch's thinking.[23] After J. Weiss and A. Schweitzer had rediscovered Jesus' eschatological understanding of reality ("die Futurisierung der Daseinserfahrung mit dem Auftreten Jesu"),[24] theology in the beginning of the 20th century by and large attempted to

---

[22] *Ibid.*, p. 24 f.
[23] Cf. Ernst Bloch, *Das Prinzip Hoffnung* (Frankfurt am Main: Suhrkamp, 1959). About Bloch's influence on P. cf. E. Frank Tupper, *op. cit.*, p. 26, ". . . Jürgen Moltmann joined the faculty there (Wuppertal), giving Pannenberg the opportunity for dialogue with a theologian of similar interests. However, unlike Moltmann, Pannenberg had not been influenced by the Marxist philosophy of Ernst Bloch. He read Bloch's massive *Das Prinzip Hoffnung* only after completing the initial draft of *Jesus-God and Man*; consequently, P. should not be indiscriminately lumped with Moltmann as "a theologian of hope" stimulated by the futuristic philosophy of Ernst Bloch. Rather than an "influence" upon P., Bloch's philosophy of hope represented a provocative "confluence" with P.'s own eschatological vision of universal history."

However, as a "confluence" Bloch's view supported Pannenberg's ontology, and as support, encouragement, and provocation it was influential on P.'s fully developed ontology as we see it in "The God of Hope", *BQiTh*, and in *ThaKoG*.

[24] Wolfhart Pannenberg, "Der Gott der Hoffnung", *Grundfragen systematischer Theologie* (Göttingen: Vandenhoeck & Ruprecht, 1967), p. 389.

bridge this gap between Jesus and the secular understanding of reality by an interpretation of "eschatological" which transformed the concrete temporal future into the presence of God's eternity within the now of existence. It is here that Pannenberg pays homage to Bloch's merits.

> Perhaps Christian theology will one day have to thank Ernst Bloch's philosophy of hope for giving it the courage to recover in the full sense its central category of eschatology. *A temporally understood future remains decisive for such a concept.* Bloch has taught us about the overwhelming power of the still-open future and of the hope that reaches out to it in anticipation for not only the life and thought of man but in addition *for the ontological uniqueness of everything in reality.* He has recovered the biblical tradition's eschatological mode of thought as a theme for philosophical reflection and also for Christian theology.[25]

While accepting Bloch's ontological conclusions from the biblical tradition and his concept of future as a mode of being ("Futurum als Seinsbeschaffenheit") for God and all of reality, Pannenberg, contrary to Bloch, firmly contends that this eschatology and concomitant ontology is *theological*.

> The primacy of the future and its novelty are guaranteed only when the coming kingdom is ontologically grounded in itself and does not owe its future merely to the present wishes and strivings of man. When the coming kingdom is designated in biblical terms as the kingdom of God, that is out of concern for the ontological primacy of the future of the kingdom over all present realities, including, above all, psychological states. . . . the being of God and that of the kingdom are identical . . .[26]

As to Bloch's atheism it is to be accepted only as regards a god who is *ein Absolutes im Modus der Vorhandenheit*. For everything existing is in principle capable of being transcended and superseded. "Therefore we must agree with Bloch that he has transposed the question of the most perfect being (*ens perfectissimum*) into a temporal mode, and turned it into 'the highest utopian problem, that of the end'."[27]

---

[25] "The God of Hope", *BQiT*, vol. ii, pp. 237f. (Italics mine)
[26] *Ibid.*, pp. 239f.
[27] *Ibid.*, pp. 241f.

C. Alfred North Whitehead

Finally, Pannenberg's ontology partially coincides with and was influenced by the process metaphysics of Whitehead.[28] Pannenberg gives credit to Whitehead and Hartshorne,

> The process philosophy of Whitehead and Hartshorne made the contribution of incorporating time into the idea of God. Theirs was an enormous achievement.

But he immediately underscores his dissent,

> But we cannot agree when Whitehead suggests that the futurity of God's kingdom implies a development in God. It is true that, from the viewpoint of our finite present, the future is not yet decided. Therefore the movement of time contributes to deciding what the definite truth is going to be, also with regard to the essence of God. But – and here is the difference from Whitehead – what turns out to be true in the future *will then be evident as having been true all along. This applies to God as well as to all finite reality. God was present in every past moment as the one who he is in his futurity.* . . . What distinguishes the present argument from Whitehead's philosophy is the *ontological priority of the future* as this priority is evident in the idea of God as the one who is coming.[29]

He furthermore states,

> We can agree with Wh. in considering the ultimate elements of reality in terms of single occasions contingently following each other. I also share his thought that every new occasion has to prehend the world it encounters, although the new occasion cannot be derived from already existing objects. Were it so derived it could not be genuinely new but only a different configuration of the old. I believe Whitehead's vision can be conceptualized in a more consistent way than Whitehead himself utilized, if the contingency of the new events or occasions which occur to the existing world is *described as a result of the futuristic power of creative love.*[30]

---

[28] P. confirmed this in a personal communication to me.
[29] *ThaKoG.*, pp. 62f. (Italics mine)
[30] *Ibid.*, pp. 66f. (Italics mine)

For Pannenberg as for Whitehead God is not only a principle (for Wh. a principle of order, for P. a principle, so to say, of eschatological fulfillment) but has a concrete temporal side, God is power. The living God is a process of synthetic unifications, his reality does not exist apart from, still is not identical with, the finite process of organic unifications, and the discontinuity between God and the creatures consists of the fact that the creative divine synthetic process has its own aim, purpose, and capacity for emergence. But the analysis will suggest that for Pannenberg God *does* have energy or being apart from the world and its components. The relation of Pannenberg's thought to Whithead's will be briefly examined in section 5 of this chapter on Pannenberg's doctrine of God.

3. The Biblical Foundation of Pannenberg's Ontology

Pannenberg's ontology rests on two presuppositions, (1) the biblical material with respect to God's self-revelation, and (2) the anthropological evidence as means of verification. An analysis of the first is presented in *Revelation as History* to which Pannenberg contributed an introductory article and his famous *Dogmatic Theses on the Doctrine of Revelation*. His analysis leads Pannenberg to the following conclusions (cf. theses i.ii, and iii):

God reveals himself indirectly through his acts in history. The real purpose of these is the demonstration that Yahweh is the true God. His acts give rise to faithful trust in him. His ultimate self-demonstration is expected by the apocalyptic only at the end of history; God's glory will become visible. Paul shares this expectation but visualizes God's glory in Christ's countenance and thus views Christ as anticipation or prolepsis of God's direct self-revelation in the eschaton.

Historical events constitute indirect revelations because they are inconclusive; God can be known only after the event, in each case. And because such revelations change their content and are but moments of a more comprehensive revelatory context, the meaning of every present happening is actually hidden. Consequently the decisive act of salvation lies in the future of all futures, i.e., in the end of history. Here the meaning of all events and the plan which comprises beginning and end will be disclosed. So God's direct revelation takes place at the end of a universal history.

> The history that demonstrates the deity of God is broadened to include the totality of all events. This corresponds completely to the universality of Israel's God who is not only the God of Israel, but will be the God of all men. This broadening of the *Heilsgeschichte* to a universal history is in essence already accomplished in the major prophets of Israel in that they treat the kingdoms of the world as responsible to God's commands.[31]

The inclusion of all nations is part of the universality of God's eschatological revelation. Now Pannenberg concludes — and *this conclusion is pivotal for his stance on what truth is,*

> Thus, it is appropriate that the proclamation of the God who raised Jesus would be tested by means of Greek philosophy and its questions about God, for philosophy is that discipline that raises the question of the true form of God for all men.[32]

A god who is the God of all men must be answerable to all men's questions, in one way or another. From the claim to the universality of God follows his universal intelligibility. ". . . the historical revelation is open to anyone who has eyes to see. It has a universal character."[33] Even God's anticipatory direct revelation in Jesus' destiny is not a supernatural but a simple truth, open for our eyes, if we only want to see it and let the facts speak for themselves in their context of *Traditionsgeschichte*, and if we only use our reason. "Theology has no reason whatsoever to ascribe the predication and rank of general rational truth to a standpoint of blindfoldedness."[34] This does not imply that revelation communicates what human reason knows anyway. Revelation mediates heretofore unknown, novel knowledge through facts; no additional secret gnosis from inspiration, no additional interpretation from a divine word is necessary.

> That these and also other events are veiled from many men, indeed from most men, does not mean that this truth is too high for them, so that their reason must be supplemented by other means of knowing.

---

[31] *RaH.*, p. 133
[32] *Ibid.*, pp. 134 ff.
[33] *Ibid.*, p. 135
[34] Wolfhart Pannenberg, ed., *Offenbarung als Geschichte* (Göttingen: Vandenhoeck & Ruprecht, 1961), p. 100 henceforth quoted OaG). This is the German original of *RaH*. Translation mine; transl. in *RaH*, p. 137, inaccurate.

... they must use their reason ... If the problem is not thought of in this way, then the Christian truth is made into a truth for the in group, and the church becomes a gnostic community.[35]

Faith is not superfluous. It rests upon the perception of the facts. One does not believe blindly but on the basis of trustworthy knowledge. Faith is trust because it has to do with the future and trust is essentially directed to the future which will justify or disprove it. True faith is not blind credulity.

> The prophets could call Israel to faith in Yahweh's promises and proclaim his prophecy because Israel had experienced the dependability of their God in the course of a long history. The Christian risks his trust, life, and future on the fact of God's having been revealed in the fate of Jesus. This presupposition must be as certain as possible to him. Otherwise who could expect to obtain a participation in the life that has been manifested in Jesus, if such a presupposition were not oriented to the future?[36]

Cognition of God's revelation is the foundation of faith. However, not knowledge but the resulting faith as trust — *if* it results — is paramount; it secures man's participation in salvation. Accordingly the proclamation of the Gospel may not call for a leap of faith into the unknown and unknowable, and no such leap may be asserted to provide certainty. It cannot. Preaching must rather seek to "assert that the facts are reliable and that you can therefore place your faith, life, and future on them."[37]

The substance of Pannenberg's theses iv and v was treated in the course of our christological discussion in chapters I–IV. But two important additional tenets Pannenberg propounds in these theses should be stated: (1) For both the Biblical and the Greek view the one true God can be revealed in his divinity only indirectly from the totality of all occurrences. But the Greeks took this totality not as a history contingently open for ever new occurrences but as a cosmos of eternally unchangeable structures of order. This Greek cosmos offered too limited a conception of reality which man experiences. The biblical experience of reality is more comprehensive; it includes the contingency of all real events. If the biblical view can incorporate the Greek insights as part of its conprehensive perception of

---

[35] *RaH.*, p. 137
[36] *Ibid.*, p. 138
[37] *Ibid.*

reality and can make it intelligible on the basis of its better presuppositions, then it is superior to the cosmos-notion. "Under this condition it is valid to say: the God indirectly revealed through the totality of history would be the superior answer to the philosophical question of God, too."[38] History as totality comes into view only at its and from its end. Therefore to speak of Jesus' destiny as the revelation of history's totality, i.e., of God, is possible only because of the eschatological, i.e., proleptic character of the Christ event. No other self-demonstration of God will lead beyond this event. "Thus, the end of the world will be on a cosmic scale what has already happened in Jesus."[39] Given the truth of the apocalyptic expectation, then in this event the God of Israel was indeed demonstrated as the one God of all mankind.

(2) But in spite of all we now know (*viz.*, that the resurrection of Jesus is God's proleptic self-revelation, etc.) Jesus' fate still reveals God as the hidden God *insofar as nobody can know and state exhaustively* what is implicated and contained in this divine self-demonstration. Much can be concretely known about the resurrection of Jesus. But at the same time, what happened to Jesus then and there for us still is future which is as yet rationally impenetrable ("noch unausdenkbare Zukunft"). "The inexhaustibility of the revelatory event as an eschatological event is very important for our understanding. Otherwise one easily mistakes what was said about knowledge of God's self-demonstration for rationalism."[40]

4. *The Corroborative Anthropological Evidence*

The apocalyptic hope, so we saw, must be corroborated by a contemporary understanding of reality in its totality. Otherwise both the concept of God's self-revelation through history and the significance of Jesus' resurrection as prolepsis of the eschaton collapse, for both depend on the truth of the apocalyptic hope. If man generically hopes for no life beyond death the apocalyptic expectation upon whose truth the definition of Jesus' divinity etc. depends could not be universally true. Christianity were irrelevant.

---

[38] *OaG.*, p. 104, my transl.
[39] *RaH.*, p. 142
[40] *OaG.*, p. 105, transl. mine.

Now on the basis of a number of anthropological studies[41] Pannenberg demonstrates man's openness for God which can find its fulfillment only in trust in God and the hope of the resurrection of the dead and life beyond death.[42] The claims most important for our theme are the following.

Man's characteristic *openness in relation to the world* through which he is distinguished from the animal (which is limited to its environment) means that he *has* a world, that he can distance himself from his environment, can have new experiences in an unlimited proportion and that his possibilities to respond to the reality he perceives are capable of almost unlimited change. Because, unlike the animal's, the direction of his drives is not steered by instincts his relationship to reality is peculiarly open. By way of experiencing the world man detects his needs which leads to his self-understanding and to the identification of his goals. However, the world never offers final information on such; man can and must decide what the world will be. Actually man is not only open in relation to the world. His openness transcends any experience, any situation, any world or world-view, even the search for world-views. This openness, reaching beyond the world, in fact is the condition of his world-experience. Neither does man find his ultimate satisfaction with his own cultural creations. What is the motor impulse of his striving into the open? Following Scheler, Gehlen speaks of man's "constant pressure of a surplus of drives".

> In contrast, the pressure of human drives is directed toward something undefined. It arises because our drives find no goal that entirely satisfies them. It asserts itself in man's characteristic impulse toward play and daring or in the detachment from the present through a smile. . . . Arnold Gehlen has spoken appropriately of an "indefinite obligation", which makes men restive and drives them beyond every attained stage in the actualization of life. He has also seen that this restlessness is one root of all religious life. That certainly does not mean that man himself creates religions by giving form to that undefined pressure through his imagination (*Phantasie*).

---

[41] Max Scheler, *Die Stellung des Menschen im Kosmos*,² 1947; A. Portmann, *Zoologie und das neue Bild des Menschen*, 1956; A. Gehlen, *Der Mensch*,⁶ 1958; H. Plessner, *Die Stufen des Organischen und der Mensch*, 1928, and *Lachen und Weinen*,² 1950; M. Landmann, *Philosophische Anthropologie*, 1955; E. Rothacker, *Probleme der Kulturanthropologie*, 1948; *et al.*
[42] This demonstration is a chief objective of *WiM*.

> Something else always precedes all imaginative activity in the formation of religions, and for that reason religion is more than merely a creation of man.[43]

This is substantiated by an analysis of the structure of man's drives. To be driven by impulses means dependence on something.

> Man's chronic need, his infinite dependence, presupposes something outside himself that is beyond every experience of the world. . . . Thus in everything that he does in life he presupposes a being beyond everything finite, a vis-a-vis upon which he is dependent. Only on this basis can his imagination form conceptions of this being. Our language has the word "God" for this entity . . .[44]

This is no proof for the existence of God. It is first of all a question of man's existence, a dependence and a quest for a ground which transcends man and his existence and supports him from out of the depth of reality.

> Only if man gains access to such a ground can he base his own behavior on a solid footing instead of on an illusory foundation that in truth lacks any basis. Only the ground of all reality, or, better, the power over all reality, is able to guarantee a security than cannot be destroyed by any other power.[45]

The core of man's openness to the world, thus, is this lack, this dependence on something vis-a-vis himself beyond the world supporting both him and all of reality. It is unknown. "Men's dependence upon God is infinite precisely because they do not posses this destiny (*Bestimmung*) from the start but must search for it. And while searching they remain dependent on God, the vis-a-vis, if it is to be found at all."[46]

This peculiarly human openness also stretches into the future. Only man can experience future before it arrives, he can anticipate novelty. Human imagination allows man to transcend his situation and picture new things creatively. He can envisage new and different states of life. The passive trait of imagination, *viz.*, that one cannot "produce" inventions or "brainstorms" but is dependent on inspiration is an indication for Pannenberg that

---

[43] *WiM*, pp. 9f.
[44] *Ibid.*, p. 10
[45] "The Question of God", p. 223
[46] *WiM*, p. 11 (my translation)

imagination has to do with man's infinite openness in a special way. And he concludes,

> This means, however, that man in his contemplative nature conceives from God by means of imagination. Of course it also means that man's imaginative life is especially affected by his perversion to evil. ... The creativeness of imagination corresponds to what is new and unforeseeable in external events. But that God constantly produces new things in man's contemplative nature as well as in external history, and that precisely in his creativity man is at the same time completely a recipient, remained concealed for a long time in Western thought.[47]
> God appears not only as the goal of man's striving in his openness to the world, but also as the origin of man's creative mastery of the world.[48]

The referent of man's dependence is the whole of reality. As such it remains imperceptible, unknown. The future is unforeseeable. Consequently man has to live in trust. Trust builds upon the reliability of its recipient and emerges from prior experiences with his faithfulness, and trust includes risk in that it is directed to the hitherto unknown future. This is true with regard to persons and the origin of the whole of reality. Both are not at man's disposal (*"unverfügbar"*) and uncontrollable, the latter also infinite in its possibilities. *Therefore one can think of it only as a person, a personal God.* "That not only trust in general but also a final, unconditional trust is unavoidable makes it clear that every man as he lives his life has his God."[49] How Pannenberg develops his argument for the personal character of God out of this and other phenomenological considerations will be investigated in the section on his doctrine of God.

The inevitability of man's hope for a life after death is anthropologically established in the following train of reasoning: All human interest focusses explicitly or by implication on the future, since it is his concern to arrange his existence and to achieve a world which promises satisfactory possibilities for life. This leads to the creation of culture and civilization. But not all things are predictable and calculable. *The quintessence of future is the*

---

[47] *Ibid.*, p. 26
[48] *Ibid.*, p. 27
[49] *Ibid.*, p. 34

unforeseeable new which can be the object of hope only since hope begins where foreknowledge ceases. Hope expects fulfillment. Now whether hope is folly or a reasonable attitude to life is decided by the question whether there is hope beyond death. For the unavoidable destiny of death threatens all provisional hopes; death destroys the future. The knowledge of death cannot be suppressed. None can turn to the present with ease unless he is certain of his future. Now it is essentially human to know about death and to extend one's hope to a life beyond death. *Man's Weltoffenheit enforces such hope and quest since man's quest for his Bestimmung*[50] *finds no conclusive answer within this life!* His *Weltoffenheit* forces him to think both God as the infinite vis-a-vis (*"das unendliche Gegenüber"*) and such life beyond death. "The two are closely connected. The God on whom man is infinitely dependent in his search for his destiny also warrants its fulfillment beyond death."[51]

This motive creates different images and conceptualizations of the life beyond death. These can be subjected to examination. *Which concept most adequately expresses the anthropological motive under consideration?* The Greek doctrine of the immortality of the soul proves to be inadequate since modern anthropology has conclusively shown the body-soul-unity so that both death or life thereafter pertain to both. But the concept of resurrection, emerging in Parsism and transmitted to Judaism and eventually to Christianity and Islam, more adequately corresponds to the anthropological findings. Anthropologically a new life is conceivable as including a physical revitalization ("Wiederaufleben") only, i.e., as a holistic new creation. Anthropologically man has his life as a link or member of a community only, and living entities and their world or their environment must be defined as a unity. The concept of resurrection corresponds to this in so far as it envisions resurrection as an event that relates to *all* men and that coincides with a new creation of the world. Thus, "The hope of resurrection from the dead consciously takes up the destiny that characterizes each person's human existence as openness beyond death."[52] "It is only an image, an earthly metaphor, for a future that is still inconceivable in its reality. Nevertheless, *it is an appropriate and indispensable image* for our understanding of man and his searching openness."[53]

---

[50] "Bestimmung" = appointed destiny, destination here includes the meaning of nature, essence
[51] *Ibid.*, p. 44   [52] *Ibid.*, p. 53   [53] *Ibid.*, p. 52 (my translation)

Moreover, this concept also meaningfully interprets man's *Weltoffenheit* which quintessentially is openness to God because it envisages a *judgment of man beyond death*. For Pannenberg, the truth of time lies beyond our experience of time and its separation into past, present, and future. "The truth of time is the concurrence of all events in an *eternal present*. Eternity, then, does not stand in contrast to time as something that is completely different. Eternity creates no other content than time. However, *eternity is the truth of time*, which remains hidden in the flux of time. Eternity is the unity of all time, but as such it simultaneously is something that exceeds our experience of time."[54] Only God can view all events in an eternal present. Now on account of sin the future obtains a special significance.

Man is meant to participate in God's eternity. Man's openness to the world drives him to see the world as objectively as possible. The most objective view is one which the eternal present offers. Man has this perspective *to the extent* that he is conscious of past and present and future. This human participation, however, is fractured by the self-centered character of man's temporality.

> Certainly, that the ego generally comes across itself between past and future is not yet an expression of sin; it is an expression of man's finitude to be tied to a particular, limited place in the stream of time. However, the perspective of our self-centered experience of time can consume our objectivity, which is open to the world. The result is that *we neglect the present by mourning over the past and by fearing the future*. Or else, in the other direction, *we forget the past and plan for the future only out of the point of view of the ego*. . . . the self-centeredness of our experience of time and space becomes a matter of being closed-off. It becomes the source of the one-sidedness of our relation to the world and the sign of sin.[55]

Man is meant to live wholly in the "moment" which is eternity in the present, i. e., out of the openness which is free for whatever is the right thing to do in each moment.

> For each instant is disclosed to man by God as a new moment of life. There is no profoundly experienced moment that is not grasped just in its uniqueness as the present of eternity.[56]

---

[54] *Ibid.*, p. 74 (Italics mine)   [55] *Ibid.*, pp. 76f. (Italics mine)   [56] *Ibid.*, p. 77

But the "moment" is always perverted into the now of self-centeredness. And because man on his own tries to expand his now into eternity, the future becomes the place of man's judgment. As long as man wanders through time judgment by eternity remains concealed to the world. *For this reason judgment is correctly envisioned as an event after death.* Even though we have to do with metaphoric language when we speak of judgment in connection with resurrection, it is only in this way that the judgment of eternity can happen to the individual.

The foregoing represents the most important yield of phenomenological anthropology for Pannenberg's theology. Pannenberg's decisive conclusions, as was obvious, were these: (1) He radicalizes man's openness in relation to the world and identifies it as openness to God as the ground and power of all known reality and the openness to the future as openness to the power of God. (2) He founds the necessity of hope for life after death upon the fact that man's search for his *Bestimmung* remains without a conclusive answer within his life and that death renders his search meaningless unless there is hope beyond death. Pannenberg departs from his profound conviction that this desire to know one's *Bestimmung*, man's zest for life and meaning, man's chase for fulfillment *cannot possibly* be meaningless folly and illusion. This is his deepest assumption with which he approaches the anthropological material. (3) From a phenomenology of the human experience of time, corroborated by Einstein's discovery of the time-space unity and the spatialization of time, Pannenberg – in concert with his rejection of the older theism and supranaturalism – develops a concept of eternity (God) as the truth and unity of time, and this truth of time as the eternal present (of God) so that the contingent and the general both have their rank and place in eternity – contrary to Greek thinking.

How does Pannenberg go about constructing his doctrine of God and being on the basis of these two complexes of facts, the Israelite-apocalyptic-Christian understanding of revelation and the anthropological evidence?

5. *The Concepts of God and Being*

Given the truth elucidated in section 3 and 4 and given the historical facticity of Jesus' resurrection, *the key to the whole of Christian theology,* Pannenberg contends, *is Jesus' message of the imminent Kingdom of God.* Jesus' resurrection confirmed Jesus' claims and endorsed this message. Then this message must found and qualify christology, the understanding of human existence, and the notions of God and creation. (The latter must also be shown as coming to terms with the discoveries and projections of the natural sciences in order to qualify as truth.)

For Jewish thought God was known through his acts in their history. Their life and piety was shaped by the Mosaic law, and the hope for the eschaton was an appendix to that only. The Kingdom of God lay in the distant future. For Jesus the Kingdom lies in the *imminent* future, and Jesus underscored the *present* impact of its imminent future – for him, Pannenberg sets forth, *the future has priority over the past and present*. He imperatively claims the present in that it alerts

> ... all men to the urgency and exclusiveness of seeking first the Kingdom of God. As his message is proclaimed and accepted, God's rule is present and we can even now glimpse his future glory. *In this way we see the present as an effect of the future, in contrast to the conventional assumption that past and present are the cause of the future.*[57]

But this does not only *seem* to be the case. For now Pannenberg significantly and decisively posits, *"This priority of the eschatological future which determines our present demands a reversal also in our ontological conceptions."*[58] He postulates that for Jesus the eschatological hope became the only source of knowledge and guide for living and that consequently – even though Jesus did not develop a corresponding theology himself, because God's existence and mode of being was not an issue then – we have *to spell out the implications of the priority of the future for God's mode of being*. The need for it, again, is twofold: there is – on account of the necessity to grasp all reality as a unity – the need to conformity with the yield of strictest historical research; there is also the fact that the way of early theology, *viz.*, its acceptance of the philosophical concept of God, is no longer tenable.

The eschatological hope in Jesus' message yields the futurization of the experience of existence *("Daseinserfahrung")*. *Pannenberg's motive when he seeks to establish the new Daseinserfahrung ontologically no doubt is his realization that without such the "god-hypostasis" would be dispensable*, as Bloch is persuaded.

---

[57] *ThaKoG.*, p. 54   [58] *Ibid.*, p. 54 (Italics mine)

Yet how would things stand if the hope of the Kingdom were only the symbolic expression of the demonstrable psychological strivings of man? ... The primacy of the future and its novelty are guaranteed only when the coming Kingdom is ontologically grounded in itself and does not owe its future merely to the present wishes and striving of men.[59]

Pannenberg agrees with Bloch's statement, "Only in relation to the 'hidden God' *(Deus absconditus)* is the *problem* of what is at stake in the legitimate mystery of the 'hidden man' *(homo absconditus)* kept open."[60] And he adds, "The primacy of the future, and therewith of the 'hidden God' who is its ground, is necessary in order that man's humanity be protected against trivialization and continue to be summoned to its future possibilities."[61]

How can this experience be ontologized? Pannenberg postulates the *identity of being with power.* "To believe in one God means to believe that one power dominates all."[62] Only if a god has power over all he is the true god. Thus the deity of God is his rule. Pannenberg contends that in Jesus' message God's claim is to be viewed exclusively in terms of his coming rule. If this is true, he concludes,

... in a restricted but important sense God does not yet exist. Since his rule and his being are inseparable, God's being is still in the process of coming to be. Considering this, God should not be mistaken for an objectified being presently existing in its fullness. In this light, the current criticism, directed against the traditional theistic idea of God is quite right. Obviously, if the mode of God's being is interlocked with the coming of his rule, we should not be surprised or embarrassed that God cannot be "found" somewhere in the present reality.[63]

Or he says,

He is God only in the execution of his lordship, and this full accomplishment of his lordship is determined as something future. To this

---

[59] "The God of Hope", pp. 239f.
[60] "The God of Hope", p. 241, quoted from Ernst Bloch, *Das Prinzip Hoffnung* (2d ed.; Frankfurt am Main: Suhrkamp Verlag, 1959) Vol. ii, p. 1406
[61] *Ibid.*   [62] *ThaKog.*, p. 55   [63] *Ibid.*, p. 56

extent, the God to whom the hope of the kingdom refers is characterized in a radical and exclusive sense by "futurity as a quality of being" *(Seinsbeschaffenheit)*.[64]

What follows from Pannenberg's identification of being with power in God reaches back to his concept of revelation. Due to this concept he had to locate God's direct self-revelation at the end of history while history is constituted by indirect self-revelations. It follows that the biblical God himself has a history. Why? Can we not hold that he merely reveals himself in different and changing ways and images? This is not the case "because the historical event of his revelation may not be thought of as something external to his essence, else it were no revelation of his essence."[65] Thus Pannenberg can say, "Although the essence of God is from everlasting to everlasting the same, it does have a history in time. Thus it is that Yahweh first becomes the God of all mankind in the course of the history that he has brought to be."[66]

Of course, he is convinced that this idea of God, drawn from Jesus' message, is valid only if the corollary conception of the extant world as expression of this power called God yields a better understanding of reality for contemporary man than any other stance. As evidence for the ontic reality of the *futurum* in question he points to our experience of reality. He focuses on man's experience of his relation to the future and sees a dark, uncertain power which threatens our lives or promises their fulfillment. ". . . this experience of the future's ambiguity points to an essential indeterminateness or vagueness in the events of nature. In this connection we speak of the contingency of events . . ."[67] Because the events are contingent, this power is personal! "What warrants do we have for saying that those contingent events are in fact acts of God from whose future they spring?"[68] The contingency of events for Pannenberg is a crucial presupposition for the *personal character* of the future and thus for the identification of the future with God. For *"to speak of God is to speak of a personal power."*[69] But has the concept of a personal God not been successfully contested long ago? No. For this concept is not the result of an

---

[64] "The God of Hope", p. 240
[65] *OaG*, p. 97, (my translation)
[66] *RaH*, pp. 133f. P. meant this statement as a *religionsgeschichtliche Feststellung*, but in other statements drew ontological consequences.
[67] *ThaKoG*, p. 57   [68] *Ibid.*   [69] *Ibid.* (Italics mine)

anthropomorphic projection of human personhood upon a divine entity, as Fichte and Feuerbach presuppose. It rather results from a primary datum of human experience with reality, *viz.*, the contingent character of the future, while the attribution of personhood to man is a derived, second step. How does Pannenberg substantiate this opinion?

> Alongside the findings of religious psychology that it really is the case that personality cannot be originally an anthropological phenomenon, there is also the primary character of the personal shape of the child's experience of his environing world, and the air of mysteriousness that cannot be erased from human personality. To this very day the human personality is still bound up with the religious theme and can be slighted where the latter disappears. The original phenomenon of the personal would then have to be sought in perhaps the impenetrability of the numinous power, which by no means remains vague but encounters one as having concrete pertinence. It is bound up with its holiness and inviolability. It is highlighted by the *freedom* of the power in relation to its form of manifestation. . . . If in this way the personality expresses itself in freedom, then freedom itself presupposes openness to the future. Man is free only because he has a future, because he can go beyond what is presently extant. And so freedom is in general the power that transforms the present. *This means, however, that futurity as a condition of freedom constitutes the very core of the personal;* it is what "resonates" through the present form of manifestation and gives it its perplexing character as a threat or enticement. . . . *In this way it is also the power of being. Being is itself to be thought of from the side of the future,* instead of as the abstract, most universal something in the background of all beings.[70]

The personal character of the power of the future (God) follows (2) from the *unity behind contingency,* i. e., the identity of the power operative in a series of events. This contended unity and identity emerges from the perception of some meaningful connection in the sequence of events. Again, human experience and its phenomenological analysis offers the material for this concept. The future is no bundle of chances nor an empty category but evolves from a concrete power which is the single future or the single power

---

[70] "The God of Hope", pp. 245f. (Italics mine)

of the future for all events. For our anxieties and hopes with regard to the future transcend the anticipation of single imminent events and, so to speak, intuit (not Pannenberg's term!) a movement of all events forward to meet a common future. There are in our experience the connections of events and the fact of corporate unities; we experience the future as a unifying power; there is, then, a definitive unity of the world.

How does the future determine the present? Pannenberg describes it phenomenologically,

> In every event the infinite future separates itself from the finite events which until then had been hidden in this future but are not released into existence. The future lets go of itself to bring into being our present. And every new event is again confronted by a dark and mysterious future out of which certain relevant events will be released.

Pannenberg concludes,

> If we, in our anxiety and hope, contemplate this power of the future, we recognize both its breathtaking excitement and its invitation to trust. . . . In every present we confront the infinite future, and in welcoming the particular finite events which spring from that future, we anticipate the coming of God.[71]

If it is sovereignty which establishes this future – for indeed only sovereignty can produce unity –, then this *experiential-phenomenological* description of the power of the future agrees with Jesus' message. The unity of all things is not the cosmos (static being) but *results from a process of reconciling* of schisms, contradictions, seemingly meaningless and contingent events. For Pannenberg unity is *"the most comprehensive characteristic of being . . . Everything is a unity to the extent it is at all."*[72] Things cannot be prior to being unified. Consequently the eschaton is envisioned as the time of achieved complete unification and reconciliation prior to which nothing is yet or, at least, is not yet definitively. The power of the future is the power of being because it unifies. Being is released from this power, thus it springs from the future. And, in a certain sense, even God *will* be and does not yet exist.

---

[71] *ThaKoG*, both passages above p. 59
[72] *Ibid.*, p. 60 (Italics mine)

From Jesus' message of the imminent Kingdom of God, corroborated by the phenomena of human experience of the future, Pannenberg further extrapolates the following for his concept of God:

(1) Today's future is the same as every past's if the future of all creatures is universally the same. The unity of the future through its unifying power *was* at work as it is now: God created the past.

(2) "The notion of the futurity of God and his kingdom most emphatically does not 'remove' God to the future. It does not mean that God is only in the future and was not in the past or is not in the present. Quite to the contrary, as the power of the future he dominates the remotest past."[73] Therefore God possesses eternity. "Because he is the power of the ultimate future God has released to each single event its actual historical future. In relation to past and present, God is constantly bringing himself back into his own eschatological futurity."[74] God "swings", we might say, construing Pannenberg's thought, from the future into each present and back into the future of each present which is the ultimate future. He creates the present, releases it, and retires to the center of his power from which all non-ultimate future emerges. It corresponds to this state of the affair that he both is and is not extant in every present, and that there is one ultimate self-revelation at the end of history and an incessant number of penultimate, provisional revelations throughout history.

(3) God's essence consequently implies time. The proof that the statement "God exists" is definitely true will be offered first by the eschatological self-revelation of God. This proof will demonstrate that God always existed. He exists to the extent that he is the future of that entity. Since he is the future of everything he exists always. "Exists" here has the ring of both *in futuro* and *in extenso* (the extant world). One is ultimate, the other provisional; God exists in one ultimately, in the other provisionally. So does everything else — with the exception of the Christ event where the ultimate future is not provisionally, but *unsurpassably anticipated*. Only on this account can we know what the ultimate future will be like, what the *essence* of God is like, the essence which does not conclusively show in the changing, evolving, historical acts of God.

In these considerations, "the present", "the past", "being", "existing" mean the designated entities only to the extent that they have been unified.

---

[73] *ThaKoG*, p. 62
[74] *Ibid.*

We must be aware of the freedom left to the creatures and their schisms, contradictions, and sin. In *this* sense God has *no* history, for Pannenberg. Essentially he is the one he always will be. But as "coming into our world", as the historical God, he is in process.[75]

(4) God not only appears to be future from our view-point (noetically) but *is* the power of the future. Pannenberg's idea of God implies that there be no future beyond God. God is the ultimate future and consequently pure freedom. When we try to understand this, perhaps ultimate future is appropriately understood as power and will (a unifying power, a will toward unity, reconciliation), temporally *and spatially* ahead of everything. For ultimate future actually seems to mean a locale, a place of origin and source of release of past and present, power and unity. It seems that by and large this coincides with much of what traditionally was meant by God's omnipotence, omniscience, sovereignty and creativity. Pannenberg's concept of God is a reinterpretation of the traditional doctrine of God so that it coheres with the message of Jesus and the human openness to God and their corollaries. The gist of his reinterpretation is the inclusion of time, eschatological orientation, and historicalness into the concepts of man, revelation, Christ, and God. The systematic linch-pin of this construction seems to be the conceivability and envisageability of ultimate

---

[75] P.'s concept of God's eternity that excludes timelessness resembles that of Isaak Agust Dorner (1809–1884) in his three articles "Über die richtige Fassung des dogmatischen Begriffs der Unveränderlichkeit Gottes, mit besonderer Beziehung auf das gegenseitige Verhältnis zwischen Gottes übergeschichtlichem und geschichtlichem Sein", *Jahrbücher für deutsche Theologie*, I/2 (1856), pp. 361 ff.; II/3 (1857), pp. 440 ff.; III/4 (1858), pp. 479 ff. For an English translation of the third of these articles cf. Claude Welch, ed. and transl., *God and Incarnation in Mid-Nineteenth Century German Theology: G. Thomasius – I. A. Dorner – A. E. Biedermann* (New York: Oxford University Press, 1965), pp. 115–180. For a characterization of Dorner's concept of God that incorporates time cf. Claude Welch, *Protestant Thought in the 19th Century*, vol. i. (New Haven and London: Yale University Press: 1972), pp. 278 f. The *result* of Dorner's application of his *spekulative Wissenschaft* to the traditional doctrine of God's immutability, in its basic vision, is quite similar to the vision of God's involvement in history (and being determined by history) which A. N. Whitehead, and process thought generally, later developed. With regard to the concrete temporal side of God (*Gottes geschichtlichem Sein*) it seems that Whitehead's vision is closer to Dorner's than is Pannenberg's who leaves not as much room for God's permitting himself to be determined.

future as a place from where the living, personal God works — to which he leads (or from where he comes). There is then a cryptic supernaturalism — which, however, is not merely asserted or postulated but all the way strictly historically and anthropologically deduced, in agreement with a satisfactory understanding of the contemporary experience of reality.

(5) God's eternity — as noted before — is his totally comprehensive present, derived from his existence as the final future. Therefore, contrary to the Greek concept of God's eternity which implies immutability, simplicity, and absence of properties in order to preserve God's unity and freedom (change implied limitation, love implied deficiency of something), Pannenberg's concept includes temporal dynamics and change.[76] The Greek attributes of God followed from a type of thinking which infers the cause from its effects and thus denied contingent acts to God. Pannenberg contests this mode of thought.

> ... if God operates contingently, acts freely, and if the properties of his effects are different from his essence, then the properties of the divine operation, because of its contingency, permit no reflection upon a similarity of the effects with the essence of God, and thus do not allow any statement that would transfer a creaturely perfection to God in a superlative sense.[77]

That is not to say that God's contingent action had nothing to do with his essence. But the connection is of a different sort than in the case of a cause that operates out of necessity. In a contingent effect, it is not a matter of an indeterminate, underlying cause *expressing* its essence by imparting itself, but rather of the agent *producing* properties for himself. He choses himself as the one who so acts in that he "decides" for such an effect rather than for another. ... The contingently operative biblical God is present in his effects ...

---

[76] Pannenberg says, "The dynamics of reconciliation are not something secondary to the creative activity of God, but unconditional, creative love characterizes the activity of the creator himself, and the evolutionary process is drawn deeper and deeper into the center of this creative dynamic notwithstanding the tendencies toward self-seclusion, self-preservation, acedia, and aggression among his creatures." cf. "Future and Unity", *Hope and the Future of Man*, ed. Ewert H. Cousins (Philadelphia: Fortress Press, 1972), p. 63.

[77] "The Appropriation of the Philosophical Concept of God as a Dogmatic Problem of Early Christian Theology", *BQiTh*, vol. ii, p. 171

in a "personal mode", i.e., by the choice of his acts he decides about the properties to which he binds himself precisely by this choice.⁷⁸

For Pannenberg, God's immutability is his *faithfulness*.

The durability of the world indeed does depend upon the fact that God does not jump from one possibility to another but abides by his creative decisions, "not changing" them or simply dropping them. But the fact that God does not change in his acts is an expression not of an immobility constitutive of his essence but rather of his free, momentary, humanly unanticipatable decision, just as much as is his creative activity.... But the faithfullness of God is realized as free act precisely in his contingent, historical action. In contrast to this, the concept of a God who is by nature immutable necessarily obstructs the theological understanding of his historical action, and it has done so to an extent that can hardly be exaggerated. It indeed constitutes the background for the idea of the impassibility of God which so fatefully determined the Christology of the early church right down to the theopaschitic controversy. Above all, however, the concept ... leads to the consequence that the transition to any innovation in the relationship between God and man has to be sought as much as possible on the side of man.⁷⁹

If God is immutable, then surely every change in man's situation in relation to salvation must be initiated by a change from man's side. One still remains close to this fundamental viewpoint even if the saving reversal from wrath to grace brought about by Christ is traced to the meritorious, free volition of the man Jesus, in keeping with a heightened diothelitism, as happened in the case of Anselm of Canterbury.⁸⁰

Statements such as these show the closely woven interrelation of all loci of Pannenberg's theology of which one should be aware also when thematizing Christ's cross in the following chapters.

---

⁷⁸ *Ibid.*, p. 172
⁷⁹ *Ibid.*, pp. 161f. In the 7th line above, *BQiTh* has "constancy" instead of "faithfullness" as translation of *Treue*.
⁸⁰ *Ibid.*, p. 163

(6) In his phenomenological analysis of the human experience of hope and future Pannenberg came to the conclusion that the power of the future from which all events eventuate has to be characterized as unifying and reconciling. *It is love.* The same results from Jesus' message. While the idea of power as such is equivocal and could have a power as its object that destroys as well as enhances and strengthens life, that distorts as well as synthesizes and "saves", Pannenberg takes "creativity" in the sense of univocal love. For Jesus, Pannenberg poignantly asserts, "suggests that the creative power of the future is conceivable only if we understand its actuality in terms of love."[81] Jesus saw God's love in the imminence of the kingdom in as much as he himself felt called to proclaim the kingdom. Such proclamation expresses love because it offers man the chance to participate in God's future instead of being inadvertently and unpreparedly overwhelmed by its precipitous arrival. Jesus' message thus reveals God's concern for man and offers salvation. When and where man accepts this message God has come into power and man has communion with God, i.e., salvation. It implies forgiveness of sin since it leads out of the past and present into the future of communion, and the forgiveness is unconditional because no condition of a certain piety is attached to God's call.

The power from the future turns out to be creative love; it embraces man in a forgiving spirit and offers new life. The present is set free to life. Love for Pannenberg is inseparably connected with future and contingency because its power is contingently creative (a tautology actually if creativity implies novelty!), giving rise to novelty, which in turn is possible for any power only it it possesses the power over the future and works from the future. In this sense the dictum of tradition that love is the ultimate motive of creation is accurate. But Pannenberg charges, "Theologians have not understood the interrelation of love, contingency, and future in its full radicality."[82] Each event is a work of creative love in (a) its uniqueness and (b) its being held by the *ultimate intention* of that love, viz., to uphold the bond between itself and the creatures.[83] Of course, this love is neither all-efficacious nor coercive. It creates autonomous forms of existence. For this reason sin is possible. Sin, we remember, is man's foreclosing of change.

---

[81] *ThaKoG*, p. 64
[82] *Ibid.*, p. 65
[83] For the compatibility of this ontology with the scientific description of natural processes see P.'s section on "Creation and Causality", *ibid.*, pp. 67f.

Man's self-assertion is good in that it reflects his assent to the particular existence God provided for him. It is evil when it forecloses the future, its promise for change, and hope in God's power. Like Henry Nelson Wieman, Pannenberg identifies this tendency as the place where "we may seek the roots of all absurdity, suffering, and evil which so grievously distort nature ... When man asserts himself against the future, he misses his authentic existence, betrays his destiny to exist in full openness toward what is to be, and abdicates his participation in God's creative love."[84] The fact that love creates autonomous forms of existence accounts for the conventional apperception of divine reality in religious experience where the future is understood as prolongation of the present rather than its creative origin. Through history as a catalyst mythical religion in which all reality is related to a primordial past is superseded by the message of the coming kingdom of God.

> History shattered mythical existence and enabled man to rise to a consciousness of his own historicity as it is interrelated with the futurity of God.[85]
>
> The process of history is God's instrument in the education of humanity, bringing man to the awareness of his historicity and thus completing his creation.[86]

(7) God as the creatively loving and unifying power of the future is the supremely, in fact singly trustworthy object of human hope and confidence. For the future has the power over the present. It can contradict the present and release such forces as are required to overcome it. For this reason this power alone can save and preserve.

> Trust in the coming reign of God now was sufficient to link one to its salvation, without any further requirements of traditional piety. Thereby the future of God — of the God of Israel, to be sure — became the measure of all things, even the measure of the history of its own past origins.[87]

---

[84] *Ibid.*, p. 69
[85] *Ibid.*, p. 68
[86] *Ibid.*, p. 69; "historicity" in these two quotations denotes what I have preferred to translate by "historicalness".
[87] "The God of Hope", p. 247

Such trust gives man freedom (a) for a truly personal life, (b) to accept the provisionality of everything, (c) in relation to nature and society, (d) to love creatively. When Pannenberg says that creative love proceeds from freedom, and its purpose and goal is the affirmation and creation of freedom in the world, freedom and unity become almost interchangeable concepts. Love proceeds from freedom in the sense that only the power which is free can love, i.e., can liberate from the enclosure and inertia of the past and present. And such freedom can be expected only from the one who is and exerts the power of the future. Unity is the opposite of enclosure, inertia, insensitive self-assertion, and blindfolded refusal to hope. Unity, unification, and freedom are interlocked in that unification presupposes freedom, and unity as repair and reconciliation of disintegrated and adverse elements is tantamount to genuine freedom. One has to infer such qualifications since Pannenberg's efforts at a comprehensive doctrine of sin (and evil) are as yet sketchy.

6. The Existence of God

The sensitive point of Pannenberg's concept of God is Bloch's concept of *Futurum als Seinsbeschaffenheit*. To conventional thinking this concept of course represents a contradiction in terms. Either something is future, then it does not now exist. Or it exists; then it is in the present, not in the future. The tension inherent in this concept leads to Pannenberg's multifarious and partially incoherent statements to the question whether or not God is extant in the contemporary world. Is Pannenberg's conception theistic or not?

The intricate problem has loomed at several places during the discussion. It comes out transparently in a statement like the following.

> The idea of future as the mode of God's being is still undeveloped in theology despite the intimate connection between God and the coming reign of God in the eschatological message of Jesus. What is the meaning of this intimate connection? For instance, is the future of his lordship, the kingdom of God, inessential to his deity, something merely appended to it? Is not God God only in the accomplishment of his lordship over the world? This is why his deity will be revealed only when the kingdom comes, since only then will

his lordship be visible. But are God's revelation of his deity and his deity itself separable from each other? The God of the Bible is God only in that he proves himself as God. He would not be the God of the world if he did not prove himself to be its lord. But just this proof is still a matter of the future, according to the expectations of Israel and the New Testament. Does this not mean that God is not yet, but is yet to be? In any case, he exists only in the way in which the future is powerful over the present, because the future decides what will emerge out of what exists in the present. As the power of the future, God is no thing, no object presently at hand . . . He appears neither as one being among others, nor as the quiescent background of all beings, the timeless being underlying all objects. Yet, is being itself perhaps to be understood as in truth the power of the future?[88]

The central statement in this text seems to be that God is yet to be. Why is that so? Because (1) God is identical with power (God is God to the extent he is powerful over the present, he proves himself to be, etc.), more precisely with his *coming* rule (reign, lordship), his *future* power, and because (2) being is this power of the future. Pannenberg's equation of God and power is decisive for his notion of God. So is the assumption that Jesus' message puts God's power into the future. Finally, his concept of God's self-revelation entails that God's indirect self-revelations in the course of history up until the eschaton *represent events internal to God's essence*. So he has a history; it is, apart from the prolepsis in the Christ event, still indefinite what God is. We would have no reliable knowledge of God's essence were it not for the proleptic character of the Christ event as direct self-revelation.

The futurity of God and all that is means that nothing is settled, nothing is completed – quantitatively and qualitatively. "Being" as the future result of a process going on in the present, "being" as an achievement rather than a presupposition is the consequence of Pannenberg's replacing the Greek concept of cosmos by the Israelite-apocalyptic historical, dynamic view of reality which gives the contingent the same rank as the necessary and the lawful. For this reason, Tillich's ontology is dissatisfactory for Pannenberg, although he shares Tillich's definition and rejection of the older theism.

---

[88] "The God of Hope", p. 242

But, contrary to Whitehead, the development leads, by "the intrinsic logic of the creative love of God himself", to an eschatological consummation. For

> ... if love is considered to represent the ultimate motivation of God's creative activity, and if it belongs to love that the one who loves communicates himself to the beloved one to the degree that is beneficial for the beloved one, then the consummation of the process of evolution in a convergent unity by participation in the unity of the creator seems intimately connected with the act of creation as such.[89]

Now obviously the power of the future cannot be thought of as exclusively *coming* or exclusively yet to be. Were this the case God would indeed have been removed out of this world and away into the future. But God is asserted to be active, creative in the past and present world. Pannenberg speaks of God's dominance. Pannenberg makes sure that he does not mean to remove God into the future — God *is* in the past and present. However, his being there does not imply all-efficaciousness. God already is in as much as he is the power which he releases into the past and present. He exists in the way and to the extent that the future is powerful over the past and present.

In other words, God's omnipotence primarily means his power as love that creates unity and freedom. It leaves freedom to his creatures. To be is to exist in fulfillment, is to exist when the process toward change, growth, novelty, hope, faith, love, freedom, unity is completed. In this sense existence is in the eschaton. Everything is not yet. The locale of being is the ultimate future. Now God is ahead of everything in this process, this history. We face a dipolarity in Pannenberg's concept of God. *Essentially* God is the same always, he is at the goal, he is the power of the ultimate future beyond which there is no new future. He is unsurpassable. He is eternal in the sense that all is present to him. On the other hand, time and history are in God also. Regarding these God is on the way, too. Historically he produces the new time and again, essentially he is the same. To the extent that God's power is efficacious in the past and present God was and is extant in the world. To the extent man accepts this power, is unified, receives freedom, openness to God, etc., he exists. But this existence is partial, incomplete.

---

[89] Wolfhart Pannenberg, "Future and Unity", p. 64

Thus God both is and is not extant in the world. He is extant for no power is thinkable unless it is. He is not extant in as much as he is coming and is and works from the future. In the final analysis Pannenberg's ideas suggest that his theology is theistic. Pannenberg refutes only the traditional theism, particularly the idea of reality according to which to exist means to be settled and closed to the future. Only in this sense God is non-extant. If, as we may assume, Pannenberg's statements posses coherence and thinkability the future has to be envisaged as a somehow supernatural reality, a locale from where God, as personal and independent being, releases his power and where the bodily risen Christ is localizable.[90]

Pannenberg's concept of God's coming and presently extant rule actually is incompatible with the concept *Zukunft als Seinsbeschaffenheit* in the strict sense. The future possesses ontological priority, not exclusiveness. It is the source, not the sole place of being.

We briefly turn to Pannenberg's position in relation to that of A. North Whitehead. Both found their systems on knowledge and some inferences. What we trust must be verifiable. While Whitehead works as an empiricist with a special mode of non-sensous perception (causal efficacy) Pannenberg, as we saw, derives the evidence from history, especially Israelite, apocalyptic, and early Christian history, and phenomenological analysis. Both extend the empirical or historical evidence speculatively. But the evidence remains the criterion of validity all along. For both God is power, not an abstraction, idea, or ideal – power with a certain aim and direction.[91] God is dipolar for both thinkers. For Whitehead, there is, on the one hand, the absolute, universal and everlasting side of God; he is an

---

[90] John B. Cobb, Jr. ("Wolfhart Pannenberg's 'Jesus: God and Man'", *The Journal of Religion*, vol. 49, No. 2, Apri. 1969, pp. 192-202) rightly suggests that in agreement with P.'s concept of resurrection Jesus' body must be localizable. It is not localizable in our familiar reality. "The alternative would seem to be to say that it is already in that future anticipated by all of us. But in that case the future must be posited as already extant or as an eternity alongside of time or abrogating the reality of time in a way that P. usually wishes to avoid." (p. 197) Cobb's conclusion is cogent.

[91] For Whitehead God does not merely provide possibilities. Cf. Daniel Day Williams, "Response to Wolfh. Pannenberg", *Hope and the Future of Man*, p. 86, "But this is not an accurate characterization of Whitehead's view in which there are no mere possibilities. All possibilities are realated to the concrete action of God and the real events in the world."

abstract form or structure, exemplified in every experience. This, his primordial nature, is "the organ of novelty, the ground of teleology, and the principle of concretion and determinateness in the world."[92] On the other hand, in his consequent nature, God is an actual concrete occasion, a process, a growth. In this aspect of his being

> God is finite and therefore limited. . . . As consequent, God is finite in his achievement of value, in the physical realization of his own conceptual nature. The consequent nature of God is composed of the world's reaction on God's primordial nature. Therefore God is physically limited by the realization of value in the world.[93]

For Pannenberg, God as the power of the future roughly corresponds to (I do not say, represents, or the like) both the primordial nature and the consequent nature of Whitehead's God. For Whitehead's consequent nature of God includes much of what Pannenberg means by God's eternity, e.g., the everlasting preservation of values. This preservation seems not to be extant in time for Pannenberg but is ascribed to the ultimate future. But Pannenberg's God as the power of the future also has the historical, temporal side. In this he roughly corresponds to Whithead's consequent nature of God who shares the principle of interdependence. Of the latter Cobb says,

> He gives himself to the world, but the world also gives itself to him. He acts in and on every entity in the world. In turn, every entity in the world reacts upon him. . . . Far from being impassible, he is perfectly sensitive and responsive to all that happens, sharing with the world in both joy and suffering.[94]

To what extent Pannenberg agrees with God's determinability and influencibility by his creatures, in his historical, temporal aspect, is a still open question. There is a tension between God's dominant power and his sharing the processive character of things, in Pannenberg. The pivotal issue seems to be: Does mutability, for Pannenberg, mean determinability or self-determined mutation? At any rate, Pannenberg upholds that there is

---

[92] John B. Cobb, Jr., "What is the Future? A Process Perspective", *Ibid.*, p. 9
[93] Bernhard M. Loomer, "Whitehead's Method of Empirical Analysis", *Process Theology*, ed. Ewert H. Cousins (New York: Newman Press, 1971), p. 81.
[94] John B. Cobb, Jr., *op. cit.*, p. 9

freedom for the creatures and room for novelty, evolution, and growth beyond anything now existing.

Some major differences are:

(1) In Pannenberg, God plays a greater part in the realization of his aim, viz., all-encompassing unity. While Whitehead's primordial nature of God, as principle of limitation and concretion, mainly supplies creativity, which is distinguished from God, with possibilities and the lure of the most relevant possibility for the occasion, Pannenberg's power of the future includes what Whitehead calls creativity and is more coercive and dominant. Pannenberg identifies God with rule, reign, lordship, omnipotence. Of course, for him God is *not now* all-dominant or omnipotent, i.e., not in the extant world. Like Daniel Day Williams, one might say, Pannenberg believes in the priority, initiative, and efficacy of the divine power. In spite of what Pannenberg by implication says about the freedom of the creatures and the emergence of sin and evil, Whitehead, because he has no concept of universal history as revelation and because he distinguishes God from creativity, can more transparently account for the fact of evil and suffering in the world.

(2) Therefore, while Whitehead's God in its consequent nature mainly suffers with, is influenced by, and even created by the creatures, Pannenberg, though establishing God's mutability and passibility, deduces no ontological consequences from this. The principal point of reference for his ontology is not Christ's cross but his proclamation of the *coming reigning* (not suffering) God and his resurrection as its proleptic fulfillment.

(3) Pannenberg and Whitehead share the intuition that meaning means fulfillment. But there are fundamental differences.

> Pannenberg's view here is close to that of Ogden. Both of them find in man's conviction that life has meaning the witness to the reality of fulfillment. But Ogden sees this fulfillment in what Whitehead has taught us to call the consequent nature of God who takes into himself and everlastingly preserves all human values. This assumes a kind of reality or completeness of each momentary experience which is then taken up into God. Pannenberg denies that there is any definite reality until the whole of the process of history is complete. Hence the fulfillment can only come at the end of history. Since it must be the fulfillment of all those who have died throughout the

ages of history, it must involve their renewal so as to participate in the end.[95]

Fulfillment for Pannenberg means concrete future revivification, redemption, and renewal of all that ever was: new creation – the ultimate victory of omnipotent love. In Whitehead's God love is *not* omnipotent. It works, like in Pannenberg's thought, toward unification but exhibits its strongest aspects in its bearing the creatures and suffering with them. The eschaton preserves only such values as were realized in the world.[96] Pannenberg takes more fully into account the centrality of hope for distinctively human life.

(4) Historicalness, one of the primary motives of Pannenberg's thought, is held more radically by Whitehead. For Whitehead "better" is better than "best" because it is open to being superseded. Pannenberg shares this view but envisions an ultimate *summum*, an eschatological fulfillment. For Whitehead the process is open-ended, for Pannenberg the ultimate future, the Kingdom is unsurpassable.

---

[95] John B. Cobb, Jr., "Wolfhart Pannenberg's 'Jesus: God and Man'", p. 196

[96] Williams contends the superiority of this view over against Pannenberg's: "But God's concrete temporal life is *more* than his essence.... What Whiteheadians do say is that the unity of the creative process is to be found *in the community of God's being with his creatures, not in absolute unity which is summed up in a final event.*" ("Response to Wolfhart Pannenberg", p. 86f; italics mine).

CHAPTER VI

THE SIGNIFICANCE OF JESUS' DEATH ON THE CROSS

Having gained an understanding of Pannenberg's presuppositions, aim, and procedure and having observed how he constructs his doctrines of God, being, and especially his christology, we now focus on Jesus' passion and death. The foregoing discussion lays the ground for the interpretation of the cross. The leading thoughts which direct Pannenberg's performance and which we will follow are:

(1) The salvific meaning of the Christ event does not establish Jesus' deity. Rather, conversely, it presupposes Jesus' identity as the Son of God. Theology has to substantiate the latter; only then can soteriological consequences be drawn. For only then is death overcome through Jesus, and only then is sin overcome on a level inaccessible to us.

(2) Just as for christology, so also for an interpretation of Christ's death the theological starting point is the "below", i.e., the historical course of Jesus' own life, action, and destiny. Only if his path to the cross contains elements of vicariousness, sacrifice, etc., can such biblical interpretations be upheld.

(3) Any such interpretation which is historically verifiable in the above sense must in addition pass the test of Pannenberg's "empiricism": Can such an interpretation of the saving significance of Jesus' death transform the common human situation of sin and can it be convincingly presented as having been transformed?[1] In other words, is it compatible with the contemporary *Wirklichkeitsverständnis*? Is it true in the sense that it makes a difference to reality?

Pannenberg now subjects the New Testament interpretations of Jesus' death to such twofold investigation.

In his programmatic statement[2] Pannenberg sets forth that Jesus' death has a vicarious and penal character and that the object of Jesus' expiation is the blasphemous existence of humanity. How does he go about establishing

---

[1] See p. 22 supra.
[2] See p. 5 supra.

this? In section I (246 ff)[3] Pannenberg preliminarily points to the image of the just man suffering vicariously for his people as the most easily accessible way for us today to understand a concept of expiation attached to Jesus. He also states that the course of Jesus' own life permits a number of historical conclusions. Finally, Paul's unique interpretation of the cross requires investigation, *viz.*, (a) What, *historically*, is the relation of Jesus' conflict with the law to his death? (b) Can his death be said to have been of a substitutionary and expiatory significance *historically*?

1. The Relationship of Jesus' Death to the Law

Since only God's own authority was superior to that of Moses, Jesus in his historical activity implicitly equated his own authority with that of God (a) when he placed his authority against that of Moses without seeking legitimation in the Torah, and (b) when he pronounced forgiveness of sin. The gift of forgiveness is implied in Jesus' message.[4] For this reason Jesus' community at table with sinners which implied absolution was so offensive and blasphemous to the Jews.[5] "What John transmits as the central point of the Jewish accusation against Jesus – he made himself equal to God (John 5:18), he made himself the Son of God (19:7) – may in this case come very close to the historical truth." (251) The whole of Jesus' activity forms the basis of his conflict with the Jews and of the resulting indictment of blasphemy. *This conflict is expressly and by implication a conflict with the Mosaic law.* By that law the Jews weigh and judge Jesus' conduct and sayings. Jesus nullified this law when he promised sinners a share in the Kingdom of God. "The reproach of blasphemy (Mark 14:64) through the claim of an authority properly belonging only to God was probably the real reason why the Jewish authorities took action against Jesus . . ." (252). Pretexts had to be sought to accuse him because the offence Jesus perpetrated was not an act explicity outlawed by the Torah. As Pannenberg

---

[3] See p. 23 supra.
[4] See p. 120 supra.
[5] Not only so, I think, because Jesus thereby assumed God's position. Jesus' attitude is as unbearable for Jews who accept Jesus' claim. For Jesus' message obliterates the essential distinction between righteous and unrighteous people and eleminates, contrary to John the Baptist and the apocalyptic, from the message of the imminent Kingdom of God the announcement of the annihilation of sinners.

astutely sees, "the offense resided in Jesus' conflict with the law, but a conflict not envisioned by the law itself." (253) Insofar as the basis of his assuming God's authority, his message, was in accord with the Jewish tradition, Jesus' conduct did not conflict with Judaism; and his proclamation *was* accepted by some of the Jews. But it conflicted inescapably *with the postexilic Jewish tradition* according to which the law had acceded to the place of the ultimate criterion of salvation. In the light of this tradition Jesus definitely acted blasphemously. His accusation *in its core* did not arise from malice or slander — whatever role this may have played for and during the trial, but it was the inevitable and understandable reaction born out of loyalty to the law, *a loyalty*, however, *which was informed by the assumption that God's and the law's authority are indistinguishably identical*. To this extent, Pannenberg holds, Paul's theologoumenon that Jesus came under the curse of the law (Galatians 3:13) coincides with the historical truth. Of course, not on account of Deut. 21:23! But because he appeared a transgressor against the law and thus against God himself. Jesus' attitude had to appear as a human questioning of God himself, and his death as the lawful penalty. In Pannenberg's view only the resurrection opened a new perspective. On account of its significance within its *Traditionsgeschichte* it could only mean that *God raised him*, and we have shown what this had to imply. Given these implications, Pannenberg argues, *Jesus' resurrection annulls and reverses the judgment of the Jewish authorities*. For now Jesus appears to be in the right. Innocent though his judges had been when they crucified Jesus, they are *post factum* revealed to have been in the wrong. Actually it was they who had committed blasphemy once their tradition of the law was shown to be godless. The Jews historically shared this understanding of Jesus' resurrection as their own condemnation when they took offense at its proclamation. Moreover, the law itself or, more precisely, the postexilic understanding of the law — the basis of Jesus' condemnation — is put in the wrong; it is "revealed to be at least an inadequate expression of God's will." (254)

The ambiguity of Jesus' pre-Easter ministry was now removed. Jesus' resurrection fundamentally undermined the law's validity and thus caused the foundation of the postexilic Jewish religion to collapse. Pannenberg later qualified, if not revoked this latter judgment.

I no longer think that way, but rather that the particular *interpretation* of Jewish religion, which is so much centered on the law, has been questioned in Christianity in light of the resurrection of Jesus. However, I would strongly emphasize the element of continuity concerning Jewish religion as such. This seems more adequate to Jesus' own proclamation, because *Jesus claimed that the God of Israel and not the law was the core of Jewish religion.* If we accept this point of view, then this would not mean to question Jewish religion as such, but *a particular interpretation of it, namely, the centrality of the law as being indistinct from that of God.* . . . there are many ways of understanding the Jewish faith. I think that even within the Jewish religion, not only on the basis of the Christian faith and the resurrection of Jesus, it could be said: the emphasis on the law is not the only possible emphasis in the self-understanding of the Jewish faith. I am going to revise my christology at that particular point.[6]

In *The Apostles' Creed* such modification is noticeable. Here Pannenberg teaches in accordance with his christological treatise,

> In the light of Jesus' resurrection, not only is the justice of the verdict passed on him condemned; so also is the legitimation of the Jewish judges to pass judgment on him in the name of the chosen people. And by the same token the legitimation of Jesus' judges to pass final judgment on him in the name of the authentic heritage of Israel (and with it the tradition which was constitutive for the Jewish people) is also annulled . . .[7]

Then he adds,

> . . . this does not affect the representative significance of the death of Jesus for the Jewish people, and thus for mankind, as chosen by God. On the contrary, the election of the Jewish people is verified by the resurrection of Jesus . . . Consequently, in the light of the Easter event, *it becomes possible for the Jews particularly to revise the verdict once passed on Jesus as unjust and as not having been passed once and for all in legitimate representation of God's chosen people.* Moreover, this possibility is open whether the revision takes

---

[6] So Pannenberg says in 1971; "A Theological Conversation with Wolfhart Pannenberg", *Dialog*, vol. xi, autumn 1972, pp. 291f.

[7] Wolfhart Pannenberg, *The Apostles' Creed. In the Light of Today's Questions* (Philadelphia: Westminster Press, 1972), p. 83 (henceforth cited AC).

place expressly on the grounds of the Christian Easter faith *or whether it is drawn from a better understanding of the Jewish tradition.*[8]

The earliest Palestinian church understood Jesus as the New Moses whom Israel had expected as the eschatological prophet[9]; he teaches in continuity with the Mosaic law. Paul was the first to interpret Jesus' death as following from the curse of the law and his resurrection as its abrogation. *But exactly what does Paul mean by the "law" in his statements?* Here utmost transparency is essential. One has to do justice to the Jewish religion, and one faces the task of investigating historically the relationship between Jesus' death and the law for the sake of a sound doctrine of the atonement. These are Pannenberg's concerns. One also has to do justice to the diverse and not clearly univocal Pauline statements whose sense, in turn, is an important element in an effort to gain a reliable historical basis for a sound position regarding the theological law-Gospel schema and the *usus legis* doctrine of the Reformers and Protestant Orthodoxy. How is Paul to be understood?

When Paul teaches that Jesus is the end of the law (Rom. 10:4) he does not mean that it is completely abrogated. In Galatians he tends to say so. The law is only the *paidagogos* in the *Heilsgeschichte*. This function allows Paul to say in Romans that we uphold the law (Rom. 3:31); Romans ch. 4 demonstrates that "this 'upholding' of the law happens in the sense of an interpretation in terms of salvation history." (255) Within this function the law fulfilled its purpose through Jesus' death.

> If the law came into human history in order that sin might become even greater (Rom. 5:20), the work of the law in general is accomplished through death. Therefore, the believers are free from the law by virtue of their being united with the death of Christ, since death emancipates from bondage to the law (Rom. 7:4). Whoever has hope in a new life beyond death is free from the law in the realm of this hope. And because believers already live out of this hope in the coming glory, their behavior is no longer subject to the law. (256)

---

[8] *Ibid.*, pp. 83f. (Italics mine).
[9] In accordance with Deuteron. 18:15. Pannenbergs follows F. Hahn, *Christologische Hoheitstitel*, pp. 380-404.

Pannenberg concludes that Rom. 10:4 means *first of all freedom from the law for those "in Christ"*, for those who are united with Christ in one body and consequently share in the fulfillment of the law through Christ in love (Gal. 5:14; 6:2; Rom. 13:10). But did Paul think that the time of the law as an *historical period* (as in Gal. 3:15 to 4:6) has come to an end also? This seems to be the case in Galatians. For here its function is fulfilled, and the law is only temporally valid (3:19) – it is not a gift given by God himself but mediated through angels. *Here the law in all probability means the specifically Israelite law.* In contrast, in Romans Paul focusses on the universal validity of the law for mankind in the interest of the universality of salvation. The law is the "law of God" himself (Rom. 7:21. 25), its validity is not of limited duration, it is called "holy and just and good" without reservation (7:12). In order to demonstrate the guilt of the Gentiles also Paul in Romans extends the concept of the law to include the law in man's conscience.

Pannenberg maintains that these two strands of statements constitute an unclearness with respect to the relation between God's eternal will (for justice) and the specific concrete law of the Old Testament. He asks, Can it be true that the Israelite law in its totality is the eternal will of God? and goes on,

> If the connection of Jesus with the law in the history of salvation – along the line of Galatians – is to be understood primarily as the concrete Israelite law, must we not say that it has come to an end in Jesus in a different sense than as God's will for justice as such, which Paul has in mind when he speaks of the law in Rom. ch. 7?

Paul's failure to clarify this relationship accounts for the fact that the theological doctrine of the law has always gone beyond Paul. Pannenberg himself, as became evident, considers the Mosaic law in its postexilic tradition to be abrogated by the resurrection; its claim to express the eternal will of God in its final formulation was refuted. However, along the line of Romans, the law does not end with Christ but is consummated, fulfilled in him. In this sense it is valid. Pannenberg believes that the position of Romans is closer to the Palestinian Jewish Christianity than Galatians. For the former Jesus is the New Moses, while Galatians questions even the divine origin and consequent authority of the Old Testament law. Paul's position in Romans is legitimate, according to Pannenberg, because – and this conclusion has eminent consequences! –

In the first place, Paul rightly saw in Rom. 2:14f. that the Jewish law has analogies in the life of other peoples in that it follows norms which are binding on the conscience. In this way it is in a certain sense representative for the situation of man generally. Further, Paul recognized that this universal significance of the Jewish law establishes the possibility of relating the salvation accomplished in Jesus' collision with the law on the cross to all humanity. (257)

The Jewish Christian position is also supported by the fact that Jesus did not in general denounce the law but reinterpreted it authoritatively. *While the freedom of this reinterpretation implied refutation of and breach with the law, later endorsed by his crucifixion and resurrection, Jesus' concentration of the law upon the commandment of love constitutes, so Pannenberg is persuaded, a continuity between Jesus' message and the law of Israel.* In Rom. 13:10 and Gal. 5:14 Paul teaches that the love which appeared in Jesus fulfilled the law. The familiar solution of the problem of the abrogation and continuity of the law according to which the Israelite law is abolished as *Heilsweg* (instrument with which to work out one's salvation) but upheld as the abiding will of God for the elect, the *justificati* (*tertius usus legis*!), is rightly deemed insufficient by Pannenberg as a representation of Paul's thought. Paul does not establish his ethical exhortation (*paraenesis*) on the authority of the Old Testament but on the history of Jesus Christ and his behavior, as, e.g., Phil. 2:5ff., and on reason and natural propriety. The power of love which Jesus' activity and path to the cross reveal will time and again generate new structures of common life and new systems and structures of justice but "they will never again be able to claim the unconditionally binding character that belonged to the Jewish law." (258)

Thus Jesus' conflict was *with the law itself as the positive legal tradition, calcified after the exile.* However, until Jesus this by and large was the historical form of God's benevolence for Israel. Now Jesus' message dethroned the validity of the law in the delineated sense. Jesus' rejection exposed his accusers, and consequently this law, as the prime obstacle to the acceptance of Jesus' proclamation and thus to communion with God. One might formulate, in line with Pannenberg: Through Jesus' resurrection God cancelled his own law in this form, function, and finality. A new covenant was made.

We note that for Pannenberg's position both conclusions proved to be pivotal: (1) The law *is* abrogated, (2) the law that is abrogated *really* was the valid expression of God's will in a certain sense. Without the first Jesus death is incapable of being interpreted as the substitutionary punishment for the blasphemy of his accusers *in keeping with the historical evidence.* No blasphemy had been committed by the Jews but for the abrogation of the law! Without the second conclusion Jesus' death merely means a collision with a preliminary Jewish particularity that has no correspondence in mankind at large. Without it Jesus' death would be incapable of being related to all humanity *in keeping with the historical evidence.* Summarily, Paul's interpretation of Christ's death as the end (curse and abolition) of the law is demanded by the demonstrated historical relation between Jesus' death and resurrection, on the one hand, and the law, on the other. Q.e.d.

2. *Can We Speak of an Expiatory Character of Jesus' Death?*

The foregoing shows that Jesus' conflict with the law does not amount to a transgression against the law when viewed *post resurrectionem Christi.* Thus his sinlessness is unimpaired by this conflict. The question of the role Jesus' sinlessness plays in his atoning death will be asked later. Suffice it to say here that Jesus' sinlessness, a biblically and traditionally important presupposition for the vicariousness and expiatory efficacy of his passion, can be historically substantiated. It is indicated by an analysis of the core of Jesus' conflict with the Israelites and it is, like his divinity, retroactively enforced by his resurrection.

Pannenberg is convinced that the concepts of vicariousness and expiation in connection with Jesus' death are not to be relinquished; they are neither unhistorical superimpositions nor untenable for contemporary thought, but historically sound, and meaningful for the present. What evidence is there for this position?

The historical evidence does not include the passion predictions.[10] Jesus, in all probability, did not actively seek his death nor understand it in an expiatory sense. He may have apprehended his passion in correspondence to the rejection and murder of prophets by the recalcitrant people (Luke 13:33; 34f.) "But we can hardly look for the point of the journey in a deliberate self-sacrifice on the part of Jesus, planned from the beginning."[11]

---

[10] Note pp. 6–10, supra, on "The Biblical Understanding of Jesus' Death."
[11] *AC*, pp. 79f.

The discovery of the vicarious and expiatory character of Jesus' death is first reflected in the Lord's Supper tradition and the ransom-saying; the latter, Pannenberg thinks, goes back to Jesus' word about his service in his disciples' midst (Luke 22:27b). This discovery came naturally. When Jesus' resurrection proved his innocence

> ... the meaning of his death could only be understood as an expression of service to humanity in the name of the love of God revealed in his message, which determined his whole mission. It could only be understood as dying for us, for our sins. (247)

Now Pannenberg introduces an important distinction. He asks, "Was his death merely the consequence of his service, or was it in itself a service?" (258f.) Only in the latter case was his death vicarious. For while Jesus' service no doubt was rendered on our behalf, is this true of his death also? One might extend Pannenberg's argument and say: Even if his death was borne, as part of his mission, on our behalf, was it *in our stead*? Primitive Christianity assumed it was as is attested in its interpretations, foremost by the application of Is. 53 to Jesus. But was this assumption appropriate, i.e., historically truthful?

Just as for his christology, so also for his understanding of Jesus' death the resurrection constitutes the fundamental historical event and provides the single adequate perspective. Now the resurrection reveals that Jesus did *not* die as a blasphemer. *De iure resurrectionis, i.e., in virtue of the inversion of standards inherent in the resurrection,* "those who rejected him as a blasphemer and had complicity in his death were the real blasphemers." (259, italics mine) By the new standard his judges deserved what Jesus received. Therefore, Pannenberg concludes — and this is the basis of his position that Jesus' death was vicarious — "*he bore their punishment.*" (259, italics mine) He suffered a substitutionary penal death.

Is this inference conclusive?

Pannenberg makes provisions for the possible objection that this argument presupposes the validity of the law after all. For only according to the law does the blasphemer deserve the death-penalty. Pannenberg meets this objection adequately when he points out that (1) Jesus' judges are not blasphemers because of the law but because they condemned him whom God has legitimated, and (2) that blasphemy universally deserved death because it means to turn against and sever oneself from the source of life, the creator. Christian forbearance toward blasphemy is justifiable only precisely on account of the vicarious significance of Christ's passion. And in this sense Jesus' death was of vicarious significance not only for his judges but all of Israel. For the judges condemned him on the basis of the law and "every Jew who was faithful to the law would have had to act in the same way or similarly had he been in the position of the Jewish authorities." (260) Jesus' resurrection shows every Jew to be a blasphemer. "The death penalty borne by Jesus is the punishment deserved by the whole people to the extent that it is bound to the authority of the law." (260)

But for two other objections that seem possible Pannenberg makes as yet no provisions.

(1) His argument rests on what he calls the *inversion of standards*, revealed through the resurrection: Jesus was disclosed to have acted lawfully, the judges are the blasphemers. However, actually the resurrection of Jesus does not establish the personal guilt of the judges. Is it morally conscionable to call them blasphemers? For if they acted in accordance with their law, one must conclude that by that standard they were innocent. A later inversion of standards can change the *evaluation* of their act but cannot establish a personal damnable guilt. *Post factum* they are revealed to have rejected the legitimate Son. Now according to the principles of civil rights, on the one hand, and ethical sensitivity, on the other, no act may be prosecuted if the law which penalizes this act was not in force at the time of the act. From this point of view which is part of our reality Jesus' judges and Israel at large appear innocent even after the inversion of standards.

Jesus' resurrection, so to say, establishes the guilt of the judges retroactively. Is this acceptable? We are not asking if such inference is *in general* theologically acceptable but on Pannenberg's own terms and premises. Just as the theological statement that Jesus was cursed by the law required to be verified by an investigation whether Jesus' historical course that led to his death can be said to have been determined by his conflict with the law, at least its *intentio*, – so also the theological judgment that Jesus' judges were the blasphemers needs substantiation not only through the resurrection but from elements in the historical attitude and decision of the Jewish authorities!

Now precisely this was Pannenberg's procedure also when he established Jesus' identity. We remember that in this instance Jesus' self-consciousness, in particular his personal community with the Father, was an indispensable element in the demonstration that Jesus was the Son of

God. The retroactive force of the resurrection in both its ontological and noetical directions for Pannenberg never amount to a superimposition of meaning on data which historically show no indication for such meaning. That, for Pannenberg, would be fiction, mere assertion, unfounded and irresponsible belief.

So we ask Pannenberg the question: Where in the decision of Jesus' judges do we historically find a datum which demonstrates the justification of the condemnation that comes over them on account of Jesus' true identity? It seems that the fact of having convicted Jesus according to the law constitutes a guilt only *if they had a chance to recognize him in his true meaning, i.e., to recognize that through him God changed or abolished his law*! Otherwise their retroactive condemnation appears offensive. Pannenberg's inference under discussion is too kerygmatic, given his premises.

To be sure, Pannenberg is correct when he says that Jesus' conflict is not with particular human failures of the particular individuals who judged him. His argument that his conflict was with the core of the law itself is cogent. But it requires to be established (1) that the judges failed to grasp that, in spite of all ambiguity in the life of Jesus, his proclamation of the imminent Kingdom of God implied an obvious change in God's standards and thus a reevaluation and abolition of the law. This would constitute their guilt historically and render Pannenberg's interpretation of Jesus' resurrection as their condemnation credible and acceptable. It needs (2) to be established that such failure of the judges is shared factually or potentially by all of Israel.

Both could be established, it seems, by use of Pannenberg's concept of sin as lack of openness to God. The God of Israel had time and again, through indirect self-revelations which were provisional and surpassable, demonstrated the historicalness of all truth, also his truth, and had designated his people for an openness to future revelations. Jesus' message and the concomitant absolution he administered in the name of God must have been persuasive for those who were open to God. This could be shown to be applicable to the whole people of Israel.

Both could also be established, it appears, by the thesis that the demand to love for any man open to the future possesses greater inherent truth than a restrictive law which generates legalistic behavior.

At any rate, in whatever way one supplements Pannenberg's argument at this point, *the guilt must become transparent which those incurred who in the face of Jesus' message could still abide by the Israelite law*. Without such historical evidence the condemnation of Jesus' judges appears a tour de force.

(2) There is another objection with which Pannenberg later deals but which should be stated at this time. Granted the guilt of the judges and Israel, how does one know that "he bore their punishment"? The innocence of one who is executed does not *ipso facto* imply the substitutionary character of his death. Strictly historically, only Jesus' service is demonstrated to have been on behalf of others. So was his death, to the extent that it was its consequence. But was it *in their stead*? Was it a vicarious penal and thus expiatory death? Of course, if we grant Pannenberg that the judges and Israel deserved to die one *could* infer that since they did not die at the time of their delict it is possible that the innocently dying Jesus bore their punishment. A possibility! – which, however, presupposes (1) the need of punishment and (2) the transferability of guilt. Pannenberg is partly aware of these questions, and we will shortly present how he deals with them. Be it said merely that the inference under discussion is *not cogent* and that for all we heard so far neither the vicarious nor the penal character of Jesus' death have been demonstrated. *Pace* Pannenberg one could argue just as well that *historically* Jesus suffered the consequence of his conflict with the law like the prophets who preached God's will to the recalcitrant people; Jesus' message entailed his death, and it was *in this sense* on our behalf. His suffering, then, represents the "price" which God in the Son pays for the abolition of his former will, the law, and, because only one who had died can be raised from the dead, for the arrival of his proleptic direct self-revelation.

3. *In What Sense Did Jesus Die for Humanity?*

Moreover, Pannenberg holds that Jesus' death has vicarious significance not only for Israel but all humanity. According to his thesis that Jesus bore the punishment of those who, by his resurrection, were demonstrated to have been blasphemers when they actually or potentially crucified him (As many are atoned for as participated in Jesus' rejection!) – according to this principle Pannenberg now must show *how all humanity shared in this blasphemy*.

It is his contention that in Jesus' conviction and sentencing the Romans participated as representatives of the Gentile nations just as the Jewish authorities as representatives of Israel. Of course, in their case it was not faithful adherence to the law which motivated their rejection of Jesus. First, in this trial before Pilate, Pilate's personal failure, his lack of courage, or the fact of the slanderous character of the accusation against Jesus, is as irrelevant as the similar circumstances in Jesus' Jewish trial had been said to be. Second, here also, behind the superficially accidental events, the conflict was one of fundamental principles: *Jesus' eschatological message assaulted the claim to ultimacy of the human political order.*

> In the sphere of the influence of Jesus' message the right of every existing state to bind its subjects to it in the innermost way is contested. The ruler may not assume the place of God. (261)

The blasphemy of the Romans is identified here as the human pride of equality with God. But Pannenberg deems this an insufficient basis for his claim.

> And yet in political power one may see only one form of the delusion of human identity with God, even though it is an especially instructive example. Therefore the conflict with political power is not yet an adequate legitimation of the universally human significance of Jesus' vicarious death. Only after it is otherwise established that Jesus in his death suffered the abandonment by God in death as the effect of the pride of equality with God, which separates man universally from God, and has taken it away once and for all, might one find non-Jewish humanity represented by the activity of the Roman procurator in Jesus' trial; then Jesus has interceded with his death for non-Jewish humanity as well. (261)

We notice that Pannenberg's aim now consists of demonstrating that Jesus "suffered the abandonment by God in death" and that this resulted from "the pride of equality with God which separates man universally from God." While in his discussion of Jesus identity as the Son of God Jesus' death was interpreted as dedication to God that became self-sacrifice when it lacked any *Verstehenshorizont*[12] Pannenberg now views it, *sub specie resurrectionis*, as abandonment by God into death. Both are historically adequate, given the historicity of Jesus' resurrection and its significance in its *Traditionsgeschichte*. That his death is effected by the universal human

---

[12] See pp. 76f. supra.

usurpation of God's rank is an idea Pannenberg introduces here for the first time; it is of biblical-kerygmatic origin, as yet unrelated to his usual definition of sin as self-centered closedness to the future and God. The idea that Jesus' resurrection inverted the standards causes Pannenberg to identify the mortal sin of Jesus' rejectors as blasphemy. Claiming salvific effect of Jesus' rejection for all nations, Pannenberg faces the task of either extending the concept of blasphemy and subsuming all godlessness under this delict as common denominator, *or* of naming alternative forms of sin as the ultimate human aversity to God and Jesus. One notices his wrestling with this problem. Another difficulty is created by this inversion of standards, it appears: In the case of Jesus' judges historically it was their loyalty to the law of God which made them reject Jesus. The resurrection disclosed their blasphemy retroactively. But with respect to humanity Pannenberg identifies the universal motive for the rejection of Jesus as the pride of equality with God. These two ideas are left unrelated. Does one not observe an unhappy consequence of Pannenberg's failure to establish and name the guilt which Jesus' judges historically incurred?

In what way did Paul attribute the salvific effect of the cross to all humanity? To this question Pannenberg now turns. Jesus, for Paul, died for the Gentiles because the cross abolishes the law that prevented the Gentiles from having free access to their participation in Abraham's blessings (II Cor. 5:14f.; Gal. 3:13f.; Rom. 11:11ff.; Acts 13:46f.) Theologically and historically the cross opened the gates into Israel's history of election to all nations. But in this sense, we might say, Jesus died on their behalf, not in their stead. Pannenberg goes on,

> The abolition of the law is, however, merely the negative condition for the Gentiles' community with the God of Israel. This also depends upon the fact that community with Israel's God is positively made possible by Jesus and all the more so since the judgment of the law over human sin, the Gentiles' like the Jews', is in no way impugned. How then is access to God for the Gentiles, in spite of their entanglement in sin, made possible by Jesus? (261)

In this statement Pannenberg has related the freedom from the law to Jesus' message which implied and therefore was accompanied by his forgiveness of sin. But, following Paul, this forgiveness must be "made possible" by Jesus still on other grounds. (Such foundation of God's forgiveness other than through and in virtue of Jesus' message was not spoken of when Pannenberg pondered the nature of God. Cf. *supra*, pp. 110 ff.). This makes sense if we assume that the abolition of the law amounts not to a wiping out of sin, an imputation of righteousness, but means its abrogation as *Heilsweg*. It is not forgiveness as such, then. Rather, access to God in spite of sin is rendered possible *through Paul's use of the Jewish Adam-speculation*. For Paul, Christ's death includes the death of man in general (II Cor. 5:14; Rom. 5 *passim*). *Human sin is universally atoned for because (1) death is the punishment for sin and (2) all die with and in Jesus' death*. The law establishes the relationship between sin and death. In this sense it remains universally true. The Gentile nations are subject to this law, too; they know it in their consciences. Consequently, both Jews and Gentiles are blasphemers, have incurred death and were freed from death because the one righteous, Jesus, died for all (including all). Paul saw Jesus' death in analogy to the death of a mystery deity. "Like a mystery deity, Jesus shared men's fate, the consequence of their sin (Romans 6:10) and in return men receive a share in his life." (262) Of the two fundamental presuppositions of this Pauline doctrine ((a) human mortality is a consequence of sin; (b) the deity dies vicariously and expiates the guilt of all) Pannenberg rejects the latter.

> Today such an explanation is no longer possible. The ideas of the mystery religions can no longer be presupposed as universally convincing truth. (262)

However, the first retains validity today on anthropological grounds.

> ... man is subject to death just because of his being closed in upon himself, while his destiny to openness to the world still points beyond death. The way in which Paul connected the Jewish law to universal anthropological conditions is also valid as an explicit example of the relation between sin and death ... (262)

On this basis Pannenberg concludes,

> When one understands the universal human significance of the Jewish law as the explicit formulation of the universally valid relation between deed and its consequences, as one form of the legal structure of social life which is realized everywhere in different ways, then the Jewish people actually represent humanity in general in its rejection of Jesus as a blasphemer in the name of the law. (262 f.)

In other words, the Gentile nations are included in the deed of the Jews since they, too, would have had to reject Jesus.

We must listen acutely. Pannenberg's suggestions are consistent only if one clearly distinguishes *the situations before and after Easter. Before* Easter Jews and Gentiles in accordance with the law of deed and consequences rightfully rejected Jesus. Here breaking the law entails death; that death is the rightful penalty for sin universally is established persuasively by Pannenberg's argument from anthropology. Jesus is guilty. So is everyone on account of his sin. *After* Easter Jesus is revealed to be innocent and the law is, by implication, abrogated. *Of what does the guilt of the Jews or the Gentiles before Easter consist when viewed from after Easter?* Is it postulated authoritatively by the resurrection alone? If we gather up what Pannenberg has said about the nature of sin and the ambivalence of the law we can say: Just as the Israelites distort the law by adhering to it without openness to God and thus crucify Jesus in the name of the (calcified, apotheosized) law (and, in so doing, seek equality with God and become blasphemers), so also the Gentiles distort the law of their consciences by adhering to it without openness to God. They too crucify Christ who challenges any closedness and legalism.

Now *if* Jesus' death atones for as many as are guilty of his rejection and are exposed as blasphemers by his resurrection, Jesus died for humanity. Again, is this principle acceptable? Pannenberg holds the use of the Adam speculation and of the myth of the dying mystery deity to possess no universally convincing truth. He has not made it transparent how else the ideas of transferable guilt and substitutionary penal suffering are thinkable today. For Pannenberg, the insight that Jesus died for our sins follows from the fact that he died (*sub specie resurrectionis*). For when he died he died the death all had incurred. Consequently it was a substitutionary death. It seems that Bible (e.g., Gal. 3:13) and tradition say the same thing when they argue: since Jesus did not deserve to die, his death must have been in place of those who deserve it. Pannenberg implicity accepts this. He verifies Jesus' ultimate openness to God (sinlessness) in his christology and man's universal closedness to the future (God) in his anthropology. And he so far mutely accepts the possibility of transference of guilt and expiation of guilt through vicarious suffering of the lawful punishment.

4. The Concept of Inclusive Substitution

Pannenberg's concept of inclusive substitution serves to explain *to what extent Jesus' death has vicarious significance, given it was vicarious.* It does not free us from the necessity of dying. But "none else has to die in the complete rejection in which Jesus died." (263) Death until and including Jesus meant exclusion from the community with God, to be expelled by the entire weight of the legitimate authority of the divine law. Jesus' death excelled, though, in that in addition it meant exclusion "from the nearness of the God in whose nearness he had known himself to be in a unique way the messenger of the imminent Kingdom of God." (263)[13] This has universally changed.

> No one else must die this death of eternal damnation, to the extent that he has community with Jesus. . . . Whoever is bound up with Jesus dies, to be sure, but dies in hope of the life of resurrection from the dead that has already appeared in Jesus. (263)

Jesus' death constitutes inclusive substitution since it includes ours and transforms our dying into a dying in hope. The concept goes back to Philipp Marheineke[14] and is derived from Paul. It presupposes, of course, the two ideas highlighted at the end of section 3 above.[15] We now turn to Pannenberg's attempt persuasively to ground this presupposition.

Pannenberg is aware that the concept of substitution, in concert with his methodological premises, requires "fundamental justification" (264). Is substitution possible in the area of personal life, with regard to moral guilt and punishment and merit? F. Socinus, D. F. Strauss, and Albrecht Ritschl, Pannenberg says, denied it. First of all he believes the basis of this denial to be an *extreme ethical individualism,* characteristic of man's self-understanding up to the 1950s, and this basis to have become doubtful "by the crisis of the social transformation of the present day." (265) Following studies by Koch and von Rad, Pannenberg points to the *very different*

---

[13] See p. 76 f., *supra*.
[14] Philipp Marheineke, *Die Grundlehren der christlichen Dogmatik als Wissenschaft* (2d ed.; Berlin: Duneker und Humboldt, 1827), para. 398.
[15] P., in a note (264), agrees with Barth who understood the vicarious significance of Christ's death as both summation and overcoming of our death (CD, IV/1, pp. 252 ff., 295 ff.).

relation between guilt and punishment in Israel.[16] According to the Israelite understanding, what follows guilt is not punishment in a moral sense. The "punishment" is neither specifically invoked nor arbitrarily determined. It is not administered as the effect of an ideal norm unrelated to the natural essence of the malefactor or his evil act. *Rather, comparable to the necessity of natural laws, an evil deed necessarily has a painful outcome as its consequence.* This explain Paul's phrase that death is the "wages" of sin.

> This means that death is built into the essence of sin as the most extreme consequence of sin's desire for separation from God, the origin of life. . . . Hebrew has a single word for the deed and its result; עָוֹן or חַטָּאת designate the evil deed as well as the misfor- misfortune following from it.

This mode of thought explains Paul's statement II Cor. 5:21:God has made Christ to be sin for us, that we might become in him the righteousness of God.

> That Christ has been made to be sin means that the misfortune following from our sin has fallen upon him. Similary, the Israelites designated the sin offering by the same word as that for 'sin'. (265)

Secondly, for the Israelite understanding of guilt and expiation the individual is heavily involved in society. Every individual fault or merit bears upon the entire society. Pannenberg explains, citing K. Koch,

> "If a serious violation of the divine law had occurred somewhere the burden that thereby fell upon the society before God stood wholly in the foreground since nothing less important than its qualification for cultic practise was thereby threatened." The evildoer was "in a completely realistic and direct sense dangerous to society" because *the wrong done had to react in one way or another on the society "unless it formally and demonstratively anulled its solidarity with the offender."* If the deed were not "turned back" on the guilty party, there was cause to fear that its inherent destructive power could strike somewhere else. This presupposes that the deeds of men,

---

[16] Klaus Koch, *"Gibt es ein Vergeltungsdogma im Alten Testament?"*, ZThK, LII 1955, pp. 1-42; Gerhard von Rad, *Old Testament Theologie* (New York: Harper & Row, 1962) vol. i, pp. 262 ff. et passim.

especially the evil deeds, pregnant with impending misfortune, have their effect to a great extent independently of the person of the doer. To be sure, they do have a tendency to fall back on the head of the doer, but so long as their destructive effect has not found its target, it can involve wider circles of society. . . . *This extensive independence of the deed from the doer* also makes it possible that the catastrophe inherent in the deed *can be directed to some other being and so be annulled.* Especially indicative of this attitude is the prescription that a young cow be sacrificed when the originator of the misdeed is unknown (Deut. 21:1-9). *The transferability of guilt is the fundamental concept underlying the Israelite institution of sin offering.* (265f., italics mine)[17]

The transference of human guilt upon animals requires divine cultic authorization which is God's gracious gift. So is the permission to punish the evildoer since his punishment wipes out the guilt which consequently can no longer threaten society.

In this mode of thought substitution is common. This understanding informs the Israelite concept of expiation and might be found in other religions as well. *But can we think in this way today?*

In response, Pannenberg first calls attention to the development in Israel's own history. When the unity of the nation dissolved 587 B. C. the ideas of transfer and substitution of guilt became difficult.

Difficulties appear, however, when it is no longer held to be sufficient that the deeds of the individual produce effects in the doer's clan, perhaps generations later, when it is demanded instead that the relation of the deed to its consequence should come to full effectiveness in the life of every individual. . . . The generation living at the time, having experienced Josiah's cultic reform, did not understand why they had to atone for the sins of earlier generations. This protest refused to accept solidarity with Israel's past. (267)

Jeremiah und Ezekiel promised or demanded the accountability of every individual for his own deeds and only for such. But this correspondence did not work out. When in the past it never worked out, this still did not cause a particular problem — the nations as the descendants would sooner or later

---

[17] For citations and page-numbers within this quote cf. Gerhard von Rad, *op. cit.*

reap the reward or bear the punishment. But when the solidarity of individual and society receded the disparity between deed and consequence became intolerable. Pannenberg thinks,

> This is surely one of the motives for the development of the apocalyptic expectation of a future judgment of the dead and of a resurrection of the rigteous. That the relation of deed and its consequences no longer worked out in the life of the individual forced one to the notion of an adjustment beyond death. (267)

Now – according to Pannenberg – this demonstrated relationship between an increasing individualism and distrust in a natural and necessary connection between an act and its consequences throws light on the modern problematic of the concept of substitution. For

> ... also the Enlightenment's criticism of the idea of substitution since the Socinians departed from an individualistic conception of guilt and responsibility: it was held that only the doer is responsible, and the deed could only afflict him.[18]

Pannenberg calls our attention to a difference between the post-exilic-Israelite and modern ethical individualism. The latter does not merely consider the disparity between deed and consequence intolerable *but deems such consequence to be externally imposed by the authority of the state or the like and in no way innate and necessary to a deed itself.* This fact is of greater importance than Pannenberg makes of it. It calls into question the very necessity of punishment and leads to the modern conviction that there can only be either *punishment* (God, the legislator) *or* forgiveness (God, the Father; cf. Ritschl's concept of God.)

Now Pannenberg sides with the vision characteristic of the older Israelite view and he does so on anthropological and sociological grounds.

> The relation between guilt and the social group is not sufficiently clarified by an extremely individualistic understanding of guilt. It is grounded in the social character of human existence that every person continually deals in responsibilities that include other people to some degree. (268)

---

[18] Wolfhart Pannenberg, *Grundzüge der Christologie*, p. 275, my translation. (Cf. *JGaM*, p. 267).

Since everybody is inescapably involved in his society, sharing both responsibility for and consequences of the deeds of everybody else, *"substitution is a universal phenomenon, both in conduct and its outcome."* (268, italics mine). Apparently Pannenberg is saying: ethical individualism cannot cope with the complexity and intricacy of the cause-effect, deed-consequence, good-reward, evil-punishment relationships. Not only are there hardly ever direct lines; most deeds spring from mixed motives, regarding both quality and origin, and most occasions when good or evil is experienced are made up of both deserved and undeserved effects. Empirically, guilt and innocence, good deeds and bad deeds are *perpetually transferred,* and both suffering and joy are perpetually substitutionary in social life.

The reality of the phenomenon of substitution thus established, *substitution is also applicable to Jesus' passion and death; it is true also of his cross.* If the premise of the Enlightenment criticism of the Orthodox doctrine of the atonement, *viz.,* ethical individualism, were correct, its criticism were accurate. Within their presupposition the Socinians were right. But this presupposition, as shown, is outdated. *Because it is outdated and because substitution is a universal phenomenen of social reality and no miraculously supernatural uniqueness of Jesus Christ it is possible to speak meaningfully of a vicarious character of Jesus' fate.* Only on such a basis is the *pro nobis* of Jesus' death defensible. And this fundamental Israelite view of reality was the presupposition, Pannenberg suggests, for the New Testament images through which the *pro nobis* of Jesus' death was expressed.[19]

We followed Pannenberg's thesis of the inversion of standards as following from Jesus resurrection and noticed his somewhat surprising inference which appeared as the postulate, "he bore their punishment." We asked, how is this known?, since it does not follow from the inversion of standards itself. We insisted that the transferability of the guilt of the universal human blasphemy upon Jesus must be made feasable and that the possibility of vicarious penal suffering required substantiation, especially the possibility or necessity of *Jesus'* passion as the penal suffering in place of all humanity. Pannenberg is convinced that the foregoing datum, the universal phenomenen of elements of substitution etc. in all social life, ade-

---

[19] P. considers this Old Testament view to be fundamental and the prophetic individualism cited above to be a side-line of the Old Testament. Cf. *JGaM*, pp. 268f.

quately answers the questions which were raised and fulfills the requirements he himself poses and we, following his theological methodology, named. He draws the conclusion and simply says,

> Under the presupposition that there is an element of substitution active in all social relationships, one is permitted to understand Jesus' death as a vicarious event in view of the unique reversal that the one rejected as a blasphemer is, in the light of the resurrection, the truly just man, and his judges, in contrast, are now the real blasphermers. (269)

Since God's own law authorized his execution, Jesus' death was a matter of God's disposition. "God himself, who raised Jesus, had laid on him the punishment for blasphemy through the actions of his legitimate officeholders." (269) Pannenberg summarizes his point,

> ... he (God) let Jesus go to his death in place of the people whose resistance to Jesus is revealed in the light of his resurrection to be rebellion against its God. In his death, Jesus bore the consequence of separation from God, the punishment for sin, not just in place of his people, but in place of all humanity. (269)

Is this basis for a defence of the *pro nobis* of Jesus' death in the sense of "in our place, in our stead" sufficient? We must scrutinize this solution with acumen. To gain further insight into Pannenberg's position an examination of his critical appraisal of some of the major historical theories of the saving significance of Jesus' death is appropriate.

CHAPTER VII

THE SIGNIFICANCE OF JESUS' DEATH
ON THE CROSS (II)

We supplement the foregoing characterization of Pannenberg's doctrine of the cross by listening closely to his statements concerning the main historical theories of the saving significance of Jesus' death, his discussion of Jesus' freedom and sinlessness, and his judgment with regard to the Old Protestant doctrine *de officio sacerdotale Christi*.

1. The Critique of Three Soteriological Theories

As we saw, for Pannenberg Jesus' death is itself a service, not merely the consequence of Jesus' service. At least it is a link in the line of a number of acts or events which together constitute Jesus' service, at most it is the culmination and climax of his service. Jesus died not merely on our behalf but in our stead. Hence as theories of the saving significance of Jesus' death Pannenberg regards those only which attribute a particular salvific function to it. Both the "classical" type of soteriology which G. Aulen called the Christ-Victor-motif[1] and the Abelardian subjective theory of reconciliation do not focus on Jesus' death soteriologically.

> These two soteriological conceptions see in Jesus' death only a particular example of that which constitutes the saving significance of his entire activity. In the "classical" theory of the atonement this is the deification that is grounded in the incarnation and consummated in Jesus' victory over death. In the subjective theory of reconciliation the death of Jesus is the ultimate consequence of God's love for man which characterizes the entirety of Jesus' activity and message. (274, n. 53)

Since for Pannenberg the cross itself is of particular saving relevance he

---

[1] Gustav Aulen, *Christus Victor. An Historical Study of the Three Main Types of the Idea of Atonement* (New York: The Macmillan Company, 1951.)

distinguishes his own doctrine from both of these. He examines three other theories in the light of his own understanding of Jesus' death. As we recall, Pannenberg looks at the death of Jesus both with regard to its historical circumstances and to the clue it receives from the resurrection. From the former view point (before Easter) it is a destiny happening to Jesus on account of his perfect dedication to God and to the commission he had from God (Jesus' sacrifice in the noncultic sense). *Sub specie resurrectionis* – due to the "inversion of standards" – it was a unique vicarious, penal suffering *pro nobis* which God had laid upon Jesus. "He bore their punishment." He bore God's judgment, rightly deserved by humanity as a whole. Thus Pannenberg attributes to Jesus' death that it was vicarious, penal, and *pro nobis* in the sense that God gave him up for us. It was not *pro nobis* in the sense that Jesus sought his death as a work of expiation in which he presented his life to God. For this would be irreconcilable with the historical evidence. Hence Pannenberg's doctrine does not attribute to Jesus' death that it was a priestly work, a sacrifice in the cultic sense, or a work of satisfaction which Jesus as representative of man performs to propitiate God. This receives further substantiation when we look at Pannenberg's evaluation of (1) the ransom-theory, (2) the Anselmian objective theory of the atonement, and (3) the doctrine of Christ's penal suffering.

Ad (1): In his brief discussion of the ransom-theory which has its biblical *verba probantia* in Mark 10:45 Pannenberg substantiates his conviction that not only for us, but also for the New Testament writers themselves the conceptions of Jesus' death as expiatory sacrifice, covenant sacrifice, Passover Lamb, etc., are *expressive illustrations of the vicarious element in Jesus' historical life and death* rather than literal, non-symbolic designations of the event. This is proved by the fact that the content of the ransom image is not realistically expanded in the New Testament; e.g., the question of to whom the ransom was paid was not raised, and that, if taken literally, the image of a ransom and the concept of an expiatory sacrifice would be mutually exclusive.

In the so-called "classical" doctrine of the Fathers the image was mythologically interpreted for the first time. Pannenberg's evaluation of the ransom-theory can be summed up as follows: (1) Like the other images of the New Testament authors it is a clarifying illustration, a symbol for the vicariousness of Jesus' death, and needs to be distinguished from the event itself which to understand adequately primitive Christianity lacked the means. The Jewish tradition "could not fully absorb the concrete circumstances of Jesus' path of suffering accessible to us, particularly his conflict with the law." (275) The mythological expansion of the ransom idea by the patristic theologians must not be overrated. "It is essentially not a theory of the inner essence of redemption, but a popular illustrative statement of its reality, the content of which is further testified by Scripture."[2] (3) Since the real soteriological interest of patristic theology is the victory over death of the believers via the incarnation and Jesus' death is merely the consequence of what was already established by the incarnation, the classical theory does not adequately interpret Jesus' death.

Ad (2): Unlike the biblical images of ransom, etc., Anselm's theory intends to offer a literal explanation of the essential significance of the cross. Anselm combined the biblical concept of ransom "which he understood not symbolically but literally in the light of the doctrine of penance" (277) with the tendency of the Gospels to — after Easter — depict Jesus' passion as the result not only of God's plan (the divine δεῖ) but also of Jesus' objective toward which he systematically directed himself. This transposition by the evangelists of the divine plan, as it could be concluded from the event of Jesus' resurrection, back into Jesus' own consciousness is unacceptable. It is contrary to the historical facts; it puts the emphasis on Christ's work as representative of man before God instead of — in accordance with Paul — on the fact that God himself gave him up as an "expiatory sacrifice". Anselm's theory is closer to the understanding which Rabbinic Judaism had of the meritorious power of the suffering of the just.[3] Moreover, Anselm neglected the relation of Jesus' death to his proclamation. The latter did not immediately imply suffering and death, neither in the context of its *Traditionsgeschichte*, nor historically in Jesus' actual human path.

If we may anticipate our criticism of Pannenberg's position for a moment, we might extend Pannenberg's reasoning here and say that while the resurrection of Jesus certainly presupposed his prior death, the apocalyptic expectation of the resurrection and its significance did not offer a *Bedeutungshorizont* within which to attribute redeeming force or consequence to Jesus' death *per se*. Rather, in this context of tradition history God's coming, his ultimate direct self-revelation itself is

---

[2] So with F. Lakner, *Lexikon für Theologie und Kirche* (2d ed.; Freiburg: Verlag Herder, 1957—1967), vol. iii, 1021 f.

[3] Here P. is following E. Lohse, *Märtyrer und Gottesknecht*, pp. 104, 105 ff., 110.

redemption. It is the beginning of the universal resurrection and of the *recapitulatio rerum omnium*. The message already implies the forgiveness of sin.

His critique of Anselm's theory again drives home Pannenberg's chief interests: a theory of the salvific meaning of Christ's death must concur with the historical facts as far as discernable in Jesus' own historical path and with the conclusions which can and must be arrived at on account of Jesus' resurrection. Pannenberg's conclusion from the "inversion of standards", "he bore their punishment", allows him to see Jesus' death as expiatory penal suffering *which God himself* offered but not as a propitiation or satisfaction of God, wrought by the man (God-man) Jesus.

Ad (3): The theory of Christ's penal suffering (Strafleiden) of course goes back to the early church which interpreted Jesus' passion by recourse to Isaiah 53. Patristic theology, Pannenberg thinks, was right when, in its main line, it saw "the cross as an action of God in and through Jesus, not as an accomplishment of the man Jesus in relation to God. Thus the character of the cross as something that happened to Jesus is maintained." (278) However, on account of its predominant interest in the incarnation the patristic doctrine of reconciliation insufficiently stresses the motif of vicarious penal suffering in Jesus' death. It was *Luther* who adequately emphasized this aspect, according to Pannenberg. Jesus as representative of all men humbles himself under God's wrath against sin and thereby is righteous before God. Pannenberg explains,

> The judgment of God stands in contrast to the judgments of men. God gives his grace to the one who is unrighteous in his own eyes and thereby shows himself to be humble before God. In this sense Christ is righteousness and so also faith in him is righteousness in a way that is derived from him (*fides Christi*). In the cross of Christ this *judicium Dei* . . . is apparent to us. In the lecture on Romans of 1515 and 1516, Luther characterized Christ in the same sense as the pattern, the prototype, of all God's actions. Because God wanted to glorify Christ and install him as king, he permitted him on the contrary to die . . . God deals in this way with all the saints. Three sentences earlier Luther described the general rule of this divine action: The work of God must be hidden and is not recognized when it happens. The grace of God is hidden under its opposite. This is the root of Luther's *theologia crucis*. (43 f.)

In later writings Luther's emphasis is most expressly on Jesus' vicarious *Strafleiden*. Pannenberg praises Luther for this. "Luther was probably the first since Paul and his school to have seen with full clarity that Jesus' death in its genuine sense is to be understood as vicarious penal suffering." (279) His error, of course, is that he justified the concept of substitution not from the human course of the event and Jesus' resurrection but – in concert with the perspective of the entire patristic and medieval tradition – on the basis of the incarnation. "Luther did not clearly see that all statements about Jesus' cross are only possible in the light of his resurrection." (279) Still, Luther came close to understanding the cross in its historical perspective when de described Jesus' penal suffering as affliction of conscience and said,

> A deo se maledictum sentiat in conscientia. . . . We must think of Jesus as enveloped in our sins, in anathema and death. God the Father speaks as it were to Jesus: 'Tu sis omnium hominum persona, qui feceris omnium hominum peccata.' . . . Non debemus ergo fingere Christum innocentem et privatam personam (ut sophistae et fere omnes Patres, Hieronymus et alii fecerunt), quae pro se tantum sit sancta et iusta.[4]

Pannenberg comments,

> According to Luther, this is an abstract point of view. One must see Jesus in his relatedness to the rest of humanity whose guilt he took upon himself in such a way that he bore it as his own guilt and suffered for us the punishment of the cross . . . (278)

It might be surprising to note that Pannenberg favors these statements because he is certain on the whole that no cognition of Jesus' psychology is accessible and that Jesus probably endured his passion, without any *Verstehenshorizont*, as an unintelligible failure of his mission. But Pannenberg is probably intrigued by Luther's showing us Jesus as a passive victim rather than an active redeemer, as a real human rather than a divine-human high priest or the like. His chief objection to Luther therefore is that here, too, the incarnation is a theological presupposition which makes "the humanity of Jesus' life problematic from the very beginning" (279) and gives to Christ's penal suffering a mythological tone.

Pannenberg chides Melanchthon and Calvin for their return to the Latin theory and praises Storr's reintroduction of the *Strafleiden* theory. He

---
[4] For place of these citations of Luther see *JGaM*, 278.

rejects the Neo-Protestant doctrines of Schleiermacher, von Hofmann, and Ritschl who, following Abelard's main train of argument, to various degrees rejected the idea of Jesus' penal suffering as expression of God's wrath against sin and against Jesus.

Regarding Karl Barth, Pannenberg says, "Barth has once more developed the doctrine of atonement as interpretation of the incarnation, not of the historical life of Jesus", but goes on,

> Nevertheless, our result stands closer to Barth's statements about the comprehensive character of Jesus Christ's vicarious suffering, which takes up and overcomes our death, than to the satisfaction theory or to the doctrine of Jesus "vocational suffering." (280)

2. The Significance of Jesus' Freedom and Sinlessness

Pannenberg's deliberations concerning Jesus' freedom and sinlessness enter into our discussion. They touch upon the question of a possible meritorious character of Jesus' passion and death.

Sub specie resurrectionis the pre-Easter Jesus is the Son of the eternal Father only in his complete dedication to the unconditionality of his historical mission. In face of the earthly failure of his mission, Jesus' dedication became self-sacrifice. "The absolute, real unity of Jesus' will with the Father's, as was confirmed in God's raising him up from the dead, is the medium of his essential unity with God and the basis of all assertions about Jesus' divine Sonship." (349) We noted that, unlike Ritschl, Pannenberg does not base Jesus' sonship on his complete vocational loyalty *as such* but on the empirically accessible community of Jesus with the Father and his historically verifiable dedication to his mission *which*, however, *are unambiguously knowable only through their confirmation*. We must conclude: Jesus' sonship rests on Ritschl's concept of Jesus' *Berufstreue* plus its confirmation at the resurrection; more precisely, the resurrection both noetically and ontologically established Jesus' identity. Since this stance forbids statements on Jesus' psychology which go beyond the *bruta facta* of his communion with the Father and his dedication to his mission, one would expect that any statement on Jesus' freedom were impossible. As a *psychological* statement it certainly is. However, even though Jesus' identity is knowable only on account of its confirmation, Pannenberg, in order to secure the genuine humanity of Jesus, must define Jesus' freedom in such a fashion as not to impinge on his humanity. In agreement with his definition of Jesus' dedication to God as absolute and unconditional (Jesus claimed nothing for himself) he now defines Jesus' freedom not as *liberum arbitrium* in the sense of freedom of choice of the man Jesus before God, a freedom of decision among several possibilities. Such a position would destroy Pannenberg's construction of Jesus' Sonship as unity of will between Jesus and the Father. We remember,

> The openness to God which belongs to the structure of human existence as such (even when it is in fact lived in contradiction to God) and that finds its fulfillment only when human existence is personally integrated in dependence upon God, is fulfilled in Jesus by the divine confirmation of his eschatological message (including its claim to authority) through his resurrection from the dead. (348)

> Hence, Jesus' freedom consisted in doing the will of the Father and pursuing his mission. . . . Jesus claimed for himself no independence of any kind from God because his freedom consisted not in independence from God but in unity with him. (349)

With his position Pannenberg opposes any doctrine of redemption which bases redemption on a meritorious deed of Jesus. For to ascribe a meritum to Jesus in the traditional sense is to presuppose freedom of choice in Jesus in relation to God's will. This freedom is the root of the meritorious character of Jesus' suffering in Roman Catholic doctrine. It is a *conditio sine quo non* in Anselm's argument. Roman Catholic theology tried to solve the conflict between Jesus' unity of will with the Father and the traditional concept of merit that presupposes an independent will of Jesus by the assumption of a *visio beatifica* which Jesus as man on earth possessed. Pannenberg rejects such assumption together with all other traditional or modern attempts at a solution as impossible.[5] For Pannenberg such a *visio beatifica* would not only exclude a *liberum arbitrium* but also Jesus' concrete historical existence in dedication. Why?

> When a mission has seized a man so unconditionally, he no longer has any choice with respect to that mission. He reserves no inner independence for himself over against his mission. Precisely this constitutes his freedom. Just in this way Jesus is one with God

---
[5] For his critique of Karl Rahner's proposition see pp. 351f. of *JGaM*.

through his dedication to his mission, through his dedication to the Father. *The thesis of a meritorious freedom of choice for Jesus' human will under these presuppositions would make his unity with God a work of his human will instead of letting that unity be something that happened to him, which he experienced as having come from God.* (351, italics by the author).

Jesus' dedication nevertheless constitutes a merit in another sense. For "the saving consequences of the mission and fate of Jesus for all humanity could be understood as merit in the sense of the harvest or result of a specific acitivity or behavior, without any relation to ultimate authorship in the sense of indifferent freedom." (351, n. 53)

But is such freedom in the sense of arbitrariness (*indifferentia ad opposita*) not part of being human? And does Pannenberg's insistence not again imperil the real humanity of Jesus? Pannenberg is aware of this. He affirms,

> It is possible to reject the assumption of a capacity of decision in Jesus' will that is in any sense indifferent to God only if we also can reject this assumption as a misunderstanding of human behavior in general. Otherwise, Jesus, without such decisional indifference, would not really be man. (352)

Pannenberg admits two elements of truth in the traditional indeterminist concept of freedom of choice. (1) Man has in fact to decide in every moment among a plurality of possibilities because he can transcend every situation by two means, (a) the posture in which he takes his distance from the impressions which pour in upon him, and (b) the questions he asks, reaching out beyond what is given in the particular moment. However, *the will does not stand indifferently above the possibilities of choice in the moment of decision* but merely prior to that, viz., at the time the possibilities are considered more exactly. "This (latter) aspect of the psychic process leading to decision is absolutized by the indeterminist theory." (352)

> Through the consideration of the possibilities of choice, however, the undecidedness of the will is to be overcome. In the process of consideration it is to be established which of the available possibilities is most appropriate to the destiny of the one who wills and which for this reason should be chosen. (352)

(2) Man's destiny itself is open to a decision since it is no fixed norm. Man is always open to a future life fulfillment that surpasses his present self-understanding.

> This openness however does not mean indifference toward the possibilities of the present situation, but such openness exists only in the hidden tendency toward something that is able to fulfill the destiny of man more deeply and richly than any present experience. (352)

The inner voice toward this tendency is identified as God's own calling which one cannot ultimately turn away from.

> The specific human capacity to keep one's distance from impressions and to transcend them, a capacity which governs man's behavior toward all surrounding finite reality, *has no function in the situation of man before God*, although in some circumstances it may well function over against certain conceptions of God. *From God's always still uncomprehended reality, from beyond all conceptions of God, the reply goes forth to that open questioning of human freedom about its destiny above and beyond every environmental situation and every self-made encasement of mind. Therefore, no one can leave God behind in the sense that one can deny other, finite possibilities of choice.* (352f., italics mine)

We cannot at length discuss Pannenberg's elaborations of this theme within this context. The decisive yield of Pannenberg's discussion of Jesus' freedom is this:

> *Thus we can also say about Jesus' mission that the clarity with which Jesus' mission claimed him must have excluded any alternative for him.* The clarity of Jesus' mission can be measured by the way in which the single idea of God's eschatological imminence permeated his message and his whole activity. (353, italics mine)

Why is this important for Pannenberg's doctrine of reconciliation? Jesus' "work" can have salvific significance only if Jesus is the Son of God. Jesus can be the Son of God only if his divinity (his Sonship) can be established in complete compatibility with his genuine humanity and the historical path of Jesus' life. *This is the case only if Jesus' dedication to God, which is the expression of his unity with God and means complete dependence on God, can be shown to be man's universal Bestimmung and if it does not contradict but fulfills man's freedom.* With this last link in the chain of the argument we had to do in this section. The old traditional understanding of freedom as *indifferentia ad opposita* and consequently *etiam ad deum* had to be refuted. Else there would have been a need to explain Jesus' dedication to God by some supernatural device which would waive his humanity and render the Christological concept mythological.[6] This position determines his soteriology. Jesus' unity with God is something that happened to him (*ein Widerfahrnis*), it came from God. The gate is open for a redemption *sola gratia* which is entirely God's own work.

As regards Jesus' sinlessness, Pannenberg faces and solves the same task as concerning Jesus' freedom, *viz.*, to define it in such a fashion as not to contradict Jesus' genuine humanity from which his entire theology, in its adherence to strict exegetical and historical scholarship and in its systematic methodology, starts. First of all, to ascribe sinlessness to Jesus is indispensable since it is only the negative expression for the reality of Jesus' dedication to God which positively is his unity with God, his identity as Son, and his freedom (openness) for God.

> If sin is essentially life in contradiction to God, in self-centered closing of our ego against God, then Jesus' unity with God is his personal community with the Father and in his identity with the person of the Son of God means immediately his separation from all sin. (355)

An exact theological comprehension of Jesus' sinlessness is consequently dependent upon the understanding of Jesus' unity with God.

For Paul Jesus' sinlessness is the presupposition for the *pro nobis* of his suffering, i.e., the vicarious bearing of our guilt and the imputation of Jesus' sinlessness to sinful man. Pannenberg's own construction – the "inversion of standards", caused by the resurrection, which is the basis for Pannenberg's judgment that Jesus died a substitutionary penal death – also requires this theologoumenon. Pannenberg points to the unanimous witness of both the New Testament authors and the christological confessions of the patristic church to Jesus' sinlessness and *asks how it was understood more exactly*. The chief points of Pannenberg's position in this quest are as follows:

---

[6] For Pannenberg's acute discussion of Jesus' temptations see pp. 353f., *JGaM*.

The Significance of Jesus' Freedom and Sinlessness 161

(1) Jesus' sinlessness cannot be left unexplained by simply stating: He in fact did not sin. The question is, why not? Did he share the actual human nature or not? If he did not his sinlessness is irrelevant. If he did, how did he overcome sin? Patristic and medieval theology soon turned to these questions with great efforts.

(2) Jesus' sinlessness cannot be adequately explained by the miraculous assumption of a sinless human nature, undamaged, not spoiled by sin coming from Adam, at the time of Jesus' birth.

(a) This concept (Basil, Ambrose, Augustine), leading to the Scholastic formula *non posse peccare*, is incompatible both with the Biblical view that sin was overcome in the flesh and the genuine humanity of Christ.

> If sin is . . . associated . . . with the structure of present human existence, one cannot conceive of a natural sinlessness of Jesus. It is inconceivable that Jesus was truly man, but that in his corporeality and behavior he was not stamped by the universal structure of centeredness of animal life that is the basis of the self-centeredness of human experience and behavior, but which becomes sin only in man. The conception that at the incarnation God did not assume human nature in its corrupt sinful state but only joined himself with a humanity absolutely purified from all sin contradicts not only the anthropological radicality of sin, but also the testimony of the New Testament . . . *The victory over sin had not been attained before Jesus' birth, but only in the entire accomplishment of the course of his existence.* Therefore, Karl Barth is right in emphasizing that Jesus "is identical with our nature under the conditions of the fall" (*CD*, I/2, pp. 167ff.). "Precisely Jesus' sinlessness was in no way a condition of his human being but the *deed* of his life that took this course from its beginning" (*CD*, IV/2, p. 102; cf. IV/1, pp. 284f.) With this interpretation Barth follows a doctrinal line that had its nineteenth century predecessors in Irving, Collenbusch, Bezzel, Menken, Böhl, and above all Hofmann. (362, italics 5th line from bottom by author)

(b) The vehicle of this concept, the doctrine of the virgin birth and, its corrollary, of the immaculate conception of Mary, is unacceptable for three reasons.

This reference to the virgin birth does not correspond to the New Testament testimony of Jesus' sinlessness, nor was it intended by the much more tenuously asserted legend of the virgin birth itself. Furthermore, such an assumption can justify Jesus' exceptional position with respect to the universal human corruption by sin only under the additional, particularly Augustinian, presupposition that original sin is transmitted through the libidinous character of human procreation. If we cannot concede to this circumstance such a deep-seated causality for the entire organic structure of human existence, especially for the centrality and egocentricity of all expressions of human life, then the assumption of the virgin birth can not accomplish what it was supposed to as an explanation of Jesus' sinlessness. *Jesus' breaking through the self-centeredness of human existence cannot be derived from a miraculous birth if the man who thus emerges is to be a man like all others.* (361f., italics mine)

(3) The other Scholastic view which interprets Jesus' *impeccabilitas* by the formula *posse non peccare* attribute this inability to sin neither to his human nature as such, nor derives it directly from the *unio hypostatica* and the dominion of the divinity over the human nature. Rather, it interprets it as a *gracious* sinlessness that leaves room for Jesus' temptability and capacity for *merita*. Pannenberg deems this to be an apparent solution only because it works with an abstract concept of human nature. But he is partly sympathetic,

> ... in view of the relation between Jesus' unity with God and his sinlessness, we can understand the concern for a sinlessness in Jesus that existed from the beginning and was not acquired at some later point. (359)

(4) Neither can Jesus' sinlessness be adequately explained by the Neo-Protestant concept of the actual ethical purity of Jesus who fully shared our corrupted nature but gained victory over it through his behavior. More precisely, the Neo-Protestant *methodology* is unacceptable for Pannenberg, we must observe. Origen was the first to explain Jesus' sinlessness as his achievement.

> The soul of Jesus, he said, is so unwaveringly dependent on God in immeasurable love that even the possibility of turning away and of sin no longer exists; through the mood which grew out of long habit, the resolution of will became nature. It is interesting that here the incapacity for sin appears as the result of Jesus' unconditional

dedication to God, even though Origen was concerned with the dedication of Jesus' preexistent soul to God, so that the sinlessness of the incarnate is no longer a problem in spite of participation in sinful flesh. (356)

For Origen, of course, the incarnation was axiomatic. For Neo-Protestantism which stars from the man Jesus it was different. The assumption of a strict or *a priori* inability to sin was relinquishes. Jesus' sinlessness was postulated on the empirical historical ground of his exemplary moral behavior that knew no exception. And "precisely the actual sinlessness of Jesus in the sense of his ethical purity, asserted merely as an experiential fact, won the significance of a basis for the doctrine of Jesus' divinity." (360) This stance, of course with modification, is found in the teaching of J. Müller, C. Ullmann, Ritschl, W. Herrmann.

As we saw, Pannenberg starts from the man Jesus also. For him, too, Jesus' sinlessness is of the essence of Jesus' identity as the Son. And for him, also, in establishing this identity, the earthly path of Jesus, his communion with the Father and his dedication to his mission as empirical historical facts play an indispensable verifying role — to be sure, it is less Jesus' individual morality, as for Ullmann and Herrmann, than his *Berufstreue*, as for Ritschl. However, the incisive difference is methodological. The historical data in turn need a verification and confirmation which establishes them beyond any ambiguity. It is, for Pannenberg, the resurrection only which establishes them both noetically and ontologically.

For Jesus' sinlessness derived from the New Testament data about his exemplary moral behavior "must be considered an extremely insecure foundation for a Christology." (361)

> Where do we get so much information about Jesus' unbroken and unique ethical grandeur? The New Testament statements that relate to Jesus' sinlessness, none of which is an authentic saying of Jesus, can in themselves surely not have so much greater authority than other New Testament statements, for example, about the miracles performed by Jesus or having happened to him. *Why the New Testament statements about Jesus' sinlessness are supposed to be particularly believable must be established on other grounds*, especially since the Jews who were his contemporaries seem to have had a quite different opinion about Jesus' sinlessness. If one finds inventing an ideal ethical image less possible than did Herrmann, it

becomes very difficult to attain the conviction of the thoroughgoing moral grandeur of Jesus' personal life through conclusions drawn from the traditions about his individual style of life. (360f., italics mine)

He concludes,

> That Jesus overcame sin under the conditions of existence of the general bondage to sin, that he lived in openness to God, *can only be asserted in the light of the resurrection*. It cannot be derived from the dedication to God that Jesus' pre-Easter existence express when taken by itself. *Jesus' earthly conduct appeared thoroughly ambiguous*. He could appear as the man who claimed for himself divine authority. In the light of the egocentricity of the condition of human existence, the claim implied in Jesus' message necessarily made the impression of unlimited pride, of blasphemy. That just this claim to authority was the expression of Jesus' total dedication to God *became visible and became reality* only through Jesus' resurrection, through the divine confirmation of Jesus inherent in it. (362f., italics mine)

God's judgment over Jesus, the judgment of his sinlessness, frees us from the impossible task of trying to penetrate into the inner life of the historical Jesus in order to establish there his sinlessness.

Pannenberg relates this judgment to the *extra nos* of the Reformation. Jesus' justification, so to speak, God's decision about his sinlessness, came from beyond and established his righteousness. But while Jesus is righteous *de facto*, our human justification, Pannenberg says, means that we only in Christ, to the extent of our community with Jesus, are justified. Traditionally speaking, our righteousness is imputed. But, one perhaps wonders, *does not Pannenberg proceed here like the kerygma-theologians after all*? When relating God's judgment over Jesus to the *extra nos*, does he not apply the *pro me* that has its proper place in the doctrine of justification to the realm of cognition, saying, We do not know anything about Jesus' sinlessness; we believe it on account of the kerygma? Particularly Pannenberg's sentence

> If we recognize in this light God's judgment upon Jesus, the judgment of his sinlessness, we need no longer attempt the

impossible task of penetrating into the inner life of the historical
Jesus in order to establish there his sinlessness (363)

and his statement that Jesus' earthly conduct appears thoroughly ambiguous seem to suggest that our faith needs no empirical, historical verification. Now this would contradict his epistemology, so far employed. But the impression is in fact mistaken. For (1) it is not the kerygma but the resurrection which confirms Jesus' claim and unity with the Father, thus his identity as the Son and his concomitant sinlessness. Note that the resurrection is conceived of as an historical fact. Remember (2) that, even though the resurrection establishes Jesus' identity not only noetically but also ontologically, the resurrection still does not "create" data that have no grounding in the actual course of Jesus' life. Note the significance of Jesus' dedication to his mission, as seen in history, for the construction of Jesus' identity. (3) The ambiguity of which Pannenberg speaks refers not to the historical *data* of Jesus' absolute claim to God's authority, his communion with God and his dedication to his mission – these are historically verifiable – but *to the evaluation of this behavior*. Is it in truth dedication *to the living God* and not to a phantom? Is it in truth *dedication* and not self-possessedness, unlimited pride, fanaticism, blasphemy? *This* is what the resurrection only decides. The resurrection clarifies the *data* but does not create them.[7] Accordingly, Pannenberg does not mean the *extra se* of Jesus'

---

[7] The distinctions in this paragraph once again show how difficult it is to decide to what extent P. really is successful in claiming an ontological efficaciousness for the resurrection beside its noetical effect. The balance between the two seems not even; the conceptuality, on the whole, is more noetical than ontological, no doubt (cf. confirmation, confirm, know, reveal, make known, remove ambiguity et al., used to describe what the resurrection does.)

Once Pannenberg was asked the following question, "I wonder if you would clarify for me why you refuse to speak of God becoming in the way John Cobb would speak of it. In *Theology and the Kingdom of God* you say that God is the power of the future. When an individual is caught up somehow in the response of faith, that future is realized. Then you specifically said, "This is not however to be understood as God becoming." At that point I no longer understood which I'm sure is because I have not read other writings by you. I wonder if you could clarify the distinctions for us." ("A Theological Conversation with Wolfhart Pannenberg", *Dialog*, vol. xi, Autumn 1972, p. 294) P. replied in detail, defending the infinity of God and his concept of eternity which is contrary to timelessness. Then he says, "Our experience of divine reality does not leave justification in an epistemological (as Bultmann) but in the soteriological sense (as Luther). And in this sense he is perfectly justified.

(5) Pannenberg concludes, with Barth and his 19th century predecessors, that

> Jesus' sinlessness is not an incapability for evil that belonged naturally to his humanity but results only from his entire process of life. Only through the entire course of Jesus' existence culminating in his resurrection is sin overcome in sinful flesh. (363)

The *culmination* of this course in Jesus' *resurrection* means that here this victory is acclaimed by God and, by God's acclamation, confirmed noetically and ontologically. It has been true all along, from the beginning. Still it had to be wrought by the man Jesus along his earthly path in that he let himself be determined by man's ultimate *Bestimmung* from God.

Now Pannenberg goes on with a weighty statement about the place of the cross within this course of victory over sin.

> In this process the crucifixion of Jesus is the decisive step – in the light of his resurrection. For through the cross of Christ sinful flesh was condemned and demolished in him who was nonetheless the Son of God, as his resurrection was to prove. Therefore, he was not himself destroyed in this judgment, but emerged the victor. Thus out of the judgment on sin, the new man was raised up in him – and only in him since all other men are destroyed together with their sin. (363)

These sentences are intelligible only, it seems, if we pay heed to Pannenberg's understanding of sin, of Jesus' dedication, and his theory of why

---

unaffected the question of the reality of God, because the very reality of God is still controversial. Only in the end, if the end should happen according to Christian expectations, will it be decided whether God is a reality. Then the reality of God will be affirmed for whatever has been. In some way, *according to our experience*, the reality of God is still in process *for every finite point of view. This does not mean that it is in the same way a process on its own terms.*" (*Ibid.*, italics mine) If this is true of God may we not assume that it is equally true of God's oneness with Jesus? If so, the resurrection (like the eschaton whose prolepsis it is) is noetically, not ontologically confirmative. *Id est*, it establishes the identity ontologically only in the sense that, for every finite point of view, only through the resurrection Jesus' identity is a decided fact.

Jesus' death was vicarious. The universal structure of centeredness of animal life is the basis of the self-centeredness of human experience and behavior, his non-openness or his protective, security-craving attitude within his openness in relation to the world (the future, God). "For whoever would save his life will lose it" (Mark 8:45a) – this saying addresses itself to this universal structure which becomes sin only in man because man can hear the call which calls him away from "God's always still uncomprehended reality, from beyond all conceptions of God ... to that open questioning of human freedom about its destiny above and beyond every environmental situation and every self-made encasement of mind." (352 f.)

> ... a man falls into sin and thereby into contradiction against God through his relation to things and men, through his refusal to transcend and *thereby* to affirm his particular finite situation or, more precisely, through insisting upon a supposed self-interest (or even on a supposed interest in others) that, focused on egocentricity, denies the openness to God of just this self. (353, italics by the author)

Jesus overcame sin in this sense in his absolute dedication to his mission which became self-sacrifice when he clung to his message even after his fate seemed to pronounce the verdict of failure and Godforsakenness over his mission and message. The saying, "whoever loses his life for my sake will find it" (Matthew 10:39), expresses this self-sacrifice of Jesus, and this word has universal ontological relevance (396) for all life because only in unconditional openness to the future (God) true being is attained to. Hence Jesus' death is his victory (which we know through the resurrection). However, that this death comes to mean *condemnation* and *demolition* of sinful flesh in Jesus is a conclusion which presupposes the identification of Jesus' death with God's judgment on sin. Yet this presupposition, as we are aware, requires Pannenberg's postulate of the transference of guilt of the real blasphemers upon Jesus who was innocent. "He bore their punishment." The contention that "thus out of the judgment on sin the new man was raised up in him" seems to be an unconvincing statement since Jesus *is* the new man already in his dedication and death, i.e., in his openness to God. What was raised in Jesus' resurrection is first of all the *revelation* that Jesus' claim and proclamation are truly from God and thus truthful and, consequently, that there is forgiveness and resurrection for all who live in communion with Jesus. "All other men are destroyed together with their sin", i.e., all will die. But on account of Jesus' confirmed message there is assured hope for fulfillment beyond death.

Pannenberg's concept of the retroactive ontic power of Jesus' resurrection again enables him to simultaneously affirm that Jesus' sinlessness was a victory over sin that had not been attained before Jesus' birth but resulted only from the entire accomplishment of his life (Jesus *vere homo*!) *and* that he was sinless from the beginning, "just as he was also the Son of God in the whole of his life and not only after a particular point in time." (Jesus vere Deus!) "However, this was decided only by Jesus' resurrection, just as in general only the future event decides the meaning of earthly events." (363f.) The strain on logic which the simultaneous validity of the two statements no doubt implies is alleviated when we remember Pannenberg's futuristic ontology in the light of which traditional modes of thought appear inadequate. His doctrine of the cross is dependent on his christology, his christology on his ontology, his ontology on his anthropology plus the exceptional position and validity Pannenberg claims for the apocalyptic concept of God's self-revelation in universal history, i.e., at its end.[8]

3. *The Evaluation of the Officium Sacerdotale Christi-Doctrine*

Does Pannenberg's discussion of the doctrine of the *munus triplex Christi* of Protestant tradition throw further light on his view of Jesus' death? Pannenberg headlines his chapter on the office (sic!) of Christ with the program-statement, "The office of Christ was to call men into the Kingdom of God, which had appeared with him." (212) Now how is this one office which Pannenberg describes functionally related to the *tria munera* of tradition? Following his methodology, Pannenberg searches for *data* in the historical course of Jesus' life and destiny which may serve to characterize his office.

Pannenberg first concludes that the justification of the threefold character of Jesus' office from the Christ title is untenable. He goes on,

---

[8] Pannenberg admits the concept of paradox to characterize this view of the incarnation and the concept of the prolepsis of the eschaton which underlies his view of the incarnation. This "way of speaking (paradox) can be justified, and only then is it meaningful." (157) Cf. also *supra* pp. 59f.

Even if it cannot be derived from the "Christ" title that the royal, the priestly, and the prophetic honors properly belong to Jesus, it still remains to be determined *whether the functions in fact apprehended by or developed upon Jesus do demonstrate him to be king, prophet, and priest. From this point of view as well, the concept of the three offices in the dogmatics of Protestant orthodoxy is subject to considerable objection.* (215, italics mine)

Without going into the evidence Pannenberg adduces for his judgment, we shall briefly state his results: Jesus did not exercise the office of a prophet in the ancient Israelite sense although he perhaps conceived of his life and destiny in the light of what was generally the fate of "the prophets" (Mark 6:4; Matt. 23:37; Luke 13:32f.). Jesus knew himself to stand in the context of contemporary prophetic traditions; these were apocalyptically influenced. Jesus was more an apocalyptic than a prophet, relatively speaking.

But he also was not an apocalyptic, although the views of the apocalyptic tradition are everywhere the presupposition of what he said and did. Jesus certainly thought in apocalyptic categories. (217)

What distinguished Jesus from the prophets and apocalyptics?

Jesus not only issued a call to repentance, but with full authority he granted to the men he met the salvation expected in the future. He was certain that in his activity the future salvation of God's kingdom had broken into the present time. (217)

In spite of these limitations, "Jesus' actual activity stands far closer to the prophetic tradition than to either of the other two 'offices'." (217)

As regards the *munus regium*, Jesus in his earthly ministry neither sought nor practised it. But "the title of King (Christ) . . . designates the position that is due to Jesus because of his resurrection, first of all with regard to the eschatological future, but then also as a present reality in heaven." (218) Contrary to the orthodox doctrine which tried to ascribe the three offices to Christ in both *status*, Jesus' "prophetic office" in reality does not extend beyond his death and his royal office does not begin on earth.

Finally – and most important for our investigation – a priestly work or office cannot be legitimately ascribed to Jesus in his pre-Easter situation.

The two roots in the New Testament of this doctrine are the explicit designation of Jesus as High Priest (Hebrews) and the conception of his death as atonement for our sins. However,

> the basis in the history of traditions for the interpretation of Jesus' death as atonement is much broader. The relation of the atonement idea to the concept of sacrifice is not found in the oldest level of the early Christian understanding of the atoning significance of Jesus' death, to be sure. It reaches back, nevertheless, into Hellenistic-Jewish-Christianity and is already attested by Paul (Rom. 3:25). The sacrificial idea easily carries with it the idea of a priesthood. (219 f.)

Again, for Pannenberg it is decisive that Jesus' death was not his work but his destiny and that the atonement was wrought by God, not by Jesus. Pannenberg here follows E. Lohse who says about the earliest Palestinian concept of Jesus' atonement,

> Christ's atoning death did not first have to create the gracious God, as was true with the pious of late Judaism who went to death in order to pay off the debts of the people and turn away the wrath of God. Rather, Christ's atoning death presupposes the gracious God who had offered up the Christ in order that he would carry the punishment of sin for us.[9]

Pannenberg is in full agreement with this exegetical judgment. One could summarize Pannenberg's efforts saying he wants to give systematic grounding to the above biblical-exegetical finding.

When Paul and the Synoptics make Jesus the subject of the offering unto death, they view Jesus' death in the light of his exaltation or the sending of the Son into the world. Pannenberg agrees that *through his fate* (!) Jesus took the place which in Israel and other religions was occupied by the priest(s) and the ritual of sacrifice. While *intercessio* is part of Jesus' *munus sacerdotale* in the orthodox system, Pannenberg — other than in the case of Jesus' passion — considers intercession a *work* of Jesus, but rather a prophetic than a priestly one.

Pannenberg points out that his disagreement with the older Protestant dogmatics on the *tria-munera-doctrine* stems from the fact that for them the God-man Christ was the bearer of the offices and "the historical reality of

---

[9] Eduard Lohse, *op. cit.*, p. 146

Jesus was bypassed." (223) The incarnation was a given; it belonged to the contemporary intellectual world of Luther's time, but "in our time it must be regarded as a mythological concept." (222) "The conscious life of such a half-god would be inconceivable for us." (223) Rather,

> *Jesus was the bearer of an office from God first as simply man; this statement is a presupposition for the discussion of his divinity.* Precisely the confirmation of Jesus in his earthly mission through his resurrection was the basis for the confession of his divinity. (223, italics mine)

In his discussion, *Pannenberg's radically historical understanding of the human character of Jesus' pre-Easter life and destiny turns out to be the ultimate motive for his insistence on the constitutively ontological, not only noetical, function and decisiveness of the resurrection.* This comes out in the following statement,

> When Jesus' pre-Easter life is conceived as having been already divine-human in a direct sense, our conception of Jesus falls back into the mythological realm. Jesus' resurrection is not only constitutive for our perception of his divinity, but it is ontologically constitutive for that divinity. Apart from the resurrection from the dead, Jesus would not be God, even though from the perspective of the resurrection, he is retrospectively one with God in his whole pre-Easter life. Here, then, is the final objection to the traditional dogmaticians' coordination of the history of Jesus with his divine human person. Whenever the tradition about Jesus is interpreted as the action of a divine-human-person without considering the indirectness of the language about God and thus about Jesus' divinity, one overlooks the incisive significance that the crucifixion and then the resurrection have for the whole of Jesus' life. The concept of the divine-human office and its unbroken extension over cross and resurrection smooths over the cleft that the cross designates in Jesus' fate. This is especially clear with respect to the royal office. If Jesus was already the Messiah, independently of the progression of his history, if his unity with God had the character of an accomplished fact, then his crucifixion can hardly be understood as anything but a mere episode or a suffering temporarily assumed by Jesus, but by no means as the catastrophe that it must

have signified for Jesus and for his disciples. With this kind of viewpoint, dogmatic Christology bypasses the real depth of meaning of Jesus' crucifixion and resurrection. (224)

In Pannenberg's view, then, to ascribe a noetical function only to the resurrection would mean to deny the genuine humanity of Jesus (thus the cleft, the depth of meaning of the crucifixion and resurrection). But precisely his humanity is the presupposition of the discussion of Jesus' divinity; it alone is non-mythological and understandable offhand. It would also take away the utter seriousness from Jesus' despair and death and hence belittle the sacrifice and "value" of the cross. It would also belittle the weight of the resurrection which — in Pannenberg's view — is a *creatio ex nihilo, redemptio ex infernis*, and an inbreaking of the eschaton. We can infer from this: (1) *Pannenberg's ontology of the future ultimately serves no other purpose than to ascertain the genuine humanity of Jesus and, precisely thereby, paradoxically, to salvage his divinity for a time in which man thinks radically non-mythologically.* Thus he renders the Christian doctrine of the person and work of Christ meaningful and intelligible to our age. By implication it also serves to answer the *problem of theodicy* when it points to the proleptic nature of the Christ event and to the promise-function of this event for the ultimate fulfillment at the end of history.

(2) If we understand Pannenberg accurately in what we just said it becomes transparent that to the question of who suffers on the cross Pannenberg's answer is: the man Jesus; not God. *In this view the genuine humanity of Jesus is the presupposition of the fact that the cross has weight, "value", and credibility, all statements to the contrary notwithstanding.* Thus Pannenberg avoids the problem of the older dogmatics as to how one can take Jesus' passion and death seriously under the assumption of his God-manhood.[10]

4. Intermediate Result

When we try to formulate the intermediate result of our investigation of Pannenberg's doctrine of reconciliation it might be advisable to articulate the particularity and idiosyncrasy of his understanding by asking the

---

[10] For the relative merits of the threefold office-topos, understood topologically and symbolically as expression of the relationship between Jesus and ancient Israel, cf. *JGaM*, pp. 224f.

question, *Exactly what kind of statement is the judgment that Jesus died a substitutionary (pro nobis) and penal (expiatory) death?*

After the foregoing discussion we now can be brief. The judgment in question differs from Pannenberg's statements about the salvific significance of God's self-revelation, Jesus' proclamation, his dedication to his mission, and his resurrection. For these there is the historical evidence, in the narrower sense, of the Old Testament and apocalyptic *Traditionsgeschichte* in whose context Jesus ministered and suffered his self-sacrifice, and the historical evidence, in the wider sense, of his resurrection as the confirmation of the former. "Confirmation" here has the peculiarly Pannenbergian ring of both "revelation" or "disclosure" and retroactive ontological establishment. We shall not criticize this construction principally. Suffice it to enumerate its sensitive points, *viz.*, the assumptions: (a) Jesus' resurrection can be verified with a historian's tools, at least indirectly; (b) Jesus' resurrection has the significance of the anticipation of the eschatological end-time and the ultimate self-revelation of God *even though only one man was resurrected*; (c) Future can be thought of as *Seinsbeschaffenheit* (mode of being) so that a later event can retroactively enforce and constitute a former being and essence of something (-one); (d) The essence of someone can simultaneously be achieved in history and at a later time be determinded to have prevailed from the beginning so that both are true: A. The man Jesus becomes the Son in the process of his communion with the Father. B. Jesus was the Son of God from the beginning. A. The one dying on the cross is the man Jesus who sacrificed himself. B. The one dying on the cross is the Son of God on whom the Father laid passion and death.

(e) The resurrection of Jesus, together with his ministry, constitutes, proleptically, God's direct self-revelation, total and unsurpassable, *even though only the future (the eschaton) will reveal what a thing is or was.* Note that the resurrection itself requires its confirmation at the end of history.

Now granting these presuppositions and bypassing their sensitiveness, Pannenberg's judgments are sound and coherent. And the historical evidence is verified by anthropology in a convincing way. But neither seems to be the case with respect to Pannenberg's judgment about Jesus' death.

This judgment does not measure up to the standards of Pannenberg's own epistemology. His judgment that, on account of the resurrection, Jesus' judges were the *real* blasphemers, was not historically verified but postulated as a consequence of the idea that Jesus' resurrection "inverted the standards." While Pannenberg, on the basis of his concept of sin which he verified by anthropology, could establish the guilt not only of Jesus' judges but also of all of Israel and humanity at large, he did not, it seems, successfully show that Jesus' judges were the real blasphemers in a historically credible fashion. Historically, they acted in accordance with the law of God. He needs this assumption, though, in order to have a basis for the vicariousness of Jesus' passion. Since they were the real blasphemers and the allegedly blasphemous Jesus was really innocent, he bore their punishment. This inference of Pannenberg's not only presupposes that the guilt of blasphemy on the side of Jesus' judges has been rendered historically credible. It also presupposes that guilt is followed by punishment, that death means punishment, that guilt and punishment are transferable, and that love and forgiveness for the sinner are connected with an expiation of guilt through punishment. With the exception of the punishment-character of death which Pannenberg could establish anthropologically, these presuppositions, however, are assumptions which do not follow from either Pannenberg's methodology or doctrinal substance, so far elaborated. It will be shown that the anthropological evidence Pannenberg adduces to verify the idea of Jesus' vicarious penal suffering is insufficient. One may venture the guess that here Pannenberg let himself be dominated by the biblical kerygma and traditional doctrine and hence did not thoroughly subject his theologizing to his own rigid epistemological and hermeneutical principles. Summarily, the judgment under consideration, contrary to most of his other interpretations, is less inferential than postulatory in character and lacks both the historical cogency and the verification from our contemporary *Wirklichkeitsverständnis* to which our author, on the whole, is devoted with candor and adamant.

Arrested in his postulation that "he bore their punishment", Pannenberg views Jesus' death predominantly as God's judgment – the judgment, apparently, that in fact follows the sin of humanity, or has to follow sin, and that wipes out the *irreversibility* and *permanence* of death as eternal damnation of those who deserved it. Now Pannenberg certainly does *not* say: Jesus caused God to lay his punishment on him, or God's love begins only after the guilt of humanity was atoned for. On the contrary, with Paul Pannenberg claims God to be the originator and inaugurator of this vicarious penal suffering of Christ. *He* lays the debitum on Jesus; *he* puts the judgment on him. His love is there first, and out of this love he creates and comes in the prolepsis of his self-revelation so that the world can know him and can know the coming Kingdom which implies forgiveness of sin. God's grace, in a word, is God's motive in his outreach to man as creator and redeemer and consummator. And it is grace alone. Jesus proclaims unconditional forgiveness when he announces the coming Kingdom to all who open up to its coming, i.e., to God. However, God's grace somehow implies the need of penal suffering for Pannenberg. And the weight of this tenet is not alleviated by the fact that the penalty is transferable to Jesus, that Jesus vicariously takes care of it and that, following from Jesus' identity, God initiates the atonement and suffers in and through Jesus. The cross appears predominantly as judgment (i. e., *sub specie resurrectionis*), not grace, because the cross is interpreted as punishment in the first place and because the need of expiation in connection with forgiveness of sin is somewhat implied.

The modern theologoumenen according to which God the Father suffers on account of man's sin and the cross represents, symbolically or literally, God's own suffering[11], plays a minor role in Pannenberg's exposition. To be sure, for Pannenberg, too, it is the Son who dies and in that much it is God who suffers. But this is an insignificant side-line in Pannenberg's construction, no doubt. As we noted above, Pannenberg's interest, with regard to the cross, in the genuine humanity of Jesus and his self-sacrifice as climax of his dedication preponderates. This is the modern, the easily accessible part of his doctrine of the cross. Now when interpreting Jesus' death as vicarious penal suffering, the *divinity* of Jesus is paramount. Without it, death were not effectively met and defeated. However, here the divinity of the *Son* is focused upon, not the passion of the *Father*.

Finally, how does Pannenberg's interpretation of Jesus' death compare with Jesus' proclamation? And how does the salvific significance of Jesus' cross relate to the function and meaning of God's proleptic self-revelation in Jesus resurrection? Pannenberg's reflexion on these questions is by and large limited to the accurate insight that the content of Jesus' proclamation does not presuppose, thematize, or necessarily lead to his death. Neither

---

[11] E.g., Jürgen Moltmann, *The Crucified God;* process theology by and large unanimously, particularly Daniel D. Williams, *The Spirit and the Forms of Love*; Paul Tillich, *Systematic Theology*, vol. ii; Frederick Herzog, *Liberation Theology*; James Cone, *A Black Theology of Liberation*; seminally in Donald Baillie, *God Was in Christ*.

does the *Traditionsgeschichte*, while it and it alone offered the interpretation of Jesus' resurrection, back up Pannenberg's interpretation of Jesus' death. His interpretation of Jesus' death as vicarious penal suffering, in place of man universally, has no grounding in the context of *Traditionsgeschichte*. Instead one must observe that Jesus' message by itself, intrinsically and inherently, as Pannenberg has shown, carries the gift of remission of sin. The message of God's coming Kingdom implies forgiveness and life (*vide supra* p. 120). *Is not the chief redemptive event God's proleptic self-revelation in his resurrecting of Jesus as such?* God's revelation is redemption. It opens the gates to salvation *sine conditione* to all who open up to the message. In a foot-note to the third of his famous Theses Pannenberg writes,

> Revelation of God means for man who is disposed to an openness toward God in its deepest sense salvation, fulfillment of his destiny, and hence of his very being. All concrete gifts of salvation grant salvation only in as much as they indirectly offer a share in God's nearness and mediate communion with the one never ending. However, God's revelation opens up to the sinner the possibility for new communion with God only as long as it gives him the strength to still turn away from his enclosure in himself toward openness for God. To this extent the salvific meaning of God's revelation is essentially tied to its proleptic character. God's revelation in the end of everything, in the judgment of the living and the dead, will mean damnation and exclusion from his human *Bestimmung* for the sinner; he at that time can no longer turn around. The proleptic revelation of God's eschatological revelation, on the other hand, essentially has the character of electing grace, the character of a granting of still available participation in salvation in the fellowship with God.[12]

According to Pannenberg's main line of reasoning, the salvation which is offered by Jesus' proclamation and its confirmation through Jesus' resurrection is in no formal or material need of its supplementation, confirmation, or enforcement through a penal expiatory sacrifice, vicariously borne, in order to be valid. Hence in a sense Pannenberg's

---

[12] *OaG*, p. 101 (my translation). Cp. *RaH*, pp. 156f. where the meaning of the German is not carried over.

elaborations in chapter VII of his christology come as a surprise and form a foreign body in the overall texture of his thought and understanding. Undoubtedly, Jesus' death is a necessary event in the coming of the Kingdom of God. Without it there were no ground upon which to construct the divinity of Christ, viewed from the resurrection. His death as ultimate *Erweis* of his *Berufsgehorsam* demonstrates his dedication to be self-sacrifice and thus "achieves" the Jesus-Son-identity.[13] And without it there were no crucified Jesus whom to raise, whose resurrecting would bring in the signal of the inbreaking eschaton. Yet this death, in order to carry such meaning and significance, needs only to be looked at from the perspective of Jesus' message and resurrection; it requires no interpretation as a penal substitutionary bearing of the curse of the law. In fact, this latter thought more puzzles than clarifies.

The cross, then, is an indispensable factor for both the *vere homo* and the *vere Deus* of Jesus. Christologically speaking, the cross is perfectly adequately valued as "Erweis der indirekten Identität Jesu mit dem Sohn Gottes." If revelation means salvation, every christological truth is soteriologically significant. Hence, as an indispensable factor for christology the cross also is indispensable soteriologically, viz., the *vere homo* and the *vere Deus* permit us to see Jesus' death as the destruction of the universal human self-centeredness, the fulfillment of the human *Bestimmung*, and thus new communion with God. Soteriologically speaking, through his self-sacrifice Jesus fulfilled God's *Bestimmung* for man in his absolute dependence upon God and his unrestricted openness to God. Only on this account is death (the consequence of man's self-enclosure) overcome, salvation at hand, etc. For Jesus did this on our behalf. Not only in his destiny in the resurrection was it enacted what man's *Bestimmung* is like, but also in his death as perfect God-openness, when viewed from Easter. What happened to Jesus was that he lived under the conditions of the universal human self-enclosure but overcame it. His death could be described as bearing the consequences of this universal human self-enclosure. However, neither does it appear to be vicarious nor penal. In concert with the "logic" of Pannenberg's theology as a whole, the salvific

---

[13] I agree with Berthold Klappert, *op. cit.* p. 61, "Dieser Grundkorrelation (historischer Jesus-Auferweckung) subsumiert bedeutet das Kreuz . . . (von der Auferweckung her) die radikale Bewährung der Persongemeinschaft Jesu mit dem Vater in der Selbstpreisgabe Jesu an Gott als der Erweis der indirekten Identität Jesu mit dem Sohne Gottes."

meaning of Jesus' cross appears to lie much more in the *Aufsprengung der menschlichen Selbstverschlossenheit* and the *"radikale Bewährung der Persongemeinschaft mit dem Vater"* (B. Klappert) pro nobis than in Jesus' bearing of the consequences of universal human self-enclosure.[14]

---

[14] In his analysis of Pannenberg's christology Klappert (*Ibid.*, pp. 54-63) argues that here the cross is subsumed under the principal correlation "of the historical Jesus" and "resurrection" and concludes, "Im Horizont der Frage nach dem vere deus hat das Kreuz nach P. keine bzw. allenfalls eine antithetische, die Notwendigkeit der Bestätigung und damit der Begründung der Gottheit Jesu verschärfende Bedeutung. Faktisch steht aber das Kreuz außerhalb des die Gottheit Jesus entscheidend begründenden Geschichts- und Bedeutungszusammenhangs von Anspruch und Bestätigung." (pp. 56f.) This view is no doubt mistaken. Klappert's error can be traced as follows. (1) He says, "Dieser Korrelation 'Jesus-Auferweckung' ist bei P. das Kreuz in seiner inhaltlichen Bedeutung subsumiert. Und zwar kommt dem Kreuz im Horizont der Frage nach der Gottheit Jesu . . . eine doppelte inhaltliche Bedeutung zu: Das Kreuz ist 1. (vom historischen Jesus her) die radikale Infragestellung des auf künftige Bewährung angelegten Vollmachtsanspruchs Jesu und 2. (von der Auferweckung her) die Verschärfung der Notwendigkeit einer Bestätigung Jesu durch Gott. Das Kreuz hat demnach bei P. im Rahmen dieser Christologie von unten nach oben und auf der Basis der Korrelation 'Jesus-Auferweckung' eine retardierende (Infragestellung des Vollmachtsanspruchs Jesu) und eine radikalisierende (Verschärfung der Notwendigkeit einer Bestätigung Jesu durch Gott) Bedeutung . . ." (p. 55) Now actually both points are true from the viewpoint *before* Easter! *Von der Auferweckung her* the cross functions, as K. himself says p. 61, as "die radikale Bewährung der Persongemeinschaft Jesu mit dem Vater in der Selbstpreisgabe Jesu an Gott als der Erweis der indirekten Identität Jesu mit dem Sohn Gottes." The ontic foundation of the *vere Deus* consists of three pillars, not two: Jesus' claim, his self-sacrifice, his confirmation. The cross cannot be regarded as subsumed under the first and third.

(2) K. correctly observes that P. is concerned with the "Konstituierung Jesu zum Prototypen der neuen Menschheit" but goes on, "Durch das Auferstehungsgeschick als der proleptischen Verwirklichung der Bestimmung aller Menschen an Jesus wird Jesus zum Repräsentanten aller Menschen vor Gott." (p. 58) K. overlooks that the *Auferweckung* confirms what appears to have been historically "achieved" by Jesus' radical and absolute dedication, when viewed from Easter. Only together with the destiny of his crucifixion is his *Auferstehungsgeschick* the *proleptische Verwirklichung der Bestimmung aller Menschen*.

(3) K. accurately says, "*Die Gottheit Jesu ist ein Implikat der Offenbarungs- und Wesensidentität des Geschicks Jesu mit der Gottheit Gottes, das vere deus Jesu ist das Prädikat der mit Gott offenbarungs- und wesensidentischen Geschichtsprolepse.*

Jesus' resurrection means, as Pannenberg says, his justification from God's side. Presumably one may also call it his *exaltatio*. For sinful man, in this theology, Jesus' resurrection, as confirmation of his message and crucifixion, *viz.*, the foundation of his identity, means salvation: forgiveness of sin is offered, total redemption will be granted. In the light of Easter Jesus' cross discloses Jesus' God-openness and man's self-centeredness. Jesus' passion manifests man's perverted existence and Jesus' *Berufstreue* in and through which he becomes (always was) the *Prototyp der neuen Menschheit*. In his relatively few statements on what the cross means when regarded as God's, the Father's work, Pannenberg, it seems, emphasizes God's punishing man by letting Jesus bear the curse of the universal human self-enclosure vicariously. *Should he not rather have interpreted it in the light of the concept of God which is implied and demonstrated in Jesus' proclamation and resurrection?*

Das Geschick Jesu als Prolepse des Endes der Universalgeschichte und damit als vollkommener Spiegel der 'Herrlichkeit Gottes' ist wesensidentisch mit Gott und impliziert damit die ontische Begründung der Gottheit Gottes." (p. 56, italics Klappert's) How, on this basis, can he uphold his opinion that the cross has no significance for the foundation of Jesus' deity? Well, he erroneously again takes *Jesu Geschick* to mean his resurrection only, excluding his crucifixion from that concept, as is obvious when he goes on to say, "D. h. die Gottheit Jesu ist ein Prädikat der Wesensidentität des Auferstehungsgeschicks Jesu mit der Gottheit Gottes . . . (p. 56).

The common fallacy of all of K.'s statements, within his analysis of P.'s christology, according to which the cross is subsumed under the correlation "historischer Jesus-Auferweckung", consists of the fact that he takes no notice of the *mutual dependence* of the noetical and the ontological foundation of Jesus' identity as Son of God (cf. supra pp. 80ff.). There is one aspect in which the cross appears to be subsumed, *viz.*, as vicarious penal suffering it is subsumed under its relevance as self-sacrifice of the man Jesus. But K. is not talking about this, as he does not discuss P.'s doctrine of atonement (reconciliation) altogether.

CHAPTER VIII

CRITIQUE OF PANNENBERG'S STAUROLOGY

Let it be recalled that Pannenberg's understanding of Jesus' death parts company with the main Abelardian and neo-Protestant view, as exemplified e. g. in Schleiermacher, von Hofmann, Ritschl, in holding the death to have been penal and substitutionary. The basis of this contention consists of three pillars. The epistemological basis consists of the resurrection of Jesus. It proves, by the inversion of standards, Jesus' death to have been the vicarious punishment for all who, directly or by representation, rejected Jesus (the blasphemous existence of humanity). The hermeneutical basis consists of two pillars which serve Pannenberg to verify that (a) humanity deserves to die and (b) that substitution with regard to guilt and punishment is possible. These two pillars consist (1) of the penal character of death, established as a universal anthropological truth, and (2) of the universal phenomenon of substitution in the total sphere of personal and social life. This last evidence is meant to invalidate and replace the position of an extreme ethical individualism from which much theology since the Socinians severely − and, on their basis, convincingly − attacked the doctrine of the vicarious penal suffering and of a satisfying, propitiating death of Christ. In Pannenberg's attempt to establish his own, modern concept of substitution the Israelite understanding of guilt and punishment played a role.

We now direct our inquiry specifically to the strength and persuasiveness of these three pillars of Pannenberg's doctrine.

1. *The Old Israelite Understanding of Expiation*[1]

Let us first turn to the use Pannenberg makes of the Old Israelite understanding of the guilt-punishment (sin-consequence) relationship. Two

---

[1] For the following cf. Klaus Koch, "Gibt es ein Vergeltungsdogma im Alten Testament?", *Zeitschrift für Theologie und Kirche*, vol. lii, 1955, pp. 1-42; Gerhard von

features of this understanding are of particular interest to Pannenberg. First, what follows from sin is its necessary consequence in terms of evil, suffering, destruction, ban, or death rather than punishment in the sense of a certain independently imposed penalty which is measured after a norm or an ideal and levied in accord with a sentence by God. What follows sin is *Schicksal*, not retaliation. It is an effect which comes about without a special sanction. An evil deed creates a sphere or aura of evil which seeks to discharge itself — comparable to electric energy. Koch prefers to call this view the concept of *"Schicksal wirkende Tatsphäre"*[2] rather than *"synthetische Lebensauffassung"* (Fahlgren).

> Das alte Israel sieht das Schicksal des Menschen in seiner Guttat oder Übeltat begründet. Durch sein Tun "schafft" der Mensch sich eine Sphäre, die ihm bleibend heil- oder unheilwirkend umgibt. Diese Sphäre ist von dringlicher Stofflichkeit und gehört zum Menschen in ähnlicher Weise wie sein Eigentum. Die Auswirkung solcher Taten tritt nicht sofort ein, sondern entwickelt sich wie die Pflanze aus dem Keim.[3]

There is no word for 'punishment' in the Old Testament, and the vocabulary of the Old Testament possesses no word for 'righteousness' in the sense of *iustitia distributiva* or vindictive justice.

Secondly, the effect of a deed is not inseparably tied to the doer of that deed but is distinguished and separable from it. It must find a place where it may unload its curse or evil power. It primarily seeks to do so on the originator of that deed but equally threatens his society.

> Through ties of blood and common lot the individual was regarded as being so deeply embedded in the community that an offense on his part was not just a private matter affecting only himself and his own relationship to God. On the contrary, wherever there had been a grave offence against the divine law, what loomed largest was the

---

Rad, *Old Testament Theology*. Vol. i: *The Theology of Israel's Historical Traditions* (New York: Harper and Row, 1967), pp. 262 ff., 385 ff.; K. H. J. Fahlgren, *Sedake nahestehende und entgegengesetzte Begriffe im Alten Testament* (Uppsala, 1932); H. Wheeler Robinson, *Corporate Personality in Ancient Israel* (Philadelphia: Fortress Press, 1964). Also *vide supra* pp. 145 ff.

[2] Koch, *op. cit.*, p. 26.
[3] *Ibid.*, p. 31.

incrimination which the community experienced in consequence at the hands of God, for because of the sin nothing less than the whole possibility of its cultic activity had become imperilled. The community had thus a vital interest in the restoration of order.[4]

This consequence or effect is transferable, then.

This concept makes perfectly clear the reason why the community had such a strong interest in an individual's sin. It was not just a matter of an imaginary moral taint which affected the community as well, and so "just" an internal disturbance of its relationship with God: rather, the evil which an action had brought into existence inevitably had effects which destroyed individual and community alike, unless the latter solemnly and clearly cancelled its solidarity with the offender. Thus, in an utterly realistic and direct sense, an offender was a danger to the whole people. Further, it becomes clear that in such circumstances the act would inevitably be looked at from one side only, under the aspect of its actual performance and, initially, without any regard being paid to its personal motivations, and also, quite apart from any questions as to the consciousness or subjective intention of the agent.[5]

What is God's role in all of this?

(1) Yahweh has ordered this relationship between deeds and consequences; it apparently is part of the convenant and must be upheld to keep the convenant in force.

(2) Yahweh "completes" the deed to the doer through a fate that belongs to it.

Jahweh wird damit zwar als eine dem Menschen *übergeordnete Größe* genannt, aber diese handelt nicht juristisch, indem sie Lohn und Strafe nach einer Norm bemißt und zuteilt, sondern sie leistet sozusagen 'Hebammendienst', indem sie *das von Menschen Angelegte zur völligen Entfaltung bringt.*[6]

---

[4] G. v. Rad, *op. cit.*, p. 264.
[5] *Ibid.*, pp. 266f.
[6] Koch, *op. cit.*, p. 5 (italics Koch's).

Jahweh greift danach in das menschliche Leben ein und bestimmt das Ergehen entsprechend den Taten. . . . Man kann *Jahwehs Handeln* . . . als *in-Kraft-setzen und vollenden des Sünde-Unheil-Zusammenhangs* verstehen . . .[7]

Unentrinnbar umgeben die dingähnlichen, raumhaften Taten das Volk, so daß selbst Jahweh hilflos zusehen muß. Ja noch mehr: kraft seiner Gottheit kann er einem solchen Volk nicht nahekommen, ohne daß dessen Sünde hervortritt und sich auswirkt. Die Taten des Volkes sind Schicksal geworden.[8]

Das Unheil, das Hosea androht, ist Züchtigung . . . ein schmerzhafter aber vorübergehender Schlag, welcher die vergangene Schuld zu Ende führt in dem zu ihr gehörigen Ergehen. . . . Wenn auch Jahweh damit nicht als "vergeltend" geschildert wird, so könnte solche Aussage doch dazu verleiten, in dem Jahweh des Alten Testaments den Garanten einer "sittlichen Weltordnung zu sehen, der überall nach dem Rechten schaut und menschliche Entscheidung als Schicksal sich auswirken läßt, einem Werkmeister vergleichbar, der den geregelten Lauf von Maschinen überwacht. Der Gedanke der Züchtigung, der bei Hosea auftaucht (und der auch in der Weisheit nicht selten ist!), führt hier weiter. Er zeigt – wie vielleicht auch der Begriff "heimsuchen" –, daß es Jahweh nicht um die Durchsetzung einer abstrakten Ordnung, sondern *um die Erhaltung des Bundes zu tun ist*.[9]

The work of Yahweh consists of the enforcement of this correspondence of deed and fate; this correspondence is "Wirkung göttlicher Treue".[10] Von Rad sums up,

> On this view, the "recompense" which catches up with evil is certainly no subsequent forensic event which the sin evokes in a completely different sphere – that is, with God. It is the radiation of the evil which now continues on: only so does the evil which the sin called out reach equilibrium. . . . the presupposition of this idea is the closest possible correspondence between action and fate: what is

---

[7] *Ibid.*, p. 7 (italics Koch's).
[8] *Ibid.*, p. 12.
[9] *Ibid.*, pp. 14f. (Italics Koch's).
[10] *Ibid.*, p. 21.

13 Neie: Pannenberg

in question is a process which, in virtue of a power alike to all that is good and all that is evil, comes to a good or an evil end. Israel regarded this as a basic order of her whole existence, to which Yahweh had given effect and over whose functioning he himself kept watch.[11]

(3) Now because the process deed-consequence does not operate quite automatically after all but requires Yahweh to watch over it and redirect the effect to its proper recipient, Yahweh can also annihilate the evil consequence (ban, curse). He can "forgive", he can forget his wrath.

> Von "Vergebung" sprechen ist deshalb mißlich, weil dadurch dieses Geschehen in das Geistige verlagert wird, was im Psalter nicht geschieht. Die Israeliten sprechen vielmehr davon, daß Sünde "weggetragen und bedeckt" . . ., "weggewischt und abgewaschen" . . ., "entfernt" . . . oder "geheilt" wird . . . Die innerweltliche, dingähnliche Tatsphäre wird durch Jahwehs "vergebendes" Eingreifen vernichtet. Der Beter kann natürlich auch darauf hoffen, daß Jahweh sein Angesicht vor der Sünde verbirgt . . . das widerspricht dem eben Gesagten nicht, denn Jahwehs Zorn ist das (dingähnliche!) movens der Tat-Vergehen-Verhaftung.[12]

So some sin could be "forgiven". What about the remainder?

(4) Yahwehs grants expiation.

> If the sin could not be forgiven, then the person concerned had to "bear his guilt". . . . The sole protection from the blow (of the almost hypostatised power of wrath) was the repeated performance of numerous atoning rites.[13]

Expiation could be effected by the vicarious death of an animal, the decisive point being that it is Yahweh who is appealed to, himself actively to effect the expiation. Von Rad concludes,

> Accordingly, the one who receives expiation is not Yahweh but Israel: Yahweh is rather the one who acts, in averting the calamitous

---

[11] v. Rad, *op. cit.*, p. 265. v. Rad also comments on Koch's analysis and thinks that Koch has not given enough weight to the element of divine declaration of guilt which works itself out in punishment.

[12] Koch, *op. cit.*, p. 21.   [13] v. Rad, *op. cit.*, p. 268f.

curse which burdens the community. ... in the last analysis it is Yahweh himself who effects or refuses expiation.[14]

What was effected in expiation was that in both cases, with persons and objects alike, Yahweh removed the baneful influence of an act ... by way of channelling the baneful influence of the evil into the animal which died vicariously for the man (or for the cultic object). Expiation was thus not a penalty, but a saving event.[15]

Where does all of this lead us?

Pannenberg is interested in this Old Israelite view of sin and its consequence and its expiation because, as he sees it, here there is substitution without the need of rationally, ethically or juridically, justifying the legitimacy of every punitive sanction as is the case when we think within the framework of an ethical individualism with a rewarding and punishing God, as the keeper of the *sittliche Weltordnung, vis-a-vis* the people as sum total of individuals. It is Pannenberg's intention to establish that the refutation of the concept of Christ's vicarious penal suffering, from Socinus to Ritschl and into the present, is irrelevant under circumstances as they obtain according to the Old Israelite view. And it is his consecutive intention to show that, because according to modern social and sociological analysis ethical individualism offers an inadequate perspective also today, that in fact it *never* was true to life, its polemic is beside the point today, too.

2. Ethical Individualism and the Ancient Hebrew Concept of Collective Liability

Let us look at Socinus' critique of the theory of satisfaction of Anselm which, to a great extent, also applies to the *Strafleiden*-theory of Luther which Pannenberg favors and follows, no doubt on other premises. The Socinian position is excellently summarized by Friedrich August Berthold Nitzsch:

> Gegen diese (doctrine of the *munus sacerdotale Christi*) wandten die Socinianer namentlich folgendes ein. 1. Es vertrage sich weder mit der Majestät noch mit der Güte Gottes, entweder Bestrafung unserer

---

[14] *Ibid.*, p. 270. [15] *Ibid.*, p. 271.

Sünden oder Genugtuung für sie zu verlangen. Denn, wenn er die eine oder andere forderte, so würde er dadurch zeigen, daß er uns unsere Sünden entweder nicht vergeben könne oder nicht vergeben wolle. 2. Vergebung und Genugtuung höben einander auf. Die Sündenvergebung beruhe auf Gottes barmherziger Liebe; durch diese werde aber die Genugtuung fordernde Gerechtigkeit ausgeschlossen (Dum debitum remittitur, condonatur; dum vero pro se satisfit, exigitur: Wird die Schuld vergeben, so wird sie erlassen; wird aber die Satisfaktion für sie geleistet, so wird die Schuld vielmehr eingefordert). 3. Übertragung von Schuld und Strafe sei undenkbar; beides sei etwas Persönliches. Dergleichen sei bei einem äußerlichen Schuldverhältnisse, wie einer Verpflichtung zu einer Geldbuße, wohl möglich, aber nicht, wo es sich um moralische Schuld handle. 4. Gott könne sich in keinem Fall eine Schuld doppelt bezahlen lassen. Dies würde aber der Fall sein, wenn Christus stellvertretend gelitten und außerdem stellvertretend das Gesetz erfüllt hätte. 5. Was Christus erduldet habe, entspreche weder quantitativ noch qualitativ dem, was angeblich wir hätten erleiden sollen. Quantitativ deswegen nicht, weil Christus als der Auferstandene offenbar nicht den angeblich uns gebührenden ewigen Tod erlitten habe, geschweige denn die Verdammnis aller einzelnen Menschen; qualitativ deshalb nicht, weil sein Leiden eigentlich nicht Strafe gewesen sei, sondern Kampf um den Preis der Erhöhung. 6. Zum tätigen Gehorsam sei Christus verpflichtet gewesen, diesen habe er also nicht stellvertretend leisten können. 7. Endlich: die kirchliche Lehre von der stellvertretenden Gesetzeserfüllung durch Christum sei schädlich, weil sie den Wahn erzeugen könne, wir brauchten eben wegen jener Stellvertretung das Gesetz nicht mehr zu erfüllen. Überhaupt sei Gott durch Christi Tun und Leiden nicht wirklich erst versöhnt worden, sondern im Tode Christi sei Gottes Gnade gegen uns zur Erscheinung gekommen, habe sich darin erwiesen; denn Christi Tod sei uns ein Vorbild standhafter Frömmigkeit bis zum Äußersten . . .[16]

---

[16] Friedrich Aug. Berth. Nitzsch, *Lehrbuch der evangelischen Dogmatik,* bearbeitet von Horst Stephan (3d ed., Tübingen: J. C. B. Mohr, 1912), pp. 554f. For an interpretation of the Socinian critique cf. especially Wolfgang Trillhaas, *Dogmatik* (Berlin: Alfred Töpelmann, 1962): "Was an kritischen Einwänden gegen das fortwirkende anselmische Schema an der Schwelle der Neuzeit zur Aussprache drängte, das findet sich wie in einem Vorgriff auf die Aufklärung bei den So-

We will now investigate the question whether the ethical individualism which forms the basis of this polemic really is inadequate to describe the reality of life and hence inapplicable to an evaluation of the Old Israelite, the modern social-sociological, and Pannenberg's own concept of substitution. Three areas have to be considered: To what extent is the Socinian critique applicable to the Old Israelite view of substitution (transference and expiation)? How, if at all, is the modern view to which Pannenberg takes recourse, congruous with the Old Israelite view? What are its specific features? And, does Pannenberg's doctrine of substitution coincide with the Old Israelite or the modern view of substitution or both? And what role does the fact play that Israel moved to a more individualistic ethicism, particularly in its apocalyptic theology? In this section we focus on the first area mentioned.

The *first* point of the Socinian criticism cited above is only partially applicable to the Old Testament view since Yahweh does not *demand* punishment or satisfaction; sin produces its own fruit. Yahweh partly forgives, covers up, or offers sinful man and his society expiation. The good or bad fruit of his deed is transfered upon the doer, someone else, or

> zinianern. Hier wurde der anselmischen Versöhnungslehre ihr rechnerischer Rationalismus Zug um Zug zurückgegeben. Hatte das Mittelalter und noch die Reformation die Versöhnungslehre in den Rahmen eines gesetzmäßigen Verhältnisses zwischen Gott und dem Menschen eingezeichnet, so dominiert bei Faustus Sozini der Gottesbegriff des Duns Scotus, nach dem Gott absoluter Wille ist und die Freiheit hat, Sünden zu bestrafen oder zu vergeben.... Der Satisfaktionsgedanke leidet aber auch an inneren Unmöglichkeiten. Er schließt nämlich die Vergebung der Schuld tatsächlich aus. Vergebung bedeutet ja den Verzicht auf Genugtuung; statt dessen lehrt die kirchliche Versöhnungslehre nur eine Vertauschung des Schuldners." (p. 292)

> "Man sieht, hier werden alle Bedenken der Vernunft ausgeschüttet. Der gebündelte Einwand ist nicht eigentlich selbst religiös, und man kann fragen, ob die religiösen Glaubensgehalte der Versöhnungslehre überhaupt noch gespürt werden. Aber hier wird der Glaube zweifellos zu einer Rechenschaft gezwungen, bei der von vornherein alle verrechenbaren Stützen weggezogen werden. Die rationalistische Kritik – und das gilt dann ebenso für ihre späteren Formen – hat die rationale Erklärung der Versöhnungslehre für immer gelähmt. Im 19. Jahrhundert finden wir in jedem selbständigen Versuch einer Bewältigung des Problems daher ebenso eine spürbare Nachwirkung der rationalistischen Kritik, aber auch den bewußten oder minder bewußten Versuch, beim Abälardschen Lehrtypus Zuflucht zu suchen." (p. 293)

an animal. God's goodness, so to say, consists in his keeping the covenant intact by directing the threats of sin to their unloading. Expiation is a saving event.

However, the Socinian critique is inapplicable only because of a different concept of God. The ancient Hebrew God cannot and does not want to set aside the deed-consequence-process. To be sure, he does not exercise judgment in the modern sense; but he instituted this process, watches over it (so that justice and salvation are upheld) and offers expiation within this scheme in which an evil deed needs to find its victim, outlet, or atonement. Now whether or not this basic schema is to be called punitive, retaliatory, recompensing is only a matter of nomenclature, it seems. Yahweh is in charge of the process – call it *Schicksal* or reward/punishment. The ultimate difference between the Old Israelite and the Socinian view *at this point* is less the difference between an ethic which obtains within a corporate personality-concept[17] and an extreme ethical individualism than between a god who works salvation within the described process and one who can abolish that circulus altogether. According to Koch this process has its own momentum; God is powerless to abolish it. In fact, in his faithfulness he keeps it going. Apparently, the covenant is inseparably tied to the efficaciousness of this process which means that God's *Gemeinschaftstreue* (צְדָקָה) includes distributive justice and grace. According to von Rad God declares guilty which declaration "works itself out in punishment". Transferability of the consequence of an evil deed upon an animal is necessary to free the doer or the society from a catastrophe. God cannot waive the "penalty" but can transfer it. Both are the object of the Socinian critique on account of its different view of God and the deed-consequence-process. For the Socinians God in his love *can* waive the guilt and apparently wants to do so. Actually they do not deny that good and evil deeds have their own good and evil consequences but that the evil consequences can be regarded as punishment. Forgiveness is spiritually understood in the Socinian frame of thought, just as guilt, and both are not transferable once a stage of ethical thought has been reached which envisions guilt and responsibility as tied to the individual – which shift no doubt occurred within later Judaism and is manifest in the apocalyptic and New Testament mode of thought. Facit: the Socinian critique at this point is not fully applicable to the Old Testament view of

---

[17] Cf. H. Wheeler Robinson, *op. cit.*

guilt and of God but is right and justified from its own concept of God and ethical perspective.

The *second* point of the Socinian criticism is absolutely cogent. Again it reveals the difference in the concept of God. Even though it was directed against the theory of satisfaction it is equally to the point with regard to the *Strafleiden*-theory. Does it apply to the Old Israelite view of God who (even if the "punishment" is not specifically demanded or sanctioned by God) runs the process? Under the condition of the irrevocable "punishment" which evil calls forth it would be unjust, of course, to demand God to stop the effect instead of merely redirecting it or atoning for it. God's hands are tied, so to speak. To this extent the God of Old Israel differs from Anselm's. The latter will not renounce payment; his forgiveness includes a foregoing satisfaction. Old Israel's God cannot revoke the effect; he did not sanction it in the first place. Israel's God does all he can do to save. Yet Sozzini's point applies wherever in the Old Testament the effect of sin is understood as work of the wrath or decision of God. And it no doubt applies as soon as and whenever we no longer consider "punishment" as the built-in effect of a sin. Once man learnt to distinguish between the consequence or effect of a good or bad act on earth and guilt before God and sin is spiritually understood, not physically-magically as a power, an aura, or a sphere, there this point does apply. And God will appear as alternatingly *revelatus* and *absconditus*, gracious and wrathful, and thus completely untrustworthy and scary, but for such a distinction.

Sozzini's *third* point leads to the question of the transferability of guilt and punishment. It no doubt applies to both the satisfaction and *Strafleiden*-theories, given an ethical individualism, as Pannenberg is in agreement. Pannenberg thinks it does not apply to the ancient Hebrew view because, on account of collective liability in Ancient Israel, transferability of guilt and consequence obtains at all time. It underlies the institution of sin offering. For this situation the Socinian objection thinks too individualistically. Now this appears to be a half-truth only. For it seems that within the corporate or collective solidarity on account of which no one minds that the fruit of a good or evil deed is harvested by someone else or the society at large or a later generation only, there is also ethical individualism. It shows itself in (1) that the evil generated by a sin primarily seeks to hit the doer himself (herself), (2) that Yahweh ordinarily is asked or functions to lead the ill back to its originator, (3) that the substitutionary bearing of someone's sin by the society is considered a threat, a catastrophe, an ill to be avoided, and (4) that the institution of sin-offering (expiation) presupposes not the transferability of guilt but of "punishment". The latter, because it is distinguished and separable from sin itself, can be transfered — a work of grace, under the conditions of a physical-spatial-powerlike concept of sin. Perhaps we can say: there is a spiritual side to sin, the guilt of the individual doer; this is not transfered but "forgiven". Hence the standards of the Socinian critique do apply partially also to the Old Israelite view; it shares them. All deviations from these standards are accounted for by the ancient view of sin and of God's limitations.

The other points (4–7) of the Socinian critique, as outlined by Nitzsch, do not occupy us here. They are exclusively directed to the understanding of Christ's death.

The result of our inquiry is as follows: the Socinian critique of the concept of God and of the transferability of guilt and punishment implied in the satisfaction and — *mutatis mutandis* — the *Strafleiden*-theories on the whole does not apply to the ancient Hebrew view; Pannenberg is right in this judgment. Instead of an ethical individualism there obtains collective liability; substitution is a common and needful phenomenon under those circumstances, indeed. Expiation of or release of the evil effect of a sin is possible through God and is not regarded as punishment, demanded by a righteous God, but as a gracious, salvific work of God who operates to the best of his ability within the frame of the irrevocable deed-effect-process. We may conclude: *Had Jesus been crucified within this ancient Hebrew society and its thinking his death would quite naturally have been considered the vicarious expiatory death of one on whom God transfered the evil curse of sins. But, of course, it could not have been considered a penal death*! For, again, in this mode of thought, suffering and death are not punishment but consequence. If von Rad is right, saying

> Death was no last enemy but Yahweh's acting upon men. . . . Yahweh decress death for a man, but in certain circumstances he also alters this decree (II Kings xx. 5f.) — it all rests with his freedom in giving and taking. . . . death too comprised many possibilities of trial but . . . in no sense became the question which threatened the foundation of all faith. Certainly, it was conceived as a question directed to men much more than to God, for because of the concept

of the fate-bringing act all disturbances of life and all illnesses had something of the effect of arousing the men concerned.[18]

and if Oehler is right, saying

> The law nowhere indicates that in sacrifice . . . an act of punitive punishment is executed; it in no way asks us to look on the altar as a place of punishment.[19]

then the Socinian critique of the concept of God implied in the *Strafleiden*-theory does not apply to the ancient Hebrew view, just as its critique of the transferability of punishment does not apply to a society in which there is no punishment and in which all evil is borne collectively anyway. On the other hand, to the extent that we find ethical individualism in the Old Testament and an understanding of God as judge who recompenses (*distributiva iustitia*) individually, the Socinian critique begins to make sense and gains momentum.

3. Ethical Individualism and the Modern View of Substitution as a Universal Phenomenon in Personal and Socio-political Life

We cannot portray the development of ethical individualism within the bounds of this treatise. It begins in the Old Testament itself. Under the impact of its development the following shifts of the ancient Hebrew view took place:

(1) The disparity between deed and consequence became unbearable. An expectation of, a hope for, and a demand for justice in the sense of individual recompense develops and replaces the former contentment with collective liability and vicarious reaping of the good by the society or nation.[20]

(2) A spiritual understanding of bliss develops which consoles the individual in face of his physical suffering and the obvious injustice in his life. With reference to Psalms 27, 36, 16 and 27 von Rad says,

---

[18] von Rad, *op. cit.*, pp. 390f.
[19] Oehler, *Theology of the Old Testament* (Edinburgh, 1874), p. 431, cited by von Rad, *op. cit.*, p. 271.
[20] For the reasons for this development cf. K. Koch, *op. cit.*, pp. 33ff.; von Rad, *op. cit.*, pp. 391-418; 443.

It is an extreme spiritualization which is attained here — a retreat into the realm of the most sublime communion with God which has made these men practically unassailable from the outside. The succinct statement 'for thy steadfast love is better than life' (Ps. LXIII. 4 3) gives a glimpse of how fundamentally the relative importance of all values had changed, for normally life and its enhancement through Yahweh's blessing was at all times the highest of good things for Israel. This discrimination between loving-kindness and life was something wholly new: it signified the discovery of the spiritual as a reality beyond the frailty of the corporeal.[21]

(3) The individualisation of the hope for and expectation of just recompense is radicalized in the Apocalyptic which expects recompense from Yahweh's acting beyond death, after a general resurrection from the dead.

> A thoroughgoing change was introduced by Apocalyptic . . . In the psalms it was the word of Yahweh addressed to the individual in a wholly personal way which bore him over the threshold of death because he abandoned himself to it completely. What was characteristic for man's situation over against death was precisely the lack of a generally accepted hope in something beyond . . . On the other hand, in Apocalyptic the resurrection of the dead is merely one act in the great apocalyptic events of the end, the main essentials of which were already fixed in anticipation. These events overtake the whole world and therefore the individual as well, who has to hold himself in readiness for them.[22]

(4) Hence in apocalyptic theology death becomes an enemy to Yahweh — an obstacle to his plan with his creation. It is expected to be destroyed by Yahweh.

These shifts seem to indicate that the trust in the efficaciousness of a good or evil deed in terms of an innately operative reward or punishment has been abandoned. At this time Yahweh was envisaged as the sovereign Lord, external to the process deed-consequence, who can and will recompense individually.

---

[21] von Rad, *op. cit.*, p. 403.
[22] *Ibid.*, p. 407f.

This ethical individualism seems to be most rationally developed in the Socinian mode of thought. *The Socinian critique is based upon such ethical individualism plus (on Scotist grounds) a faith that takes the proclamation of Jesus that God is love and forgives us our sin utmostly seriously.* On this basis Christ's suffering could not be understood as either penal (punishment and forgiveness are mutually exclusive) or vicarious (substitution in the moral personal realm is ethically untenable.) Ritschl and, by and large, all the other neo-Protestant theologians share this understanding of God and of Jesus' passion. For Sozzini, "the relation between guilt and punishment is merely external, residing in no way in the nature of the matter and becoming a reality only through the force of the state." (268)

Now does the element of substitution in all of man's personal and social life rescind this ethical individualism and permit us to once more understand Jesus' death as penal and vicarious? What are the specific features of this general phenomenon of substitution?

Pannenberg's explanations[23] seem sketchy, general, and brief, and they are undocumented; they lack precision. This surprises the more one realizes the importance of this point for his doctrine. For the sake of more precision we have to introduce two distinctions, it seems: (1) the distinction between the *realm of cause and effect*, on the one hand, and the *moral area of guilt and its consequence* (evil, suffering), on the other. This distinction has already occupied our attention. (2) There is a distinction between *participation (sharing) in responsibility, guilt, etc., and substitution (vicarious bearing in place of someone (-thing). Now there no doubt is a great amount of substitution in the sense of bearing the evil and fruition of the good in the cause/effect-realm.* How many guilty live comfortably, how many innocent suffer and die! Many doers of highly beneficent deeds do not fruit the benefit of their accomplishments; others benefit who did nothing to achieve the good, on the contrary. The modern view coincides with the ancient Hebrew that there is substitution in the sense that the outcome of deeds is perpetually transfered, that the consequence is not tied to the particular deed or its doer but works itself out upon someone else, too, or others, or the group, society, nation, manking. Modern man puts up with this reality like the ancient Hebrew, as far as the this-worldly cause/effect-nexus is concerned. *But unlike the ancient Hebrew modern*

---

[23] Cf. *JGaM*, p. 268; *The Apostles' Creed*, pp. 87f.

man does not accept collective liability, vicarious responsibility or guilt. In the area of responsibility and guilt there actually is no transference, in modern life. No doubt, there is sharing and participation in the moral realm. Rarely ever is one man alone guilty of something — there is the corporate factor, the kingdom of evil, corporate sin. But this does not permit us, strictly speaking, to speak of *transference* of *guilt* or bearing of *guilt* in place of others. For even if someone else has had to bear the consequences of my sin, I surely am not acquitted thereby.

This makes a profound difference. Personal guilt and responsibility, in spite of all sharing with others who contributed to my failure through their sin of commission or omission, is not transferable. No one can vicariously bear my guilt even if he (she) bears the consequences of my failure. This, it seems, is central to modern man's self-understanding. In Christian thinking, this modern ethical individualism reflects the development from the Old Testament through Apocalyptic and Enlightenment to the present. The emergence of the radicalization of ethical individualism in the Apocalyptic and the concomitant development of hope for adjustment beyond death is a step of no return. Pannenberg himself verified the truth of this view anthropologically, and it plays a major role in his attempt to prove the relevance of the apocalyptic expectation of the resurrection of the dead for our modern *Wirklichkeitsverständnis*. The quest and yearning for fulfillment of individual life testifies to the lack of truth in the concept of collective liability. The development in the direction of ethical individualism should, from Pannenberg's perspective, be regarded as a "product" of the indirect self-revelation of God in history instead of as rescinded by whatever factor in the personal and sociopolitical reality of life. If this development were a flaw in history, the apocalyptic expectation, a consequence of the intolerable character of the disparity between *Verhalten* and *Ergehen*, conduct and outcome, were in the wrong, too, and the anthropological-phenomenological analysis of hope should and would result in a picture very different from Pannenberg's.

In the realm of life universally there is no substitution of responsibility and guilt. If, as does the traditional doctrine, one man, viz. Christ, is said to take over my guilt, *then this has to be accounted for on other grounds, as the traditional doctrine indeed does*. Then Christ's substitution becomes a miraculous, unique phenomenon, a special grace.

Precisely those phenomena which Pannenberg conjures up to illustrate his thesis, viz., the "vicarious" suffering of the population of such German provinces as were annexed by Poland who expelled millions of German citizens so that, indeed, those millions of refugees bore the consequence of Hitler's war much more severely and fiercely than say the population of Hesse or Bavaria, do not constitute a transference of punishment but of effects. The guilt and (if one believes in the need of punishment) punishment of those who caused this disaster is not taken away thereby. Precisely such phenomena spur the sighs *de profundis* and the hope for adjustment beyond death just as they give rise to despair and nihilism in people who do not share such hope.

There is substitution everywhere in the realm of deed and consequence; there is no such thing in the field of ethics, it appears. For example, Kirchenpräsident Dr. Martin Niemöller's famous post-war thesis of the collective guilt of the German people in Hitler's crimes can only mean that many, perhaps several millions of men and women share in that guilt – not on account of transference but on account of their very own commission or omission to do something about it, or else this concept becomes absurd.

Let us summarize the difference and agreement between the Hebrew and the modern view. By the modern view we do not think of a general secular understanding of ethical responsibility but of the view which emerged from Pannenberg's own anthropology and phenomenological analysis of hope. The chief elements of divergence may be listed schematically.

Ancient Hebrew View	*Modern View*
Death is accepted	Death is the enemy
Collective liability and transference of guilt (substitution) are accepted.	Complexity of cause and guilt is recognized; substitution in the realm of consequences is accepted. In the area of responsibility and guilt ethical individualism is held.
God works salvation within the process of guilt = cause/"punishment" = effect. God's will and *Schicksal* are identical. No individual recompense is expected.	God is sovereign Lord over this process. Fate (consequence) and recompense (reward, punishment) are distinguished. Sin is spiritualized. Forgiveness and individual redemption are hoped for beyond death.

As regards the *common element* of the two views we can point to two phenomena. (1) For both views substitution is common *in the realm of consequences of good and evil deeds*. Every deed gives birth to a corresponding effect or fruit quite independent of the particular doer and apart from considerations of punishment and reward. This is accepted. But while the Hebrew rests content with this fact — "somehow and sometime justice will be restored" —, the modern viewer either expects *no* adjustment or, if Pannenberg is correct in his anthropology, hopes for adjustment beyond death. In either case the disparity between conduct and its outcome is considered intramundanely definitive. (2) Also for both views God is not the punisher in terms of the *ius talionis* or vindictive justice within the individual's life on earth. For the ancient Hebrew the deeds themselves punish man or are met by expiation or "forgiveness" through God's grace. According to the modern view man's intrinsic hope for adjustment coincides with and is even superseded and surpassed by Christ's proclamation of the coming kingdom and the implied message of forgiveness of sin. God forgives all who are open to the communion with Christ. The concept of God implied by Jesus' proclamation of the imminent kingdom of God coincides with Ritschl's concept of God as the Father, at least to a great degree.[24] In this perspective no evil (consequences of deeds) can be regarded as God's punishment anymore;[25] *das Übel* is a discipline and test of trust, on the one hand, and an opportunity to prove *die christliche Vollkommenheit*, viz., love and service, on the other. The main difference here appears to consist of the fact that for the ancient Hebrew God's love is *intra legem*, for the modern view *contra legem*.

Particularly alien to the modern view is the Hebrew understanding that God offers expiation so that the evil resulting from sin is intramundanely removed. According to the modern understanding of reality not evil as the intramundance effect of sin, but the spiritual consequence of sin, guilt, is removed by God's grace, viz., it is forgiven.

4. Pannenberg's Doctrine and the Phenomenon of Substitution

If our preceding observations are accurate, the universal phenomenon of substitution does not apply to guilt and punishment. Vicarious suffering or fruition merely implies that we encounter the consequences of good and bad deeds unrelated to our desert.

---

[24] Cf. Albrecht Ritschl, *op. cit.*, para. 8-18.
[25] This does neither obliterate man's consciousness of sin nor condone his sin.

Consequently the phenomenon of substitution does not serve the purpose it is supposed to render for Pannenberg's doctrine of Jesus' death on the cross. Pannenberg, in this systematic locus, presupposes a concept of God which is dominated by the image of a legislator. In its train Jesus is seen to suffer the punishment due to the blasphemous existence of humanity. But his concept escapes verification. Since substitution of guilt or punishment is no universal phenomenon Jesus' death can be construed only as the vicarious suffering of consequences of the sin of others, viz., of their closedness to Jesus' message, of man's universal self-enclosure toward God. Even this is only partially true. Empirically his death is the consequence of his absolute *Berufstreue* to his mission and proclamation. The modern discovery of the disparity between *Verhalten* and *Ergehen* and the concomitant vicarious character of much suffering of evil as well as enjoyment of good cannot serve to establish the penal character of Jesus' passion and death. Jesus' passion and death does by no means imply man's acquittal. Man remains responsible for and guilty of his transgression. In other words, ethical individualism is not disproved, though no doubt it is broadened by modern insights. Thus the *pro nobis* of Jesus' cross in the vicarious penal sense cannot be substantiated in virtue of the phenomenon of substitution in the area of personal or socio-political life.

Neither can it be established *historically*, it appears. Let it be recalled how Pannenberg established his doctrine historically. Historically Jesus' resurrection and the light it throws on his passion and death are the cornerstone of Pannenberg's thesis. For the resurrection demonstrates Jesus' death to have been his self-sacrifice to God (Jesus' sinlessness!) and his judges (Israel, humanity) to have been the true blasphemers. They deserve death. God laid upon Jesus what humanity deserved and deserves.

In his interpretation of the *vicariousness* of Jesus' death Pannenberg employed the concept of "inclusive substitution" which Marheineke coined: Jesus died the death all have incurred. We share in Jesus' death, i.e., our death is taken up into the community of Jesus' dying. Jesus' dying includes ours in itself and thereby transforms the latter into a dying in hope.

We raise two question. (1) *Is there sufficient evidence to back up this view?*

As we observed, in a very general sense Jesus' passion is substitutionary as bearing the consequence of others' sin. In this Jesus shares the common lot. Yet his passion is not *in our place* specifically. Why not? First, because every man still has to die his own death. Second, the new which arises from Jesus' resurrection is that our death no longer means curse, damnation, punishment. This distinguishes our death from Jesus'. *However, it is not Jesus' death which wrought the new hope in which we may live and die but Jesus' proclamation of God and his imminent kingdom as confirmed by his resurrection.* To be sure, Jesus' death plays an indispensable part in this,[26] *but not on account of its vicarious or penal character*! Rather, from the historical viewpoint, his death is ὑπερ ἡμῶν as the price and sacrifice paid in the process of revealing and establishing the new "convenant", the new *Heilsordnung (ordo salutis)*, the new design of life: *redemptio contra legem, remissio peccatorum sola gratia*. Third, our redemption, i.e. the hope in which we die, rather than to depend upon a vicarious penal death of Jesus, is tied to our communion with Jesus. This communion includes trust in Jesus' message, trust in the openness to God which Jesus demonstrated when he died (this openness being a real possibility now), trust in his resurrection as God's promise that what happened to Jesus will happen to us also, and discipleship in such openness and hope. Fourth, Jesus' death, seen from the resurrection, is the *paradigm par excellence of open existence* and assured the disciples of Jesus' love and faithfulness which, in the light of Jesus' resurrection, turned out to be God's own love. Historically, in Jesus' death the love, not the punishment, of God rises up. His death was not in man's place except in the very general sense in which it does not possess a particularity and in which it is of no salvific avail. No doubt, precisely in this general sense his was a unique exemplar in that he, and he alone, died completely innocently. But his innocence does not establish the vicariousness of his death. Historically his death was *on our behalf, a sacrifice of love for us.*

(2) *Is the historical evidence sufficient to establish the penal character of his death?* Our negative answer actually once more repudiates the vicarious character as well if this tenet, as in Pannenberg's case, is derived from the "inversion of standards". This inversion, necessitated by Jesus' resurrection, does not imply that "he bore their punishment", as we tried to demonstrate. To repeat, God changed the standards of his judgment, he abrogated the law. Thereby the accusation of that law including its penal measures are abrogated also. Pannenberg of course realizes this and argues that the guilt of Jesus' judges consisted of their condemning him whom

---

[26] *Vide supra*, pp. 176f.

God had legitimated and that blasphemy deserves death because it means to turn against and sever from the source of live, the creator.²⁷ What happened here is that Pannenberg tries to establish the guilt of Jesus' judges in a way that is compatible with the retroactive abrogation of the law. They committed blasphemy, and blasphemy deserves death. Neither of these two contentions is historically convincing, though. As was pointed out, the abrogation of God's law occurred *after* Jesus' condemnation; at the time of Jesus' condemnation the judges acted lawfully, not blasphemously. The retroactive nullification of the law cannot retroactively establish guilt. Neither can the judges' guilt be established independent of the law, as Pannenberg tries to do. Jesus' legitimation happened *post factum*, too. To proceed historically, the guilt of the judges, it seems, must be established in terms of their closedness vis-a-vis an advanced indirect self-revelation of God in Jesus prior to his death and resurrection. In other words, they share the universal human self-enclosure which hampers man's openness to God. But why does this behavior deserve death? Is it because the law penalizes such behavior by the death-penalty? However, the law is abrogated by Christ's resurrection! An act which abrogates the law cannot at the same time condemn by means of the law. Pannenberg, aware of this, argues that such behavior deserves death because it means to sever from the creator himself (the anthropological argument for the penal character of death), and this looks conclusive at first glance. However, Pannenberg overlooks the fact that in this interpretation — contrary to the concept of God he develops in his theology as a whole — he employs a notion of God which has its orientation in the image of the legislator *in spite of the fact that precisely this concept received its retroactive nullification with Jesus' resurrection, through which the law was abrogated and a new concept of God was revealed and retroactively validated.* In this case, in accordance with ethical and juridical standards, the retroactive efficacy of the abrogation of the law is fully acceptable for this time a debitum is cancelled, not constituted.

In other words, the concept of God, rising from Jesus' resurrection and confirming his proclamation, nullifies not only the law and its death penalty on blasphemy or separation from God. In addition, it makes it impossible to speak of any consequence that sin might have, as of God's punishment. Even death, anthropologically conclusively shown to be the consequences of un-open existence, appears as penal only as long as the law and its frame

---

²⁷ *Vide supra*, pp. 137 ff.

14 Neie: Pannenberg

of reference is valid. The law invalidated and God demonstrated to be the Father who loves and forgives, death is no penalty any more. Hence the judges of Jesus do not deserve the penalty for blasphemy — neither in accord with the law (in this case they did not commit blasphemy) nor in view of the law's abrogation; in this case their sin, as man's universally, leads to death but a death in hope on account of God's forgiveness.

Now once the judges have not incurred death in the *penal* sense there is no penalty which could be transfered to Jesus. Hence Jesus' death cannot be considered to possess penal character either. Q.e.d.

We come to the conclusion that neither the historical evidence nor a recourse to the phenomenon of substitution in life generally support the position that Jesus' death was vicarious and penal. Jesus' resurrection and its significance replaces the concept of God who judges *intra legem* by a concept of God who forgives. Its corrollary, the conceptuality of expiation or satisfaction or penal suffering *pro nobis*, is replaced by the conceptuality of sacrificial love, of love to the point of self-sacrifice unto death *on our behalf*. Such love of God achieves what we cannot achieve, without rendering our own love in Jesus' footsteps superfluous. On the contrary! Only in community with Jesus is death as our eternal, irrevocable *Schicksal* overcome; we can die *in hope*. Jesus was the last who *had* to die a death which meant condemnation and curse in his own understanding of it.

Some strands of Moltmann's position support our conclusion. Following Pannenberg, Moltmann holds,

> By his resurrection Jesus is qualified in his person to be the Christ of God. So his suffering and death must be understood to be the suffering of the Christ of God. Only in the light of his resurrection from the dead does his death gain that special, unique saving significance which it cannot achieve otherwise, even in the light of the life that he lived. . . . The resurrection 'does not evacuate the cross' (I Cor. 1:17), but fills it with eschatology and saving significance.[28]

But regarding an understanding of that saving significance, he says,

> . . . the early Jewish-Christian idea of the dying Christ as an ex-

---

[28] Jürgen Moltmann, *The Crucified God. The Cross of Christ as the Foundation and Criticism of Christian Theology* (New York, Evanston, San Francisco, London: Harper & Row, 1974), p. 182.

piatory offering for our sins, which has constantly been repeated throughout the tradition in varied forms, *cannot display any intrinsic theological connection with the kerygma of the resurrection.* One can hardly talk of the resurrection of an expiatory offering, any more than one can talk of the resurrection of the Son of God who sacrificed himself to satisfy the injured honor of God. Within the framework of the idea of expiatory offerings, both individuals and the people as a whole need expiation for their sins, so that the righteousness of the law of the covenant may be restored. The expiation was offered in the sacrificial cult of the Jerusalem temple. The exemplary martyrs' death of the righteous had atoning force for the whole community. The idea of the special expiatory power of the 'blood of Jesus' (Rom. 3:25; I. Cor. 10:16 etc.) has its root here. The phrase 'died for our sins' means that the cause of his suffering was our sins, the purpose of his suffering is expiation for us, the ground of his suffering is the love of God for us. *It is very difficult to harmonize the resurrection of Jesus with these interpretations of his death and very difficult to harmonize these interpretations of his death with his resurrection from the dead. For the ideas of expiatory offerings move consistently within the framework of the law:* sin transgresses the law, expiation restores the law. By sin man falls short of the righteousness of the law and comes under the accusation of the law; by expiation he is restored to the righteousness of the law. Its future concern is the *restitutio in integrum,* not the *beginning of a new life.*[29]

---

[29] *Ibid.*, p. 183 (italics mine). With regard to the appropriateness and appropriatability of the conceptuality of expiation and substitution in our context, Moltmann's position is ambivalent, though. On the one hand, he defends the *Sühnevorstellung* as useful. It can show "1. how little unrighteous man can achieve his own righteousness, how there can be no new future for him without the acceptance of guilt and liberation from it, at least through good intentions by which he only denies himself; 2. that as the Christ of God, Jesus took the place of helpless man as his representative and in so doing made it possible for man to enter into communion before God in which he otherwise could not stand and survive; 3. that in the death of Christ God himself has acted in favor of man." (p. 183) These statements are basically in agreement with Pannenberg. Point 1 matches with P.'s emphasis on an essential christology as over against a merely functional christology. Point 2 applies substitution to the whole of Jesus' existence *pro nobis.*

5. The pro nobis of Jesus' Death

We have tried to interpret the *pro nobis* of Jesus' death as *on our behalf* or *in our favor* against Pannenberg's conception of it as in our place in his staurology. The factual and historical element of substitution in Jesus' fate is negligible in the context of the question whether or not his passion is a vicarious penal one. That Jesus bore the consequences of human sin in the

---

Moltmann's predilection for the vocable *Stellvertreter* and *stellvertretend* (substitute, vicarious) may not distract from the fact that basically he means that Jesus is our *representative* (Thus the English transl. is accurate, even though philologically wrong). Pannenberg speaks of Jesus as our *Repräsentant*, chapt. 5 of *JGaM*. Hence *stellvertretend* means on our behalf, here. And in point 3 M. *expressis verbis* says that God acted *in favor of man* (not "of this man", as the tranl. erroneously renders "zugunsten dieser Menschen", but of humanity). We can agree with these points but do not believe that they render the *Sühnevorstellung* useful or justifiable. For this image always suggests God as the legislator. Then M. goes on, "But if we want to understand the cross strictly as the cross of Christ, that is of the risen Christ, we must go beyond the ideas of expiatory sacrifice which we find here." (p. 184)

In his following discussion of the meaning of Jesus' cross, to which we will refer more often, M. develops the following: (1) In accordance with the eschatological *Zeitsinn* (Apparently adopting Pannenberg's ontology, M. speaks of "the reversal of the noetic and ontic order", p. 184) Jesus died as the risen one and was incarnate as the coming one. (2) Hence his death gives meaning to his resurrection, not vice versa. "Thus the saving significance of his cross manifests his resurrection. It is not his resurrection that shows that his death on the cross took place for us, but on the contrary, his death on the cross 'for us' that makes relevant his resurrection 'before us'." (pp. 182f.) (3) In this *Zeitsinn* Jesus is the incarnation of the coming God into our flesh and into the death on the cross. Chiding P., I believe, M. goes on, "It is one-sided and a mistaken interpretation of his death on the cross if on the basis of the proleptic resurrection of Jesus one looks only into the future of God and to the end of history." (p. 184) (4) Only through his death does Jesus become the Christ for us. "Through his suffering and death, the Christ who was raised from the dead *before us* becomes the Christ *for us*, just as the 'God before us' becomes the 'God for us'. This anticipation of the resurrection of the dead in him gains its saving significance for us only through his offering for us on the cross. His prolepsis forms the basis of his pro-existence and in it becomes significant for us. Only when the one who was raised proleptically takes our place and dies does his prolepsis have saving significance for us. The basic New Testament idea of Christ as the representative ("Stellvertreter"!) for us, 'for all', must therefore be

sense that he was killed because his judges were blind to Jesus' proclamation, closed to God's message, does not take away their guilt. Rather it reveals Jesus' love: rather would he let himself be killed than abandon his mission and proclamation.

But Jesus' death was in our behalf because (1) his service, which led to his death as a consequence, brings us God's message of his coming kingdom inspite of our sin and thereby forgiveness of sin; (2) because his death is a

---

developed systematically from the concept of prolepsis used for the resurrection. The theology of Easter hope must be changed into the theology of the cross if it is to set our feet on the ground of the reality of the death of Christ and our own death." (pp. 184f.) (5) M. speaks of "stellvertretende Leiden". "Through his suffering and death, the risen Christ brings righteousness and life to the unrighteous and the dying. Thus the cross of Christ modifies the resurrection of Christ under the conditions of the suffering of the world so that it changes from being a purely future event to being an event of liberating love. Through his death the risen Christ introduces the coming reign of God into the godless present by means of representative (*stellvertretende!*) suffering. He anticipates the coming righteousness of God under the conditions of human injustice in the law of grace and in the justification of the godless by his death." (p. 185) Summarily, "therefore we must say that Christ's death on the cross is 'the significance' of his resurrection for us." (p. 186) (6) The concept of God implied in the *resurrection* of the crucified and in the *cross* of the risen one includes passion and death as an *opus Trinitatis ad intra*. But observe in what way! With reference to Paul, but apparently approvingly, M. says, "The suffering and dying of Jesus, understood as the suffering and dying of the Son of God, ... are works of God toward himself and therefore at the same time passions of God. God overcomes himself, God passes judgment on himself, God takes the judgment on the sin of man upon himself. He assigns to himself the fate that men should by rights endure." (p. 193) And, "He took upon himself the unforgivable sin and the guilt for which there is no atonement, together with the rejection and anger that cannot be turned away, so that in Christ we might become his righteousness in the world. Taken to its final consequence this means that God died that we might live." (p. 192)

How is this position to be characterized?

(1) M. adopts P.'s ontology, it seems, but not his epistemology and hermeneutic. Consequently he can take over Paul's emphasis on the *Heilssinn* of the cross as clue to the meaning of the resurrection *without having to look for the historical evidence in the pre-Easter life and conduct of Jesus which supports such salvific meaning*. He is spared the difficult task which P. undertook to prove the historical reality of the "vicarious" and "penal" with regard to Jesus' death by way of the inversion of standards and the blasphemy of Jesus' judges etc. We

service to us in its own right in as much as only Jesus' utter dedication to his mission unto death constitutes the self-sacrifice to God which in turn is the basis for the incarnation (more precisely: the co-supposition of the incarnation, viz. together with his resurrection). In his self-giving to the Father the man Jesus is the Son. Without it he would not be the Son and his resurrection would not constitute God's self-revelation. Were it not God's self-revelation, Jesus' work, death, and resurrection would be inconclusive and of no salvific avail. It would not be pro nobis.[30] One simply cannot

> think P. did not succeed in this task. But his effort was right and necessary. M., contrarily, takes the primitive Christian understanding of the *pro nobis* of the cross in the sense of *in our place* for granted. Because he does not follow P.'s hermeneutic M. also spares himself the task of *establishing* the *Umkehrung des Zeitsinns*, the ontology from the future. What does *Umkehrung des Zeitsinns* for M. mean? How is it known for him that reality is attached to such shift of perspective?
>
> (2) For M., against the historical evidence, the resurrection merely shows the Christ *before* us, not the Christ *for* us. Only his death turns his resurrection into *euangelion*. Only on its account Jesus' *Voransein* turns out to be his *Proexistenz* and thereby the God *prae nobis* is shown to be the God *pro nobis*. Pannenberg more accurately establishes the salvific character of the Christ event *on the basis of Christ's proclamation of the coming kingdom of God, confirmed by the resurrection* and by what the resurrection means in the context of its *Traditionsgeschichte*. Jesus' death is an indispensable soteriological moment in this but not, as for M., the sole ground on which the Christ event appears to be *Heilsgeschehen*.
>
> (3) In some statements of M.'s *Stellvertretung*, *stellvertretend* means representation, in others substitution, vicariousness. If I am not mistaken there is in his thought an unsolved – an insoluble – tension between the Christ and God who suffer out of love on our behalf and the God who suffers penally and vicariously the judgment on the unforgivable sin and the unexpiable guilt. In spite of his assertion that the *Sühnevorstellung* is inadequate he attempts to retain it to a degree over and beyond what he says about its kernel of truth (the three points above). Why? Because, it seems, he too is arrested by the concept of God as the legislator who redeems *intra legem*. It appears that M. has not explicated his concept of the *Recht der Gnade* thoroughly. Perhaps a judgmental connotation is ineradicably part and parcel of the understanding of Christ's suffering within the framework of Luther's *theologia crucis*. This impression does not take away from M.'s genuine achievement: his attempt to understand Jesus' passion as the Father's to which we will refer later and through which he improves upon P.
>
> [30] To this extent M. is right, "The basic New Testament idea of Christ as the representative 'for us', 'for all', must therefore be developed systematically from

agree with Pannenberg that

> The particular vicarious significance of Jesus' fate "for us" can be defended only on the basis of an understanding of human behavior generally which . . . sees individuals interwoven with one another in their actions and in the results of their actions and *certainly also in the ethical problem. Only in the tradition of such an understanding could the New Testament concepts about the vicarious significance of Jesus' fate have been construed.* They all presuppose the fundamental Israelite view of a relation of the deed to its consequence that goes far beyond the individual. (268, italics mine)

Actually, such New Testament interpretations of Jesus' death and their images as convey its substitutionary meaning no doupt presuppose the ancient Hebrew view of the transferability of guilt, but not the modern view which sees substitution in the realm of consequences, not of guilt.[31]

---

the concept of prolepsis used for the resurrection." (Jürgen Moltmann, *op. cit.*, p. 185). But it is preferable to say that the *pro nobis* of the Christ event must be systematically developed from this point of departure whatever it might mean, without *Festlegung* on the New Testament equation 'for us' = *Stellvertretung*.

[31] This ethical personalism also lies in the background of Dorothee Sölle's *Stellvertretung. Ein Kapitel Theologie nach dem "Tode* Gottes" (Stuttgart 1965), English *Christ the Representative* (SCM Press, 1967). She attacks the traditional doctrine of Christ's *Stellvertretung* by focussing on the untenableness of the ethical implications of the Old Protestant doctrine of the *oboedientia activa Christi* (munus sacerdotale). The identity and self-responsibility of the ones represented must be preserved. Consequently, as Moltmann puts it in his discussion of Sölle's main thesis, "To represent anyone therefore means to intercede for him for a time. Otherwise representation (*Stellvertretung*) is inconceivable in the personal age of modern times. In this way all magical and materialistic conceptions of the expiatory sacrifice and the substitute in God's judgment come to nothing when applied to Christ." (Moltmann, *op. cit.*, p. 262) We agree with Sölle's ethical position but must also endorse Moltmann's critique of S.'s main thesis. A clue lies in the distinction between representation and replacement. S. rightly sees that if representation is to preserve the longing for identity and is not to destroy it, it must not become replacement (Ersatzleistung). It seems accurate to say that Christ is our *Repräsentant* before God (Pannenberg's term in chapter V of *JGaM*,) not our *Ersatzmann*. But, against S., he *never* is man's Stellvertreter, not even temporarily, and he *always* is man's Repräsentant, not merely temporarily. Cf. M.'s critique of S.'s position, *op. cit.*, pp. 262–264.

Even if Pannenberg were right and transference of guilt were a common element of contemporary understanding of reality, it still could not serve to explain the early Christian position. For the primitive church Jesus' passion was a unique incident of substitution, a mystery of miraculous grace, not an example of a universal phenomenon.

CHAPTER IX

THE CROSS AS GOD'S PASSION – FURTHER QUESTIONS
AND SOME CONSTRUCTIVE SUGGESTIONS

1. The Rank of the Cross in the Christ Event

As our analysis suggested, Pannenberg sees the Christ event as subdivided into three pivotal events: Jesus' mission and proclamation, his cross, and his resurrection.[1] How are these related to each other? The contention that Pannenberg's christology rests upon the basic correlation of historical Jesus and resurrection and that Pannenberg subsumes the cross under this correlation had to be repudiated.[2] The ontic foundation of the *vere deus* and the *vere homo* consits of three pillars, not two: Jesus' claim, his self-sacrifice, and his confirmation.[3] Here Jesus' proclamation in its formal significance as claim is particularly relevant. The historical which includes Jesus' dedication and self-sacrifice, and the eschatological in its proleptic *Ereignung* condition each other and are co-suppositions in Pannenberg's christology.

Regarding their soteriological significance, our whole investigation leads to the conclusion that here, too, all three events under discussion are perfectly correlated in Pannenberg's theology. If we want to describe this correlation abstractly it could be called apocalyptic-*universalgeschichtlich*-

---

[1] B. Klappert, *op. cit.*, p. 54, speaks of the three *Größen* "historischer Jesus-Kreuz-Auferstehung".

[2] *Vide supra*, pp. 178ff. In Klappert's conceptualy "historischer Jesus" means the proclamation and mission of Jesus, mainly his *claim*, excluding his dedication and self-sacrifice.

[3] Pannenberg's statement, "Measured by the imminent nearness of these events, it must have been of secondary significance for Jesus whether he himself would have to endure death before the end came. The truth of his proclamation did not need to depend on this" (66, *JGaM*), is – contrary to Klappert, *op. cit.*, p. 57 – no objection to this. The absence of a conscious inclusion of his death as a salvific work in Jesus' self-understanding does in no way question the soteriological rank of the cross. On the contrary, it is its condition! For only because Jesus did *not* possess such a vision was his death a complete and absolute self-giving. The absence of any comprehension is the presupposition that permits us to understand his death as a self-sacrifice in which Jesus sought nothing for himself. Cf. *supra* pp. 77.

incarnational.[4] Within this correlation no factor is soteriologically conclusive without the other two, and the factors are of equal weight. The rank of the cross, while representing the climax and apex of Jesus' dedication to God, has – under the aspect of its *Heilsbedeutung* – no higher rank than the other two factors, just as it is of no lower.

The mutual interdependence of the factors of this correlation is obvious when we once more, briefly, name the yield of Jesus' death. We do so in three sentences, each followed by two sentences which show this interdependence.

(1) Jesus' *death* achieves his identity, thus confirms his proclamation that imparts forgiveness, new life, and hope for the ultimate total redemption. *But*: Jesus' identity is in need of verification by his *resurrection*. What Jesus *proclaimed* throws light on why he suffered.

(2) Jesus' *death* achieves the open existence, the new life before God to which man is called, and shows Jesus the prototype of man. *But*: Only Jesus' *resurrection* clarifies that his death was a sacrifice to God. Without his *proclamation* his death would not be capable of being interpreted as the realization of that existence to which Jesus leads.

(3) Without his *death* the law would not be abrogated, and its abrogation is the negative side of the law of love which Christ proclaims as God's own attitude toward us and will for us. *But*: Only the *resurrection* shows Jesus to have been the innocent victim of the law and the law to be abrogated. Such abrogation makes sense only in the light of the new law of grace which is implied in Jesus' *proclamation*. It is evident that in each of these three instances it is not his death alone but *his death as encompassed by his proclamation and his being resurrected that form the matrix of meaning to determine the salvific relevance of his death*.[5] In other words,

---

[4] Klappert, *op. cit.*, p. 55, argues that the *Grundkorrelation* in P.'s christology is the *apokalyptisch-universalgeschichtliche Korrelation "Jesus-Auferweckung"*. In his understanding, *universalgeschichtlich* includes the element of incarnation as *Derivat* from the theologoumenon of God's proleptic self-revelation in the resurrection. We propose to add "incarnational" to determine this correlation in order to point to the element of dedication and self-sacrifice in the "achievement" of the incarnation.

[5] Therefore Moltmann is wrong when he says, "Through his suffering and death, the Christ who was raised from the dead *before us* becomes the Christ *for us*, just as the 'God *before us'* becomes the 'God *for us'*. The anticipation of the resurrection of the death in him gains its saving significance for us only through his

Heilssinn also pertains to Jesus' prolepsis (resurrection); not first or only his death constitutes his *Proexistenz*. *Even if one concedes that his prolepsis as such is ambiguous to the extent that resurrection in its Traditionsgeschichte may mean damnation as well as life, this ambiguity is surely cleared away not first by Jesus' death on our behalf but already by his proclamation and its implicit granting of forgiveness.*

2. The Christ Event as Revelation

The cross has its saving significance as one factor among three of equal rank which together form the Christ event which is God's proleptic self-revelation. In this, Jesus on the cross both reveals and creates *das Heil* — within the described correlation. Jesus' death creates in that it reveals and reveals in that it creates the breakthrough of the *homo incurvatus in se* and his hopeless existence. To describe its telos, its *pro nobis*-character, we have not used the concepts *Stellvertreter* or representative (in the sense of substitute, deputy) for Jesus Christ. Preferable is Pannenberg's concept of *Repräsentant* in the sense of prototype of the new humanity. For these first

---

offering for us on the cross. His prolepsis forms the basis of his pro-existence and in it becomes significant for us. Only when the one who was raised proleptically takes our place and dies does his prolepsis have saving significance for us." (*Op. cit.*, pp. 184f.) While M. remarkably clearly recognizes that the cross has no meaning without Jesus' resurrection, understood as proleptic eschatological event, he does not see the salvific significance implicit in the resurrection from the dead itself which is constituted (a) by its meaning in the Jewish-apocalyptic *Traditionszusammenhang* and (b) by what *Auferweckung* means in the context of what a phenomenological analysis yields with regard to human hope. Moreover, M. completely disregards the *message* of the one who was raised. If one interprets Jesus' resurrection as confirmation of his message in its content and implicit claim, which is cogent, how can one deny his resurrection a *Heilsbedeutung für uns?* Cf. also foot-note 29, pp. 201–204, *supra*.

And why should first and only Jesus' *death* for us solve the problem of theodicy (cf. M., p. 184)? At any rate, it is not better answered by M. than by P. It equally applies to P.'s thought when M. says, "If resurrection has already been anticipated in him, then 'resurrection, life, and righteousness' come through the death of this one man in favor of those who have been delivered over to death through their unrighteousness" (op. cit., p. 185) However, these gifts rise not from Jesus' *vicarious* death and not from his death alone.

terms suggest that he represents us before a court, a forum, a parliament or the like and thus fulfills requirements or demands in our place. In every such instant looms the concept of God as the legislator. Our analysis suggests that we pass up the traditional forensic mode of thought in our soteriological thinking. God is the Father, and a father does things for me out of love. The question of my own obligation is not raised in this context. What Christ does is in man's behalf, not in his place. To the extent that I *could not* or *cannot* do it myself, it cannot be in my place. To the extent that I am expected to do it myself, it may not be vicariously taken care of. For a non-legalist, non-juridical understanding, Christ's grace is not imputing righteousness but provides enabling and liberating grace.[6] The resurrection reveals Jesus to be man's *Urbild* and *Vorbild*. He breaks the way which we are to follow. His breaking this way is *pro nobis*; we cannot do it. His opening of this liberation for us in the sense of forgiveness and new existence, open to God, is his work. But to go this way is ours. He who sees it (viz. the love of God, the human existence open to and for God's love) will trust it and follow it. For — in Pannenberg's sense — seeing is believing.

As regards the nomenclature of the Reformation doctrine of justification, it seems appropriate to retain the concepts of *pro nobis/pro me* and, with reservations, *extra nos* as expressions of God's unconditional love and forgiveness and of *in Christo, in ecclesia*, and *per Spiritum sanctum* as expressions of the fact that only in communion with Jesus we attain to the fulfillment of our existence, viz., when our existence is personally integrated in dependence upon and dedication to the Father, as was Jesus'.[7]

The concept of *justificatio impiorum* is ambivalent in that it well expresses the unconditional love of God for the sinner as a *creatio ex nihilo* while the term *justificatio* itself unfortunately suggests a legal relationship. However, the concepts of *iustitia aliena* and *propter Christum* should be relinquished, it seems. They suggest the traditional emphasis on the *vicarious penal suffering* or *vicarious* active obedience of Christ which distorts the concept of God as the Father to which Jesus' proclamation and resurrection and the concomitant abrogation of the law give rise. This also

---

[6] Cf. Moltmann's (*op. cit.*, pp. 263 f.) emphasis on the innovative, irreplaceable work of Christ liberating in his debate with Dorothee Sölle.

[7] "Through the Spirit of sonship, the Son of God wants to become person-building, existence-integrating power in all men." (*JGaM*, p. 346)

applies to some degree to the concept *extra nos*. Also these concepts emphasize the "inspite of" − nature of God's love while actually God's love is so deep and so forgiving not inspite but precisely on account of man's sin and failure.[8] The inspite of-ness requires emphasis in a legal frame, not in a personal one. When personal love abounds one will not mention the fact that the other is so little worthy of love. One will reassure the other rather than put him (her) down.[9]

3. What is Love?

Our view proposes that the cross does not represent God's judgment but sheer love.

This view is often countered by the opinion that sheer love be tantamount to permissiveness, a laissez-faire-attitude of weakness, a condoning of sin. God's love in order to be precious and trustworthy has to include his holiness in the sense of justice and wrath, it is held. Love as indulgence would result in man's taking God not seriously and in a loss of man's responsibility before God. E.g., Paul Tillich says, ". . . justice is the structural form of love without which it would be sheer sentimentality."[10] And, ". . . there are no conflicts in God between his reconciling love and his retributive justice."[11] Now one expects him to share Pannenberg's understanding of the atonement as the vicarious penal death of Christ and is prepared to counter that justice in the sense of retribution (*iustitia vindicativa*) and forgiveness as remission are mutually exclusive. But Tillich's further statements show that he does not share Pannenberg's position; atonement for him, too, means divine removal of guilt and punishment. Justice for him is "the act through which God lets the self-destructive consequences of existential estrangement go their way. He cannot remove them because they belong to the structure of being itself . . ."[12] One probably must agree that God lets the consequences of evil go

---

[8] I am indepted for this insight to Prof. Bernard M. Loomer.
[9] According to Paul, not the law but God's goodness leads man to repentance. Luther's doctrine of the *secundus usus legis* is incompatible with Paul at this point.
[10] Paul Tillich, *Systematic Theology*, vol. ii: *Existence and the Christ* (Chicago: University of Chicago Press, 1957), p. 174.
[11] *Ibid.*   [12] *Ibid.*

their way, but only to a certain extent! For these consequences are countered by the healing, renewing, transforming forces of love. Should one not call the goal of these forces, healing and restoration, justice rather than apply this concept to God's letting evil produce its consequences? Tillich may have this in mind in the following sentence. "The exercise of justice is the working of his love, resisting and breaking what is against love."[13] This is agreeable except for the image of coercion which the verbs convey. How can one break injustice without destroying rather than transforming the sinner? The impression is that God's justice as letting the consequences of evil work themselves out, which God cannot stop, and as the work of love that aims at healing and removal of such consequences contradict each other, in Tillich's statements. Be that as it may, Tillich ultimately does not view justice as *justitia* in a forensic sense in spite of his use of the concept of retributive justice. His point is that God does not merely overlook evil and leave things as they are.

The position according to which love and punishment belong together is consistently represented in contemporary theological literature by Emil Brunner. He says, "The message of the Cross is first of all the revelation of the incomprehensible, unconditional love of God. . . . Secondly, the revelation of righteousness is combined with love. God takes his own law seriously."[14] He goes on,

> Forgiveness *sans phrase*, without further ado, is exposed to a terrible misunderstanding, namely, that "it doesn't matter" if we do break the law, because God can easily overlook it! Forgiveness is not only something undeserved, but it is "unjust". Everything that shakes the idea of merit, shakes that of righteousness too, it throws doubt on moral earnestness, on responsibility. *The moral shock which the idea of acquittal from all guilt evokes in the ethically "serious" person is justified.* "Mere" forgiveness may lead to a careless disregard of moral obligation. Hence the Atoning death of His Son is a "sign" that God sees this moral danger, and thus gives us a "proof of His righteousness", lest we should doubt His Wisdom.[15]

Or he says, "The removal of the reality of wrath is the Atonement."[16]

---

[13] *Ibid.*
[14] Emil Brunner, *The Christian Doctrine of Creation and Redemption* (Philadelphia: Westminster Press, 1952), p. 295.
[15] *Ibid.* (italics mine).   [16] *Ibid.*, p. 297.

It seems that here two positions are opposed to each other in a way that is in principle unbridgeable. The reason for this understanding possibly lies in a very different intuition of what love, goodness, and trust consist of. Maybe in the final analysis only biography can account for this intuition in terms of what concepts of God, father, justice, and love have determined the consciousness of a theologian in his upbringing through the standards of his parents, school, church, and society at large. For the position we try to propose it is not retaliation, punishment, retributive justice which safeguards sheer love from being mistaken for cheap and inconsequential indulgence, but the suffering of the one who loves from his love which bears the weakness, sin, and rebellion of the beloved one. Only such sheer love invites trust, is ethically trustworthy and a refuge for *das angefochtene Gewissen*. It seems that for contemporary sensitivities the kind of love Brunner ascribes to God actually is something one will be highly distrustful of. Here the Abelardian intuition better meets our modern sensitivity, and Schleiermacher and Ritschl are more contemporary than Brunner.[17] This unavenging love of God which freely gives and no one has to "pay" for but God himself "pays", effectively invites us not to concentrate on our sin and guilt but on his forgiveness and thus makes trust psychologically possible. Nothing that happens can be considered to be of penal character anymore in the Christian's consciousness. As Conzelmann puts it,

---

[17] This is true also of J. C. K. von Hofmann who abandoned "the accepted substitutionary satisfaction theory with its concentration on the death of Christ and the overcoming of divine wrath. Rather, for Hofmann, Christ appeared as man on earth as the historical actualization of the eternal inner-divine will of love to restore the fellowship with God, broken by sin. He did this not so much by an act of dying as by a human form of being and willing and doing that throughout (thus also unto death) was characterized by obedience to the divine call. Thus the love and fidelity of Jesus to the Father, reflecting the inner-divine love of Son to Father, mediates a new relation of God and man, and those who receive this divine act in faith become participants in the new humanity of which Christ is the head. Christ is not a substitute in the sense of doing something for man that man is therefore not obliged to do. Rather he restores a relationship which is, in him as the new Adam, restored in man." So Claude Welch, *Protestant Thought in the 19th Century, vol. i: 1799-1870* (New Haven and London: Yale University Press, 1972), p. 225. The resemblance to Pannenberg's position is striking except for P.'s staurology which we tried to identify as *Fremdkörper*. A position like this would follow from P.'s presuppositions if consistently applied.

Wrath is not an ingredient of the gospel. Its content is not that God is gracious, but also angry. It does not say anthing about what God is in himself . . . Conclusion: the church does not have to preach judgment and grace. It cannot use the wrath of God as a pedagogical means of forcing men to faith through fright. The wrath of God is not to be played with, even pastorally. Preaching has to offer unconditional salvation, which is there in the cross. The fear that grace will then be too cheap is unfounded. It only arises if grace is not defined exactly as grace, if it is debased and made the indulgence *des lieben Gottes*.[18]

It is the *suffering of love itself* which distinguishes grace from mere indulgence *des lieben Gottes*. Since everyone knows through experience how painful love is, it is no real option for anyone to take grace as un-costly indulgence.

In his discussion of the doctrinal types of atonement theories Tillich ascribes the power of the satisfaction theory to its penal and vicarious character.

Whenever he (the Christian) prays that God may forgive his sins because of the innocent suffering and death of the Christ, he accepts both the demand that he himself suffer infinite punishment and the message that he is released from guilt and punishment by the substitutional suffering of the Christ. This point gave the Anselmian doctrine its strongest psychological effect and kept it alive in spite of its dated legalistic terminology and its quantitative measureing of sin and punishment. The discovery of an often deeply hidden guilt feeling has given us a new key for an explanation of the tremendous effect of the Anselmian theory on personal piety, hymns, liturgies, and much of Christian teaching and preaching. A system of symbols which gives the individual the courage to accept himself in spite of his awareness that he is unacceptable has every chance to be accepted itself.[19]

---

[18] Hans Conzelmann, *An Outline of the Theology of the New Testament* (New York and Evanston: Harper & Row, 1969), p. 241. Contrary to Conzelmann and following Pannenberg we take the Christ event to reveal not only what God *does to us* but as God's *essential self-revelation* – with the reservation that it is proleptic.

[19] Paul Tillich, *op. cit.* p. 173.

Tillich's view is undoubtedly accurate. It demonstrates the psychological attractiveness of Anselm's theory within a certain framework of thought. In his principles of a doctrine of the atonement Tillich himself leaves this framework behind.

If it is our deepest intuition that *Strafe muß sein!*[20] (popular German saying!) and guilt cannot be got rid of unless it is paid for, the Anselmian or any theory of vicarious *Strafleiden* will be most attractive indeed. The church's proclamation no doubt underlined this intuition; the Anselmian theory, at any rate, implies and confirms it. Given this intuition, the data to which Tillich calls our attention carry weight. However, this intuition can be and should be replaced by a gospel that does not reaffirm but rescind man's deep guilt feelings by pointing out that man is acceptable. God accepted man. Theories like the Anselmian and their implications add to, do not heal, selfhatred, guilt feelings, ultimately hate of life and of God.[21]

What is love? John Macquarrie's understanding of the cross supports the direction our analysis has taken.

> *The self-giving of Christ is continuous with the self-giving of God . . . the self-giving of Christ, understood as the new sacrifice in which priest and victim are one and the same, brings God's constant self-giving for his creation right into the creation. Here that absolute self-giving, which is of the essence of God, has appeared in history in the work of Jesus Christ,* and this work is a work *on behalf of* man, a work of grace. It not only makes a demand (as an example does) but it lays hold on the human race, empowers a change of direction, brings the dynamic activity of God into the midst of human society.[22]

---

[20] "There must be punishment!"

[21] Cf. Edward V. Stein, *Guilt: Theory and Therapy* (Philadelphia: Westminster Press, 1968); David E. Roberts, *Psychotherapy and a Christian View of Man; an Examination of the Relations between Two Complementary Traditions of Spiritual Health* (New York: Charles Scribner's Sons, 1950); Karl Augustus Menninger, Man Against Himself (New York: Harcourt, Brace and Company, 1938); Oskar Pfister, *Christianity and Fear; a Study in History and in the Psychology and Hygiene of Religion* (London: G. Allen & Unwin, 1948); John Hick, *Evil and the God of Love* (London: Macmillan, 1966).

[22] John Macquarrie, *Principles of Christian Theology* (New York: Charles Scribner's Sons, 1966), p. 289. According to Macquarrie, "One model (of the atonement) that, as it seems to me, has usually been developed in such a way that it becomes

The concept of sacrifice well expresses the permanent unavoidable activity (passion) of love itself. Macquarrie uses it in the noncultic sense although he does not say so *expressis verbis*. To give means to extend something to someone gratis. *Sacrificial* giving includes, in addition, the element of pain or loss in such giving. This is essentially what sheer love is doing. Love always is sacrificial in that it includes pain from the lack of love and response of the beloved one as well as the pain on account of love's sharing the pain of the beloved one because it identifies with him/her. The disappointment in love, viz. the rejection of the loving one by the loved one, constitutes the "loss" in sacrificial love. On the human level love's self-giving might include the loss of one's physical life also.

4. *Christ's Suffering in Relation to God the Father's*

Macquarrie sees the self-giving of Christ as continuous with the self-giving of God. So do we. How can we relate the suffering of the Son more closely to that of the Father? It has been our contention that, in opposition to Pannenberg's presentation in chapter VII but in concert with the main line of his christology and soteriology, the suffering of Jesus is not to be understood as a vicarious penal suffering which God laid on Jesus but as the passion which Jesus endured in consequence of his absolute dedication to the Father and unconditional dependence upon and openness before God.

Disregarding Pannenberg's staurology in chapter VII of his christological treatise, could we relate Jesus' cross to God the Father in a way different from Pannenberg's course but still in keeping with his main line of reasoning, i.e., on his terms? Pannenberg himself is in favor of further developing this aspect[23] and considers Moltmann's concern with the

---

sub-Christian in its thought of God and its idea of reconciliation, is the notion of substitutionary punishment . . . But this view of the atonement, . . . even if it could claim support from the Bible or the history of theology, would still have to be rejected because of the affront which it offers to reason and conscience." (p. 284)

[23] In a postscript to E. Frank Tupper, *The Theology of Wolfhart Pannenberg* (Philadelphia: Westminster Press, 1973) Pannenberg says (p. 305), "When a revised version of my Christology . . . is undertaken, I will supplement the interpretation given in the chapter of the crucifixion by a discussion of the

'crucified God' as a supplementation to his own deliberations.[24] Trying to supplement his doctrine at this point, how shall we proceed?

First of all, such supplementation is justifiable only if it is necessary. It may not be a theological *akademische Pflichtübung*, a game, l'art pour l'art, a formal nicety. There should be a systematic need for it. Moreover, an understanding of Jesus' suffering as an act or a passion of God needs to pass the same epistemological and hermeneutical criteria as the other doctrines. Now a formal necessity for an attempt at such a supplementation seems to

> action of God in the cross of Jesus. That seems to be precisely what Dr. Tupper is asking for. Beause of my approach from the anthropological-historical perspective ('from below'), I concentrated my attention on the inherent meaning of the events rather than on a divine intention attributed to them, although I did relate the historical events to the activity of God. Only after the Christology was published was I able to clarify certain aspects in the doctrine of God to my own satisfaction so that I could dare now to speak of a divine intention in historical events. As a consequence, in relation to the crucifixion, as in other respects, the self-explication of God in the history of Jesus will get closer attention when I am able someday to revise the text of that book."
>
> Dr. Tupper accepts P.'s understanding of Jesus' passion as penal and vicarious. For his critique cf. pp. 299f. He chiefly criticizes that "the interpretation of the crucifixion ... fails to clarify the material relationship of the cross to God's coming kingdom". He goes on, "If the relationship of the cross to the Kingdom were clarified, perhaps the interpretative significance of the cross for the resurrection itself would emerge – without making the cross the central interpretative category for Jesus' mission on the one side or for the resurrection on the other. To be sure, Pannenberg's interpretation of the cross is of considerable soteriological significance; however, the theological rationale for the 'must' of the cross between Jesus' proclamation of the Kingdom and its anticipatory arrival in the resurrection is lacking. Why did God allow Jesus to endure the Godforsakenness of the cross . . . ? Was the cross prerequisite to the eschatological appearance of God's Kingdom? P. fails to answer these crucial questions." (*op. cit.*, p. 300)
>
> If our understanding was accurate, this critique is unfounded. Firstly, Tupper overlooks that the cross is an indispensable cosupposition of the resurrection in its "achievement" and demonstration (the ontological and noetical importance) of Jesus' identity as the Son, without which the Christ event were no proleptic self-revelation of God, etc. Secondly, P. understands, so we gathered, the cross as materially related to the Kingdom of God in that it opens, by Jesus' utmost openness and dedication, the gate to the kingdom for us. Cf. *supra*, p. 208.

[24] Personal communication, November 14, 1975.

emerge from the fact that, since Pannenberg's staurology is neither historically verifiable nor intelligible to the contemporary *Wirklichkeitsverständnis*, the cross might speak more profoundly to man if Jesus' passion is related to God the Father's love in a way which matches with the experience of suffering, death, and love on the human level.[25] If such supplementation yields a profounder understanding of Jesus' message, it is not only permissable; it is indeed called for! And if such understanding works with elements of our contemporary *Wirklichkeitsverständnis* and is verifiable in this context, it has passed Pannenberg's hermeneutical test from the start. But how about the historical evidence for an extrapolation of the Father's passion from Jesus'? Has not Pannenberg said all one can say on those grounds when he pointed to the self-sacrificial love of the man Jesus which realizes what his message proclaims as regards the openness of existence before and for God?

It appears that the historical evidence not only permits but requires us to envisage God the Father's love and passion in, with, and under Jesus' love and passion. There is an inner systematic compulsion for such an extension of our perspective. For the historical Christ event proffers a concept and self-definition of God which, compared to the concept of God in Jewish apocalyptic, contains a novel element. If we take seriously Pannenberg's concept of the historicalness of truth, even of God's indirect self-revelations, and the corollary futuristic ontology whereby all revelation is open to be surpassed and no reality is final prior to God's ultimate selfrevelation, then the prolepsis of God's ultimate self-revelation through Jesus' resurrection in the Christ event *must not be interpreted so as to match with*

---

[25] This direction has been taken most comprehensively in a compelling way by Daniel Day Williams, *The Spirit and the Forms of Love* (New York and Evanston: Harper & Row, 1968), chapter IX: The Atonement. W. remarks, "There is a remarkable fact which appears when we look at the history of the doctrine of the atonement. It is this — that none of the traditional theories has taken as its point of departure and its key an experiential analysis of the work of love. . . . in interpreting the how of redemption the question has too rarely been asked, 'What is the meaning of atonement as love doing its distinctive work in dealing with guilt and self-destruction?' If God's work is reconciliation . . . one would suppose that the profoundest insight into the 'how' of reconciliation would come from the experience of reconciliation between persons." (p. 176) W.'s method, based on Whiteheadian metaphysics, is compatible with Pannenberg's use of anthropology for purposes of verification.

the ancient Hebrew or the apocalyptic concept of God but, conversely, becomes the point of orientation for a better, more truthful understanding of God. The proclamation of Jesus with its implied message of forgiveness of sin and Jesus' resurrection as abrogation of the law abrogated the concept of God the legislator as well and heralded in God the Father who is passible, who operates *extra legem*, and who provides his own conditions of operation. And if we take seriously Pannenberg's course of establishing Jesus' identity as the Son of the Father and if, on account of God's self-definition as love through Jesus' proclamation and resurrection, Jesus' passion is no longer intelligible as penal or in place of man, *then it must be interpreted so as to be compatible with this novel self-definition of God. That is, then it may, and must, be understood as the suffering of God who suffers because he loves man. Because he loves man, he shares*[26] *man's suffering from and under man. God bears and endures what man does to him and what man does to and endures from one another.*[27]

Now from Pannenberg's thesis of God's proleptic self-revelation in the Christ event, does there not follow the participation of the Son in the fate of the man Jesus, when viewed from hind-sight? Moreover, do not the Father and the Spirit suffer also? We briefly turn to such statements of Pannenberg's which construct the basis of a trinitarian doctrine and permit us to see the framework within which Pannenberg might explicate the cross as an act of God once he sets out to do so.

It has been shown ... that Jesus' person cannot be separated from God's essence if Jesus in person is God's self-revelation. However,

---

[26] Similarly Paul Tillich, *op. cit.*, p. 976. Substitutional suffering is "a rather unfortunate term and should not be used in theology. God participates in the suffering of existential estrangement, but his suffering is not a substitute for the suffering of the creature. Neither is the suffering of the Christ a substitute for the suffering of man. But the suffering of God, universally and in the Christ, is the power which overcomes creaturely self-destruction by participation and transformation. Not substitution, but free participation, is the character of the divine suffering." – One would take issue with T. only on the "free". For love *necessarily* participates in the suffering of the other.

[27] For the history of this idea in theology and philosophy of religion, beginning with the Biblical prophets, cf. J. Moltmann, *op. cit.* pp. 267–278, and the literature cited there. Especially important for the development and use of this idea is Jewish religious philosophy and theology and process theology. M. does not inform about the latter's achievement.

Jesus understood himself as set over against the God whom he called Father. He distinguished the Father from himself. (158)

If Jesus' history and his person now belong to the essence, to the divinity of God, *then the distinction that Jesus maintained between himself and the Father also belongs to the divinity of God.* (159, italics by the author)

God's essence as it is revealed in the Christ event thus contains within itself the twofoldness, the tension, and the relation of Father and Son. The deity of Jesus Christ cannot therefore have the *sense of undifferentiated identity with the divine nature, as if in Jesus God the Father himself had appeared in human form and suffered on the cross.* (159f., my italics)

That the distinctiveness of Father and Son is a distinction in the essence of God himself is the beginning point for the doctrine of the Trinity systematically as well as historically. (169)

We must proceed from the knowledge of Jesus' divinity attained from the message about Christ if we want to understand the divinity of the Spirit. . . . Because Jesus Christ, as the revelation of God, is one with the essence of God himself, the Spirit of Christ dwelling in Christians and going out from Jesus is the Spirit of God himself. (174)

The independence of the Spirit, which became increasingly clear with increasing distance from the Easter event and with the decreasing expectation of the nearness of the *eschaton*, can be taken as an indication that a third independent moment in God's essence is to be assumed only when a personal relation and thus also a difference of the Spirit from the Son can be demonstrated. . . . it is the basis for our knowledge of the independence of the Spirit as a person over against the Son and the Father, *because he leads us to glorify the Son and the Father*, and thus demonstrates himself to be distinct from both. (179, italics mine)

If Father, Son, and Spirit are distinct but coordinate moments in the accomplishment of God's revelation, then they are so in God's eternal essence as well. But how are they one single God in spite of such differentiation? (180)

Christ's Suffering in Relation to God the Father's

Of the three most important theological paths to solve this problem (doctrine of procession; relational theory; Hegel) Pannenberg favors the third which he calls the "theory of the self-sublimation of the three Persons in the unity of God." (180)

> In his treatment of the doctrine of the Trinity in his *Philosophy of Religion* Hegel was the first to so elaborate the concept of "person" in such a way that God's unity becomes understandable precisely from the reciprocity of the divine Persons. (181)

> The God who reveals himself is essentially person. . . . as Hegel says, it is "the character of the person, of the subject, to relinquish its isolation, Morality, love, is just this: to relinquish its particularity, its particular personality (Persönlichkeit) to extend it to universality – friendship is the same. . . . The truth of personality is just this: to win it through immersion, through being immersed in the other." Through this profound thought that the essence of the person is to exist in self-dedication to another person, Hegel understood the unity in the Trinity as the unity of reciprocal self-dedication, thus, as a unity that only comes into existence through the process of reciprocal dedication. Thereby he conceived God's unity in an intensity and vitality never before achieved, not by striking off the threeness of persons, but precisely by means of the sharpest accentuation of the concept of the personality of Father, Son, and Spirit. . . . With the exception of the problematic derivation of the Trinity from the concept of Spirit which Hegel shared with tradition, his idea is especially suited to the relation of Jesus to the Father and of the Father to him, as well as to that of the Spirit, who glorifies both, to the Father and the Son, as it is expressed in the New Testament. (182f.)[28]

> An intimation of this perception of the unity of the three persons grounded in complete reciprocal dedication is already to be seen in the patristic doctrine of the perichoresis, the reciprocal indwelling of the Three Persons in one another. (183)

What does Pannenberg say here, and his christology altogether, regarding our present concern? Firstly, does he teach that the Son suffers

---

[28] The citation from Hegel is to be found in *Lectures on the Philosophy of Religion* (Humanities Press, Inc., 1962), vol. iii, pp. 24f.

on the cross? To say so in a traditional mode of thought, *viz.* within a two-natures-concept, would compromise Pannenberg's understanding that the subject of passion and death is none other than the historical Jesus in his authentic humanity. To jeopardize the latter would also render the tragedy of his genuine God-forsakenness, and thus his self-sacrifice, unreal. But for Pannenberg, as we recall, the Son-identity is achieved precisely in and through the self-dedication of the man Jesus to God the Father, and precisely and only in this Jesus *is* the Son. Hence the eternal Son *did* suffer on the cross because exactly as suffering man Jesus is the Son. Jesus' complete self-dedication achieves the unity with God (Hegel), as the resurrection shows and establishes.

Secondly, does Pannenberg teach that the Father suffers on the cross on account of that unity? The Father does not suffer or die on the cross because the historical distinction and over-againstness of Jesus and God in Jesus' consciousness is part and parcel of God's essence. This distinction is *in* God. The Father laid the suffering on the Son. Pannenberg does not say more. The brute fact of the historical distinction Jesus-God which, if the history and person of Jesus is God's self-revelation, must be in God, forbids Pannenberg to see the Father as the subject of the passion. The subject of the passion is the man; from hind-sight it is the Son. It is not the Father. *Because he takes the historical reality so seriously he avoids speculation on the participation of the Father in the passion of the Son* which Hegel's concepts of reciprocal self-dedication of the Persons of the trinity would have opened up, and in fact, *does* open up. For, following Hegel, the distinction does not preclude the unity but, conversely, enables it. And since "Jesus' history and his person now belong to the essence, to the divinity of God" (159) this must be true of the passion in this history and person as well.

For within Pannenberg's trinitarian thinking one could argue that the Father suffers with the Son (or *from* the Son's suffering) in as much as he dedicates himself to the Son just as the Son dedicates himself to the Father. This dedication (a) *necessarily includes participation in, identification with, and assumption of the passion* of the Son and conversely. Precisely in his love-dedication that includes such participation the Father is the Father of the Son. Moreover, this dedication, as Hegel says, (b) *extends to universality (Allgemeinheit). Thus Father, Son, and Spirit do not only live in reciprocal self-dedication among themselves but each of them also in dedication to universality, i.e., to the creatures.* This concept of the trinitarian God would permit Pannenberg, and permits us, to speak of the suffering of the Father on the cross. For it is an *opus trinitatis ad extra* in which the three Persons participate, and this love is at the same time an expression of their reciprocal self-dedication as it is an expression of their common dedication to the creatures. In this way God, on account of his love as dedication to the creatures, immerses into and participates in their passion, suffering, and forsakenness, as we have tried to understand God's acting on the cross above.[29]

In this fashion the tension between the immanent and economic trinity is overcome, just as the separation of what God is for us and what he is in himself.

The fact that the Son and the Father realize themselves in their unity precisely by their reciprocal self-dedication and common dedication to the creatures, which includes participation in the others' suffering, would enable Pannenberg to teach that God in his love for humanity and all creatures suffers on the cross the passion of love — *without compromising his principle, historically established, of the distinction of Father, Son and Spirit in the essence of God itself*. To say, then, that God suffers on the cross means that the Persons of the trinity participate in Jesus' passion on the cross — as in *all* suffering of *all* creatures on *all* crosses.

The direction of our constructive effort is supported by Pannenberg's

---

[29] *Vide supra*, p. 219. That P. plans to work in the same direction is expressed in his latest article (*vide infra* pp. 224ff.) and in his postscript to the still unpublished 5th German edition of *JGaM*. I am indebted to Prof. Pannenberg for providing me with its text. Here he says, "Die sich an der Geschichte Jesu orientierende Betrachtungsweise ist durch ihre Begründungsleistung für Aussagen, die sonst nur als unvermittelte Behauptungen auftreten können, hinlänglich ausgewiesen. Aber eine Erweiterung der traditionsgeschichtlichen Reflexion der 'Christologie von unten' erweist sich an dieser Stelle in der Tat als nötig. Es genügt nicht, Gott nur als *Voraussetzung* der Christologie zu denken. Vielmehr erfordern es die Aussagen, zu denen die Christologie gelangt, Gott als sich in Jesus Christus offenbarend zu denken. . . . *Dabei stellt sich die Aufgabe, die Christologie im Zusammenhang des Weltverhältnisses Gottes und besonders im Zusammenhang seiner Beziehung zur Menschheit in ihrer Geschichte zu denken, so aber, daß die Geschichte Jesu sich dabei als Schlüssel zum Verständnis der Geschichte der Menschheit und zum Weltverständnis Gottes überhaupt erweist.*" (*Grundzüge der Christologie*, 5., um ein Nachwort erweiterte Auflage 1976, p. 422; Italics, except 6th line, mine)

latest article in which he says,

> Die künftige Herrlichkeit Gottes bestimmt die gegenwärtige Welt da, wo man nach Gerechtigkeit hungert und dürstet, wo Gewaltlosigkeit, Friedfertigkeit und Barmherzigkeit regieren, wo Bedürftige, Trauernde, Leidende und Verfolgte ihren Trost in der Zukunft Gottes finden. *Eben das ist auch am Kreuze Jesu offenbar.* Gott ist im Bunde mit denen, die — meist gegen den Strom ihrer Zeit und darum in Leiden, Schwachheit und Verfolgungen — reinen Herzens Gerechtigkeit, Frieden und barmherzige Liebe suchen. Darum ist *die Gemeinschaft Gottes mit solcher menschlichen Schwachheit nicht als Entäußerung, als Ablegen einer Macht und Gewalt, die Gott bei sich selbst eigentlich schon besäße, zu verstehen.* . . . (Christliches Gottverständnis) muß Gottes Gottheit aus seinem in Botschaft und Geschichte Jesu von Nazareth offenbaren Verhalten denken. Es kann darum das Sichverbinden Gottes mit dem, was in dieser Welt schwach ist und scheitert . . . nicht als eine Art temporären Verzicht Gottes auf seine wahre Natur deuten, nicht als Selbstentäußerung, *sondern vielmehr gerade als Selbstverwirklichung Gottes* in der Ausübung seiner Herrschaft über seine Schöpfung.[30]

The pivotal point here is that the *cross, understood as expression of God's love and bearing with those who suffer, must inform the Christian concept of God*. This thought supplements Pannenberg's procedure to gain a concept of God exclusively from Jesus' message of the immenent Kingdom of God, and his resurrection. The character of God's power as explicated in this article is not different from what our analysis in chapter V, 5 and 6, set forth. The second pivotal point in the above passage is that God's love, displayed on the cross, is *no condescension but self-realization of God*. For

> Die Allmacht des christlichen Gottes steht nicht im Gegensatz zu seiner gewaltlosen Liebe, sondern erweist sich gerade in der Macht der scheinbar (nämlich in den Augen des von Gott isolierten Men-

---

[30] Wolfhart Pannenberg, "Christologie und Theologie", *Kerygma und Dogma*, vol. xxi, 3/1975, pp. 159—175; above quotation pp. 170f. (italics mine). Contrary to P., the cross displays God's oneness with *all* who suffer, not merely with those who suffer for righteous causes and are "reinen Herzens", I think. However, it is certainly true that God's future glory is *determinative* of the present world only where, briefly, love is exercised or yearned for (cf. first sentence).

schen) ohnmächtigen Sache des Rechts, des Friedens und der Liebe unter den Menschen.³¹

Die Selbstverwirklichung Gottes läßt sich nicht als punktuelles Ereignis denken, sondern, wenn anders es sich dabei um die Selbstverwirklichung *Gottes,* der alles bestimmenden Wirklichkeit, handelt, ist alles Geschehen hineingezogen in diesen Prozeß, so daß alle Dinge durch ihn schöpferisch konstituiert und bestimmt werden.
... Der noch nicht abgeschlossene Prozeß der Versöhnung der Welt gehört also als konstitutives Moment mit zum Prozeß der Selbstverwirklichung Gottes in Jesus Christus hinzu.³²

While Moltmann focuses chiefly on man's forsakenness, misery, and suffering Pannenberg focusses on its cause, man's self-enclosure toward God, his lack of openness to the future.³³ As regards redemption, both theologians envision it eschatologically; still, for both, the coming God is redemptively at work in the present. Pannenberg conceptualized this redemptive work on the one hand as forgiveness, on the other as unifying.³⁴ Christ as the prototype of the new humanity opens up the possibility of existence in openness to God; the new Adam "achieves", fulfills and "makes available" man's *Bestimmung* in communion with himself. Moltmann, on the other side, chiefly asks what the recognition of the crucified God means *für den ohnmächtigen und leidenden Menschen:* God's solidarity with man *im Leiden* enables man to stick to love. His forsakenness is *aufgehoben* in Christ's forsakenness. Man finds the strength to remain in love and hold on to it. The suffering on the cross becomes for him God's own history which contains the history of the world; this *Gottesgeschichte* is open to the future and opens the future to the believer. Our own construction tried to supplement Pannenberg's soteriology, similar to Moltmann, but on Pannenberg's terms, by an emphasis on the vulnerability of God's love. This love is self-giving, self-dedicating, vulnerable; suffering is of its essence. It invites our unrestrained trust.³⁵

---

³¹*Ibid.,* p. 171 ³² *Ibid.,* p. 173
³³ Cf. Jürgen Moltmann, *op. cit.,* chapters V,3–VI,9 (pp. 178–291)
³⁴ *Vide supra,* pp. 114 ff.
³⁵ Thus the yield of the cross can be formulated in complete agreement with Calvin in terms of its consequences: "The important point (of Christ's sacerdotal office) is that the significance of this exclusive priesthood of Christ is not cultic, but rather the 'favor with God' from which 'proceeds not only confidence in

It is interesting to note that for both Pannenberg and Moltmann the concept of reconciliation plays almost no role to identify the yield of God's love in the present. This may follow from the fact that for both theologians the acute problem is not God's enmity toward man or man's enmity toward God but *how God's love can be made arguable and convincingly comprehensible in today's world*.[36]

Moltmann's paramount concern with the cry for God's justice in the midst of injustice, torture, and martyrdom of millions of humans (without which, no doubt, no theology will do!) is powerfully present in Pannenberg's doctrine also. Namely, his anthropological *Ansatz* that man's *Bestimmung* to openness to the world, radicalized as openness to God, finds no fulfillment in the world and *points beyond death*, derives from the experience of the disparity between *Verhalten* and *Ergehen*. The concept of this disparity contains all of what Moltmann is concerned with at this point.[37]

We tried to apply the unconditional love of God, as it is displayed in Jesus' proclamation and resurrection, to the interpretation of Jesus' cross as an act of God in order to unlock an understanding of the crucifixion which

---

prayer, but also tranquillity to the consciences of the faithful; while they recline in safety on the paternal indulgence of God, and are certainly persuaded, that he is pleased with whatever is consecrated to Him through the Mediator'." Paul L. Lehmann, *Ethics in a Christian Context* (New York and Evanston: Harper & Row, 1963), p. 115; quotes from Calvin's *Institutio*, II, 15, 6. Lehmann explains, "The accent falls upon the redemptive consequences for behavior or, in Calvin's words, the redemptive 'benefits which he confers on us'." While we share Calvin's view of the consequences of the cross, the traditional understanding of *what happened on the cross* is no longer tenable, it seems.

[36] Where P. uses this concept it denotes the idea of God's creative unification (cf. *supra*, pp. 120ff.) and the healing of man's suffering as well as the reconciliation *among* men, as when he says, "The kingdom of God ... is God's own ultimate reality and brings with it the reconciliation of all men in a society of peace and justice ... Only that future can substantiate faith in a loving God when his love will attain satisfaction in reconciling all suffering and aberrations of his creatures." ("Future and Unity", *Hope and the Future of Man*, p. 65)

[37] Cf. *supra*, pp. 104ff., especially 107f. P. himself does not explicitly relate the rise of man's hope that extends to a life beyond death to man's experience of the disparity between deed and consequence. But it seems cogent to think that the experience of injustice, which entails suffering, is part of "death" which prevents man from finding a conclusive answer to his quest for his *Bestimmung* within this life.

agrees with and deepens the concept of God as such love. In his most recent article Pannenberg has moved in the same direction. The unifying power of the future is seen, in this article, in the light of Jesus' cross as the love which is "im Bunde"[38] with the suffering creatures. The cross displays this love's depth and non-coerciveness. In such love God realizes himself. One might say that this is Pannenberg's version of saying what we meant when we interpreted the cross as God's *opus proprium, viz.* the work of love, and when we, following Pannenberg's suggestion and utilizing Hegel's insight, applied Hegel's theory of the self-sublimation of the three Persons in the unity of God also in this direction: the Father *is* the Father only in his self-dedication to the Son.

What makes up Christ's redemptive work in the present, namely, his leading men to open existence in communion with himself, Pannenberg, in this article, calls *Selbstverwirklichung des Menschen*. Here the work of God reaches its goal, i. e., *the self-realization of God and man are identical.*

> Die Selbstfindung Gottes geschieht, indem die Menschheit das Selbst Gottes findet. In dem Masse wie die Menschen Frieden und Recht und Liebe üben, verwirklicht sich durch ihr Handeln Gott: Die Selbstverwirklichung des Menschen und die Selbstverwirklichung Gottes sind also identisch; sie vollziehen sich in ein und demselben Prozeß.[39]

This *identity* of the divine and human *Selbstverwirklichung* is the meaning of the sentence: God suffered on the cross, *in nuce*.

Looking at the cross as an act of God, Jesus' *message and resurrection* display the love of God as forgiveness and as the power from the future which transforms the chaos into the new cosmos. Jesus' *cross* displays the love of God as *vulnerable misericordia* and invincible long-suffering with the sin of man that opens the possibility for us to attain to the human *Bestimmung*.[40]

---

[38] Wolfhart Pannenberg, "Christologie und Theologie", p. 170 (cp. *supra*, p. 224).
[39] *Ibid.*, p. 174
[40] Without wishing to exposit Moltmann's monumental design of *The Crucified God*, a few remarks, in addition to what was said above through text and notes, may indicate the proximity to and difference from P. and our suggestions. M. is profoundly motivated by the challenge Max Horkheimer's 'atheism of protest' raises against both traditional theism and atheism with their distinctive separation of God from suffering and by the oppressive human search for God's *Gerechtig-*

keit in the midst of human misery, "But how can deliverance and liberation for godforsaken man lie in the figure of the godforsaken, crucified Christ?" (242) M. answers: (1) The cross is in God. While the Son suffers death, the Father suffers the dying of the Son. The cross is the basis of the trinitarian understanding of God, trinitarian theology must be theology of the cross of the Father, Son, and Spirit. (2) M. expands the Father's suffering from the dying of the Son so as to encompass the suffering of the creatures. (3) The cross demonstrates the suffering love of both Father and Son; this love is essentially *Feindesliebe* (unconditional love of the enemy). (4) This is redemptive in that (a) it gives rise to the Spirit who creates love in man; thus it does not only promise a future alleviation of and salvation from evil and death (hope) but also a present power which creates freedom. M.'s concept of freedom unites freedom from guilt (Jesus bears the punishment, the *Gottverlassenheit*), from idolatry (*Menschenvergottung im Atheismus*), legalism, *Zwänge*, lovelessness.

Like P.'s, M.'s doctrine of the cross has to do with the cross of the risen one. Like P., M. deems a solution of the christological problem as impossible within the two-natures-doctrine; the passion is *personales Geschehen* between Jesus and God. Like P., M. utilizes Hegel's concept of dedication but combines it with Luther's new epistemological principle; "as the cross of the outcast and forsaken Christ it (the cross) is the visible revelation of God's being for man in the reality of his world" (208). While for Luther it was strictly the cross of the Son, for M. it is the cross of the trinity. But why is the passion of the Father salvific? M.'s premise reads, "Only if all disaster, forsakenness by God, absolute death, the infinite curse of damnation and sinking into nothingness is in God himself, is community with this God eternal salvation, infinite joy, indestructable election and divine life." (246) God's love is proved, so to say, by his sharing the human predicament. Why does this help? The dialectic of human life is this, "we live because and insofar as we love, – and we suffer and die because and insofar as we love. In this way we experience life and death in love (*an der Liebe*)." (253) "Therefore anyone who enters into love, and through love experiences inextricable suffering and the fatality of death, enters into the history of the human God, for his forsakenness is lifted away from him in the forsakenness of Christ, and in this way he can continue to love, need not look away from the negative and from death, but can sustain death." (254)

For M. the crucifixion of Jesus is the basis for a trinitarian concept of God. But why choose the *crucifixion* of Jesus or Jesus at all? Even Jesus' resurrection does not define God as one who raises from the dead universally, unless one first has a concept of God which permits, via anthropology and the *Traditionsgeschichte* of the idea of resurrection from the dead, to discern Jesus' resurrection as God's proleptic self-revelation. M.'s theology is one of the Word. P., in a different way, starts with the historical and anthropological phenomena.

SELECTED BIBLIOGRAPHY

I WORKS BY WOLFHART PANNENBERG

Pannenberg, Wolfhart: *The Apostles' Creed. In the Light of Today's Questions.* Translated by Margaret Kohl. Philadelphia: Westminster Press, 1972. Translation of *Das Glaubensbekenntnis, ausgelegt und verantwortet vor den Fragen der Gegenwart.* Hamburg: Siebenstern, 1972.

—: *Basic Questions in Theology. Collected Essays.* 2 vols. Translated by George H. Kehm. Philadelphia: Fortress Press, vol. i 1970, vol. ii 1971. Translation of *Grundfragen systematischer Theologie.* Göttingen: Vandenhoeck & Ruprecht, 1967.

—: *Christentum und Mythos. Späthorizonte des Mythos in biblischer und christlicher Überlieferung.* Gütersloh: Gerd Mohn, 1972.

—: "Christologie und Theologie". *Kerygma und Dogma* 21 (July/Sept., 1975), 159–175.

—: "Dogmatische Erwägungen zur Auferstehung Jesu." *Kerygma und Dogma* 14 (April, 1968), 105–118.

— und Müller, A. M. Klaus: *Erwägungen zu einer Theologie der Natur.* Gütersloh: Gerd Mohn, 1970.

—: "Future and Unity". *Hope and the Future of Man.* Ed. Ewert H. Cousins. Philadelphia: Fortress Press, 1972, 60–77.

—: *Gegenwart Gottes. Predigten.* München: Claudius Verlag, 1973.

—: *The Idea of God and Human Freedom.* Philadelphia: Westminster Press, 1973. Translated by R. A. Wilson. Translation of *Gottesgedanke und menschliche Freiheit.* Göttingen, Vandenhoeck & Ruprecht, 1972.

—: *Jesus – God and Man.* Translated by Lewis L. Wilkins and Duane A. Priebe. Philadelphia: Westminster Press, 5th ed., 1974. Translation of *Grundzüge der Christologie.* Gütersloh: Gerd Mohn, 1964.

—: "Response to the Discussion." *Theology As History.* Eds. James M. Robinson and John B. Cobb, Jr. New York et al.: Harper and Row: 1967, 221–276. Translated by Kendrick Grobel.

— et al: *Revelation as History.* Translated by David Granskou. New York: The Macmillan Company, 1968. Translation of *Offenbarung als Geschichte.* Göttingen: Vandenhoeck & Ruprecht, 1961.

—: "The Revelation of God in Jesus of Nazareth." *Theology as History.* Eds. James M. Robinson and John B. Cobb, Jr. New York et al.: Harper & Row, 1967, 101–133. Translated by Kendrick Grobel.

— et al: *Spirit, Faith, and Church*. Philadelphia: Westminster Press, 1970.

—: "A Theological Conversation with Wolfhart Pannenberg." *Dialog* 11 (Autumn, 1972), 286—295.

—: *Theology and the Kingdom of God*. Philadelphia: Westminster Press, 1969.

—: *Thesen zur Theologie der Kirche*. München: Claudius, 1970.

—: "Weltgeschichte und Heilsgeschichte." *Probleme biblisher Theologie. Gerhard von Rad zum 70. Geburtstag*. Ed. Hans Walter Wolff. München: Chr. Kaiser. 1971, 349—366.

II OTHER LITERATURE

Anselm von Canterbury: *Cur Deus Homo. Warum Gott Mensch geworden*. Lateinisch und deutsch. Translated by Franciscus Salesius Schmitt O.S.B. München: Kösel-Verlag, 1956.

Aulen, Gustav: *Christus Victor. An Historical Study of the Three Main Types of the Idea of Atonement*. Translated by A. G. Hebert. New York: Macmillan, 1951.

Baillie, Donald M: *God Was in Christ. An Essay on Incarnation and Atonement*. New York: Charles Scribner's Sons, 1948.

Barth, Karl: *Kirchliche Dogmatik*. vol. IV/1: *Die Lehre von der Versöhnung*. Zollikon-Zürich: Evangelischer Verlag, 1953.

Barth, Karl: *Die Protestantische Theologie im 19. Jahrhundert*. Zollikon-Zürich: Evangelischer Verlag. 1952.

Berten, Ignace: *Histoire, Revelation, Foi. Dialogue avec Wolfgang Pannenberg*. Bruxelles: Centre d'etudes pastorales, 1969.

Betz, H. D.: "The Concept of Apocalyptic in the Theology of the Pannenberg Group". *Apocalypticsm* (Journal for Theology and the Church, vol. VI), ed. R. W. Funk, 1969.

Bloch, Ernst: *Das Prinzip Hoffnung*. 2 vols. Frankfurt am Main: Suhrkamp, 1959.

Bomann, Thorleif: *Das Hebräische Denken im Vergleich mit dem Griechischen*. Göttingen: Vandenhoeck & Ruprecht, 1952.

Bornkamm, Günther: *Paulus*. Stuttgart et al: W. Kohlhammer, 1969.

Braaten, Carl E: "The Current Controversy on Revelation. Pannenberg and His Critics". *The Journal of Religion* 45 (July, 1965), 225—237.

—: *The Future of God. The Revolutionary Dynamics of Hope*. New York et al.: Harper & Row, 1969.

—: *History and Hermeneutics* (vol. ii of New Directions in Theology Today). Philadelphia: Westminster Press, 1966.

Brunner, Emil: *The Christian Doctrine of Creation and Redemption* (Dogmatics, vol. ii). Translated by Olive Wyon. Philadelphia: Westminster Press, 1952.

Bultmann, Rudolf: *Jesus and the Word*. Translated by Louise Pettibone Smith and Erminie Huntress Lantero. New York: Charles Scribner's Sons, 1958.

—: *Jesus Christ and Mythology*. New York: Charles Scribner's Sons, 1958.

—: *Theologie des Neuen Testaments.* 5., durch einen Nachtrag erweiterte Auflage. Tübingen: J. C. B. Mohr (Paul Siebeck), 1965.
Buren, Paul van: *Christ in Our Place. The Substitutionary Character of Calvin's Doctrine of Reconciliation.* Grand Rapids. Michigan: W. B. Erdmans, 1957.
Cave, Sydney: *The Doctrine of the Work of Christ.* Nashville, Tenn.: Cokesbury Press, 1937.
Cobb, John B., Jr.: *A Christian Natural Theology. Based on the Thought of Alfred North Whitehead.* Philadelphia: Westminster Press, 1965.
Cobb, John B., Jr.: *Living Options in Protestant Theology. A Survey of Methods.* Philadelphia: Westminster Press, 1962.
— and James M. Robinson, eds. *Theology as History* (vol. iii of New Frontiers in Theology). New York et al.: Harper & Row, 1967.
—: "Wolfhart Pannenberg's 'Jesus-God and Man'." *The Journal of Religion* 49 (April, 1969), 192–201.
—: "A Process Systematic Theology". *The Journal of Religion* 50 (April 1970), 199–206.
Come, Arnold Bruce: *An Introduction to Karl Barth's Dogmatics for Preachers.* Philadelphia: Westminster Press, 1963.
Cone, James H.: *Liberation. A Black Theology of Liberation.* Philadelphia and New York: J. B. Lippincott, 1970.
Conzelmann, Hans: *An Outline of the Theology of the New Testament.* New York and Evanston: Harper and Row, 1969.
Crawford, R. G.: "The Atonement in Karl Barth." *Theology* 74 (August 1971), 355–358.
—: "Is the Penal Theory of the Atonement Scriptural?" *Scottish Journal of Theology* 23 (August 1970), 257–272.
Cullmann, Oskar: *Die Christologie des Neuen Testaments.* Tübingen: J. C. B. Mohr (Paul Siebeck), 1957.
Cuncliffe-Jones, H.: "The Atonement in Karl Barth". *Theology* 74 (November, 1971), 536.
—: "The Meaning of the Atonement Today". *Theology* 74 (March 1971), 119–123.
Dantine, Wilhelm: *Die Gerechtmachung des Gottlosen.* München: Chr. Kaiser, 1959.
Dawe, D. G.: "Christology in Contemporary Systematic Theology". *Interpretation* 26 (July, 1972), 259–277.
Delling, Gerhard: "Der Tod Jesu in der Verkündigung des Paulus." *Apophoreta* (Festschrift für Ernst Haenchen zu seinem 70. Geburtstag). ed. Walter Eltester. Berlin: A. Töpelmann, 1964.
Dillistone, F. W.: *The Christian Understanding of Atonement.* Philadelphia: Westminster Press, 1968.
Dillistone, F. W.: *Jesus Christ and His Cross. Studies on the Saving Work of Christ.* Philadelphia: Westminster Press, 1953.

Dilthey, Wilhelm: *Pattern and Meaning in History. Thoughts on History and Society.* Ed. and introduced by H. P. Rickman. New York: Harper & Brothers, 1961.

Ecke, Gustav: *Die theologische Schule Albrecht Ritschls und die evangelische Kirche der Gegenwart.* vol. i. Berlin: Reuther & Richard, 1897.

Fohrer, Georg: "Das Geschick des Menschen nach dem Tode im Alten Testament." *Kerygma und Dogma* 14 (October, 1968), 249–262.

Forsyth, Peter Taylor: *The Cruciality of the Cross.* London: Hodder and Stoughton, 1910.

—: *The Work of Christ.* With a Foreword by John S. Whale and a Memoir of the Author by Jessie Forsyth Andrews. London: Independent Press, 1938.

Friedrich, Gerhard: "Die Auferweckung Jesu, eine Tat Gottes oder ein Interpretament der Jünger?" *Kerygma und Dogma* 17 (1971), 153–187.

Foster, A. Durwood: "Albrecht Ritschl". *A Handbook of Christian Theologians.* Eds. Dean G. Peerman and Martin E. Marty. Cleveland and New York: World Publishing Company, 49–67.

Gollwitzer, Helmut: *Von der Stellvertretung Gottes. Christlicher Glaube in der Erfahrung der Verborgenheit Gottes. Zum Gespräch mit Dorothee Sölle.* München: Chr. Kaiser, 1967.

Grass, Hans: *Christliche Glaubenslehre.* 2 vols. Stuttgart et al.: Kohlhammer, vol. i 1973, vol. ii 1974.

—: *Ostergeschehen und Osterberichte.* Göttingen: Vandenhoeck & Ruprecht, 1962.

—: *Theologie und Kritik. Gesammelte Aufsätze und Vorträge.* Göttingen: Vandenhoeck & Ruprecht, 1969.

Hahn, Ferdinand: *Christologische Hoheitstitel. Ihre Geschichte im frühen Christentum.* Göttingen: Vandenhoeck & Ruprecht, 1963.

Harder, Helmut G. and Stevenson, W. Taylor: "The Continuity of History and Faith in the Theology of Wolfhart Pannenberg: Toward an Erotics of History." *The Journal of Religion* 51 (January, 1971), 34–56.

Harvey. Van A.: "Secularism, Responsible Belief, and the 'Theology of Hope'". *The Future of Hope. Theology as Eschatology.* Ed. Frederick Herzog. New York: Herder & Herder, 1970, 126–153.

Hefner, Philip: "Questions for Moltmann and Pannenberg." *Una Sancta* 25 (Michaelmass, 1968), 32–51.

Hegel, Georg Wilhelm Friedrich: *Lectures on the Philosophy of Religion.* Translated by E. B. Speirs and J. Burdon Sanderson, ed. E. B. Speirs. 3 vols. London: Kegan Paul, Trench, Trübner & Co., 1895.

Herzog, Frederick: *Liberation Theology: Liberation in the Light of the Fourth Gospel.* New York: Seabury Press, 1972.

—: *Understanding God. The Key Issue in Present-Day Protestant Thought.* New York: Charles Scribner's Sons. 1966.

Hesse, Franz: "Wolfhart Pannenberg und das Alte Testament." *Neue Zeitschrift für systematische Theologie und Religionsphilosophie* 7 (1965), 174–199.
Hick, John: *Evil and the God of Love*. New York: Harper & Row, 1966.
Hirsch, Emanuel: *Geschichte der neuern evangelischen Theologie im Zusammenhang mit den allgemeinen Bewegungen des europäischen Denkens*. Vol. v. Gütersloh: C. Bertelsmann, 1954.
Hodgson, Peter Crafts: *Jesus-Word and Presence; an Essay in Christology*. Philadelphia: Fortress Press, 1971.
—: "Pannenberg on Jesus." *Journal of the American Academy of Religion* 36 (December, 1968), 373–384.
Jeremias, Joachim: *Abba. Studien zur neutestamentlichen Theologie und Zeitgeschichte*. Göttingen: Vandenhoeck & Ruprecht, 1966.
—: *New Testament Theology*. Translated New York: Scribner's, 1971.
Käsemann, Ernst: "Erwägungen zum Stichwort 'Versöhnungslehre im Neuen Testament'." *Zeit und Geschichte*. Ed. Erich Dinkler. Tübingen: J. C. B. Mohr (Paul Siebeck), 1964.
— et al: *Zur Bedeutung des Todes Jesu. Exegetische Beiträge*. Ed. Fritz Viering. Gütersloh: Gerd Mohn, 1967.
Kaiser, Otto: "Dike und Sedaqa. Zur Frage nach der sittlichen Weltordnung. Ein theologisches Präludium." *Neue Zeitschrift für systematische Theologie und Religionsphilosophie* 7 (1965), 251–273.
Kendall, E. L.: *A Living Sacrifice. A Study in Reparation*. Philadelphia: Westminster Press, 1960.
Klappert, Berthold: *Die Auferweckung des Gekreuzigten. Der Ansatz der Christologie Karl Barths im Zusammenhang der Christologie der Gegenwart*. Neukirchen-Vluyn: Neukirchener Verlag, 1971.
Klein, Günter: *Theologie des Wortes Gottes und die Hypothese der Universalgeschichte*. München: Chr. Kaiser, 1964.
Kluback, William: *Wilhelm Dilthey's Philosophy of History*. New York: Columbia University Press, 1956.
Koch, Klaus: "Gibt es ein Vergeltungsdogma im Alten Testament?". *Zeitschrift für Theologie und Kirche* 52 (1955), 1–42.
—: *The Rediscovery of Apocalyptic. A Polemical Work on a Neglected Area of Biblical Studies and its Damaging Effects on Theology and Philosophy*. Translated by Margaret Kohl. Naperville, Ill.: Alec R. Allenson Inc., no year.
Kümmel, Werner Georg: *The Theology of the New Testament. According to Its Major Witnesses: Jesus-Paul-John*. Translated by John E. Steely. Nashville and New York: Abington Press, 1973.
—: "Πάρεσις und ἔνδειξις". *Heilsgeschehen und Geschichte. Gesammelte Aufsätze 1933–1964*. Ed. Erich Grässer, Otto Merk, Adolf Fritz. Marburg/Lahn: N. G. Elwert, 1965.

Lawson, John: *Comprehensive Handbook of Christian Doctrine.* Engelwood Cliffs, New Jersey: Prentice Hall Inc., 1967.

Lehmann, Paul: *Ethics in a Christian Context.* New York and Evanston: Harper and Row, 1963.

Lohse, Eduard: *Märtyrer und Gottesknecht. Untersuchungen zur urchristlichen Verkündigung vom Sühnetod Jesu Christi.* Göttingen: Vandenhoeck & Ruprecht, 1963.

Loomer, Bernard M.: "Christian Faith and Process Philosophy." *The Journal of Religion* 29 (July, 1949), 181–203.

–: "Whitehead's Method of Empirical Analysis." *Process Theology.* Ed. Ewert H. Cousins. New York et al.: Newman Press, 1971.

Marxsen, Willi et al: *Die Bedeutung der Auferstehungsbotschaft für den Glauben an Jesus Christus.* Ed. Fritz Viering. Gütersloh: Gerd Mohn, 1966.

McClendon, James W., Jr.: "How is Religious Talk Justifiable?" *American Philosophy and the Future. Essays for a New Generation.* Ed. Michael Novak. New York: Charles Scribner's Sons, 1968, 324–347.

–: *Biography as Theology. How Life Stories Can Remake Today's Theology.* Nashville: Abington Press, 1974.

Macquarrie, John: *Principles of Christian Theology.* New York: Scribner's, 1966.

–: *20th Century Religious Thought. The Frontiers of Philosophy, 1900–1970.* London: SCM Press Ltd., 1971.

–: "Demonology and the Classic Idea of Atonement". *The Expository Times* 68 (Oct., 1956–Sept., 1957), 3–6 and 60–63.

Meeks, M. Douglas: *Origins of the Theology of Hope.* Philadelphia: Fortress Press, 1974.

Menninger, Karl A.: *Man Against Himself.* New York: Harcourt, Brace & World Inc., 1938.

Miller, Randolph Crump: *The American Spirit in Theology.* Philadelphia: United Church Press, 1974.

Moltmann, Jürgen: *Theologie der Hoffnung.* München: Chr. Kaiser, 1964.

–: *Der gekreuzigte Gott. Das Kreuz Christi als Grund und Kritik christlicher Theologie.* München: Chr. Kaiser, 1972.

–: et al: *The Future of Hope: Theology as Eschatology.* Ed. Frederick Herzog. New York: Herder & Herder, 1970.

Müller-Schwefe, Hans-Rudolf: *Christus ist größer. Der Weg der Theologie zu einem neuen Bild von Christus.* Hamburg: Agentur des Rauhen Hauses, 1968.

Nicholls, William: *Systematic and Philosophical Theology* (The Pelican Guide to Modern Theology). Hardmondsworth, England: Penguin Books, 1971.

Nitzsch, Friedrich August Berth: *Lehrbuch der evangelischen Dogmatik.* 3d ed. Ed. Horst Stephan. Tübingen: J. C. B. Mohr (Paul Siebeck), 1912.

Osborne, Kenan B: *New Being. A Study on the Relationship between Conditioned and Unconditioned Being according to Paul Tillich.* The Hague: Martinus Nijhoff, 1969.

Outler, Albert C.: *Psychotherapy and the Christian Message.* New York: Harper and Brothers, 1954.

Perrin, Norman: "Putting Back the Clock." *The Christian Century* 85, (Dec. 11, 1968), 1575–1576.

Pfister, Oskar: *Christianity and Fear. A Study in History and in the Psychology and Hygiene of Religion.* Translated by W. H. Johnston. London: George Allan & Unwin, 1948. Translation of *Das Christentum und die Angst.* Zürich: Artemis, 1944.

Pittenger, W. Norman: *Theology and Reality. Essays in Restatement.* Greenwich, Conn.: Seabury Press, 1955.

Rad, Gerhard von: *Old Testament Theology. vol. i: The Theology of Israel's Historical Traditions.* Translated by D. M. G. Stalker. New York: Harper & Row, 1967.

Rashdall, Hasting: *The Idea of Atonement in Christian Theology.* London: Macmillan & Co., 1920.

Ratschow, Carl Heinz: *Gott existiert. Eine dogmatische Studie.* Berlin: A. Töpelmann, 1966.

Reist, Benjamin A.: *Theology in Red, White, and Black.* Philadelphia: Westminster Press, 1975.

—: *Toward a Theology of Involvement: The Thought of Ernst Troeltsch.* Philadelphia: Westminster Press, 1966.

Rhine, Joseph Banks: *New World of the Mind.* New York: William Sloane, 1953.

Richardson, Alan: "The Resurrection of Jesus Christ." *Theology* 74, (April, 1971), 146–154.

Ritschl, Albrecht: *The Christian Doctrine of Justification and Reconciliation. The Positive Development of the Doctrine.* Translated by and ed. H. R. Mcintosh and A. B. Macaulay. 2d. ed. Edinburgh: T. & T. Clark, 1902.

Roberts, David. E.: *Psychotherapy and a Christian View of Man.* New York: Charles Scribner's Sons, 1950.

Robinson, H. Wheeler: *Corporate Personality in Ancient Israel.* Philadelphia: Fortress Press, 1964.

Rössler, Dietrich: *Gesetz und Geschichte. Untersuchungen zur Theologie der jüdischen Apokalyptik und der pharisäischen Orthodoxie.* Neukirchen Krs. Moers: Neukirchener Verlag, 1960.

Sauter, Gerhard: "Angewandte Eschatologie. Überlegungen zu Jürgen Moltmanns 'Theologie der Hoffnung'". *Diskussion über die 'Theologie der Hoffnung' von Jürgen Moltmann.* Ed. and intr. Wolf-Dieter Marsch. München: Chr. Kaiser, 1967. 106–121.

Schäfer, Rolf: *Ritschl. Grundlinien eines fast verschollenen dogmatischen Systems.* Tübingen: J. C. B. Mohr (Paul Siebeck), 1968.

Seils, Martin: "Zur sprachphilosophischen und worttheologischen Problematik der Auseinandersetzung zwischen Existenztheologie und Geschichtstheologie." *Neue Zeitschrift für systematische Theologie und Religionsphilosophie* 7 (1965), 1–14.

Sölle, Dorothee: *Christ the Representative; an Essay in Theology after the Death of God.* Translated by David Lewis. Philadelphia: Fortress press, 1967.

Steiger, Lothar: "Revelation History and Theological Reason: A Critique of the Theology of Wolfhart Pannenberg." *History and Hermeneutic* (Journal for Theology and the Church, 4). Ed. Robert W. Funk. New York: Harper & Row, 1967. 82–106.

Stein, Edward V.: *Guilt: Theory and Therapy.* Philadelphia: Westminster Press, 1968.

Taylor, Vincent: *The Atonement in New Testament Teaching.* London: Epworth Press, 1940.

—: *New Testament Essays.* London: Epworth Press, 1970.

Tillich, Paul: *Systematic Theology*, vols. i–iii. Chicago: The University of Chicago Press, 1951–1963.

Trillhaas, Wolfgang: *Dogmatik.* Berlin: A. Töpelmann, 1962.

—: *Das Evangelium und der Zwang der Wohlstandskultur.* Berlin: A. Töpelmann, 1966.

—: "Felix culpa. Zur Deutung der Geschichte vom Sündenfall bei Hegel." *Probleme biblischer Theologie. Gerhard von Rad zum 70. Geburtstag.* Ed. Hans Walter Wolff. München: Chr. Kaiser, 1971. 589–602.

—: *Glaube und Kritik.* Göttingen: Vandenhoeck & Ruprecht, 1969.

—: "Pannenberg, Wolfgang: Grundzüge der Christologie." (Reviewarticle). *Theologische Literaturzeitung* 91 (1966), 207–211.

Tupper, Frank: *The Theology of Wolfhart Pannenberg.* Philadelphia: Westminster Press, 1973.

Viering, Fritz: *Der Kreuzestod Jesu. Interpretation eines theologischen Gutachtens.* Gütersloh: Gerd Mohn, 1969.

Weber, Otto: "Das dogmatische Problem der Versöhnungslehre." *Evangelische Theologie* 26 (1966), 258–272.

Welch, Claude: Ed. and translated. *God and Incarnation in Mid-Nineteenth Century German Theology: G. Thomasius – I. A. Dorner – A. E. Biedermann.* New York: Oxford University Press, 1965.

—: *Protestant Thought in the 19th Century*, vol. i.: *1799–1870.* New Haven and London: Yale University Press, 1972.

Whitehead, Alfred North: *Religion in the Making.* New York: Macmillan, 1926.

—: *The Function of Reason.* New York: Macmillan, 1929.

Williams, Daniel Day: "Response to Wolfhart Pannenberg." *Hope and the Future*

of Man. Ed. Ewert H. Cousins. Philadelphia: Fortress Press, 1972. 83—88.
—: *The Spirit and the Forms of Love.* New York and Evanston: Harper & Row, 1968.
—: "'What Is Man?' by Wolfhart Pannenberg." (Review) *Theology Today* 28 (April, 1971), 107—109.
Wolf, William: *No Cross, No Crown. A Study of the Atonement.* Garden City, New York: Doubleday & Company, Inc., 1957.